I

Knowing the Unknowable God

"Jim Lucas analyzes the mysterious paradoxes of God and shows us how we can trust and believe what God says, even if it seems contradictory. *Knowing the Unknowable God* challenges Christians to understand, appreciate, and celebrate our holy, mysterious Creator. This book shows how biblical paradoxes strengthen our faith."

> —DR. BOB and YVONNE TURNBULL, conference speakers and coauthors of *TeamMates: Building Your Marriage to Complete, Not Compete*

"With contagious passion, Jim Lucas leads us on a quest for God that is ruthlessly honest and deeply fulfilling. His thoughtful exploration of the paradoxes of faith will help you hear God's voice with more clarity than you ever have before."

> —LES PARROTT, PH.D., Seattle Pacific University, coauthor of *Love the Life You Live*

"God invites us to come and reason with him. In a world of intellectual confusion that presumes the fallacy of faith, Jim Lucas presents God's self-revelation as it exists in powerful paradox. Pondering this collection of divine portraits, you will appreciate anew the wonder of the Almighty."

> —BOB SHANK, founder/CEO of The Master's Program

"Writing in the language of the layman, Jim Lucas tackles the fascinating paradoxes of our amazing, mysterious, wondrous God, reminding us that with God it's not a matter of either/or but a paradox of both/and. I highly recommend stretching your mind and your spirit with *Knowing the Unknowable God*."

> —GAYLE ROPER, author of *Autumn Dreams, Summer Shadows,* and *Spring Rain*

"Paradox is a necessary expression for anything profound. *Knowing the Unknowable God* is a necessary expression of the profound."

—PHIL HOTSENPILLER, teaching pastor at Jacksonville Chapel,
Lincoln Park, New Jersey

"Living in a culture characterized by ten-second sound bites and bumper-sticker philosophies, we often miss the fact that Truth according to the Creator of the universe is much, much bigger. Jim Lucas's book teaches us how to embrace biblical paradoxes for a deeper, more accurate understanding of a mighty God. *Knowing the Unknowable God* is insightful and timely."

—BRETT POSTEN and ROBERT D. TENEYCK, founders of DeoVibe:
The Pulse of Popular Culture

"James Lucas carefully studies and explains difficulties in Scripture that thoughtful believers need to understand both for themselves and to be able to help others."

—DR. PATRICK O. CATE, president of Christar

"Mystery surrounds God, and it should come as no surprise to anyone who reads the Bible attentively to find mystery there wrapped in paradox. Paradox is intrinsic to the Bible because the Bible is of God. God does not speak to us in dumbed-down, obvious truisms, but in truths that will touch and awaken our imaginations. This book has made me aware of an illuminating principle to which one ought to pay closer attention when reading Scripture."

—REV. DR. JOHN MAXWELL KERR, Oxford University,
former warden of the Society of Ordained Scientists

KNOWING *the*
UNKNOWABLE
GOD

OTHER BOOKS BY JAMES R. LUCAS

PERSONAL GROWTH

Walking Through the Fire: Finding the Purpose of Pain in the Christian Life

FAMILY AND OTHER RELATIONSHIPS

Am I the One? Clues to Finding and Becoming a Person Worth Marrying
The Paradox Principle of Parenting: How to Parent Your Child Like God Parents You
1001 Ways to Connect with Your Kids
Proactive Parenting: The Only Approach That Really Works
The Parenting of Champions

FICTION

A Perfect Persecution
Noah: Voyage to a New Earth
Weeping in Ramah

LEADERSHIP AND ORGANIZATIONAL DEVELOPMENT

The Passionate Organization: Igniting the Fire of Employee Commitment
Balance of Power: Fueling Employee Power Without Relinquishing Your Own
Fatal Illusions: Shredding a Dozen Unrealities That Can Keep Your Organization from Success

KNOWING *the* UNKNOWABLE GOD

How Faith Thrives on Divine Mystery

JAMES R. LUCAS

WATERBROOK
PRESS

KNOWING THE UNKNOWABLE GOD
PUBLISHED BY WATERBROOK PRESS
2375 Telstar Drive, Suite 160
Colorado Springs, Colorado 80920
A division of Random House, Inc.

Library of Congress Cataloging-in-Publication Data

Lucas, J. R. (James Raymond), 1950–
    Knowing the unknowable God : how faith thrives on divine mystery / James R. Lucas.— 1st ed.
    p. cm.
Includes bibliographical references.
    ISBN 1-57856-600-2
  1. God. I. Title.
    BT103.L83 2003
    231—dc22

                              2003015782

Printed in Canada
2004

10 9 8 7 6 5 4 3 2

To the One God,
the Father, Son, and Holy Spirit,
the Living Lord of Paradox.

And to Laura,
who has cared for and enhanced this project
and made everything around her better.

And to David,
who has loved the life of paradox
and the paradox of life.

CONTENTS

Acknowledgments

Many thanks to Ron Lee, my terrific senior editor at WaterBrook Press. Ron, your vision for this project has been critical to its development, and you have personally been both enlightening and inspiring as we've worked on it together. I appreciate both your professionalism and your friendship.

The rest of the team at WaterBrook has done a fabulous job on this project. I want especially to thank Laura Wright and all those involved with the final details. I have also appreciated the passion of Ginia Hairston of WaterBrook and Jeane Wynn of Wynn-Wynn Media for getting this book into the hands of seekers.

As on other projects, when it came time to make sure that the book was, in every detail, relevant, accurate, and worthy of a reader's time, I turned the manuscript over to my daughter, Laura Lucas. She read through every word and every line multiple times, and made an incredible number of improvements to the work. Laura, you bring a strong love for God, people, ideas, and paradox to this work, and it is a much better book because of your involvement.

I also want to thank Laura's colleague and friend (and my friend) Jenn Prentice for taking time out of a packed schedule to bring her great insights and suggestions to the work. Jenn, you're something!

And to my longtime friend, researcher, and editor, Janette Jasperson, I owe further thanks. Janette, your long devotion is much appreciated.

A number of people have been the source of great encouragement, not the least my son David. Dave, I've enjoyed all of our many conversations on this subject. My other son, Peter, contributed his thoughts as well. Pete, I appreciate your love for paradox. Your prize-winning calligraphy on paradox was inspirational. I am also grateful for the encouragement of many others, including Pastor Rob Brown, Heather Ellsworth, and Jack and Lori Houghton.

Maryl Janson, a key part of our staff at the Relationship Development

Center, has worked hard to make this project a reality. Maryl, you have definitely kept this idea on my front burner and full of fire. Many thanks also to the rest of the RDC team.

My family has been, as always, exceptionally supportive. Thank you.

Finally, my thanks to G. H. for your inspiration and encouragement.

The Shocking Truth

I want to level with you. This book has a simple goal: to shake you to your roots, to push you to think more deeply about God.

Now, truth be told, I feel very much like a first grader trying to write a biography of Albert Einstein, an astoundingly complex person. But not nearly so complex, nor so paradoxical, as God. As together we seek knowledge of our unknowable God, I hope you will remember that I'm only a first grader in the kingdom of God.

Still, there is a great advantage to approaching the mystery of God with wide-eyed wonder. One shocking paradox of the kingdom of God is that only little children can actually "get it." Jesus tells us that only those with a childlike faith can understand and enter the kingdom of God.[1] I am asking you to have the faith of a child, to hold on to a child's willingness to accept things that don't at first make sense to a logical adult. If you renew your sense of curiosity and a willingness to believe that with God all things are possible, there is no limit to how much your faith can thrive.[2]

The many paradoxes that we find in Scripture are part of the mystery of God. At first glance, they either make absolutely no sense or they scream out a seeming contradiction. But this shouldn't surprise us. In the Bible we read: "It is the glory of God to conceal a matter; to search out a matter is the glory of kings."[3] Still, if God is *hiding* things, where does that leave us ordinary mortals?

Actually, we already have a good start on unraveling these mysteries. Our first tool is a faith that is willing to believe what God says even if it seems contradictory. The second is the ancient rabbinic method of interpreting Scripture, which we find that Jesus used.[4] It's called *halakic reasoning*. This is the approach to Scripture that holds both strands of a paradox in tension and balance, know-ing that with God both sides must be true. It's the process of firmly grabbing *both* ideas in a paradox and then merging the two into a greater understanding of the character and nature of God. We'll discuss specific biblical paradoxes and the halakic method of interpreting these paradoxes throughout the following chapters. The good thing—the really jump-up-and-down-exciting thing about all of this—is that you and I can know a whole lot more about God than we know today.

Jesus said, "You will know the truth, and the truth will set you free."[5] But truth is not defined by what *people* think it is (no matter how many agree on a certain point). Truth is what *God* says it is, even if no one else believes it to be true, even if it seems contradictory at first glance.

In this book, I invite you to join me on an extraordinary journey into the apparent contradictions of the Bible. I'm confident you will find this exploration of biblical paradoxes to be a breathtaking journey—a pilgrimage to the center of God.

Why bother with biblical paradoxes? Because the cost of not examining and understanding these opposing ideas is confusion. Or worse, ignorance will lead us to grab one of the two strands and swing to an extreme, unbiblical belief. But the reward for thinking about these things deeply, looking at them as Jesus and other rabbis have done in their practice of halakic reasoning, is a much bigger faith in a much bigger God.

This book is designed to expand both your faith and your view of God. As you read the pages that follow, you will see that delving into paradox is not just an interesting intellectual exercise. Paradox is the king's highway to understand-ing the character of God and to knowing how to relate to this straight-forward, mysterious Being.

And this brings us to the paradox at the core of this book, the paradox of head and heart, of thought and feeling: As you explore the world of paradoxes with the rabbinical tool of halakic reasoning, you will find yourself with a more practical and reassuring relationship with a God who is even more transcendent and mysterious than you ever before imagined. This is the paradox of paradoxes:

to grow exponentially in knowledge of God, only to discover—because we have grown so much—how unfathomable this God really is.

This study calls upon both your head and your heart, your intellect and your emotions. If you want rational arguments that help explain what's hard to understand about God, you'll find them here. And if you want to sense the mystery and the transcendence of our sovereign God, drawing on your emotions and lifting your soul, we'll explore these, too. Here's the bottom line: If someone gives you only one or the other, they haven't given you half the story—they've given you the *wrong* story.

So let's venture forward to see and know more deeply the God of all of life. Let's ask him to lift our relationship with him to higher ground. As you join me on this daring adventure, you will find a few of your ideas challenged and a few of your assumptions about God shaken. Perhaps many. But there's also a very good chance that you will complete this journey with deeper love for God, greater reverence for him, and stronger faith in him.

May it be so for you.

PART I

Paradoxes *in the* BIBLE

One

Contradiction or Paradox?

GOD IS BOTH/AND...NOT EITHER/OR

~~~~~~~

The paradox is the source of the thinker's passion...the thinker without a paradox is like a lover without feeling: a paltry mediocrity.
SÖREN KIERKEGAARD

Unthinking faith is a curious offering to be made to the creator of the human mind.
JOHN HUTCHINSON

Religious skeptics have long used apparent contradictions in the Bible—and there are many—to discredit Christian faith. "How can a rational person believe something that is so full of holes?" they continue to ask, even after centuries of debate.

In some cases, those who challenge the reliability of Scripture have to search diligently to locate a clear case of one verse contradicting another—or at least, *seeming* to contradict each other. Verses that appear to be at odds with one another often were penned by different writers and were recorded hundreds of years apart. But consider the following passage in Proverbs. Here are two consecutive verses that, from all outside appearances, tell us to do completely opposite things.

When arguing with fools, don't answer their foolish arguments, or you will become as foolish as they are.

When arguing with fools, be sure to answer their foolish arguments, or they will become wise in their own estimation.[1]

So which is it: Answer a fool or don't answer a fool? We are commanded to do both!

Adding to the drama are the consequences for ignoring either command. The price for ignoring the first command is that we become just as foolish as the fool. This one exacts a personal cost. However, disobeying the second command also brings a serious consequence: The blockheads end up thinking they're geniuses, and the whole world withers a little more. This hurts the foolish one as well as those who follow that person.

Unlike most biblical paradoxes, these are written consecutively, the first taking us in one direction, the second slamming us to a stop and spinning us 180 degrees. It's as if God wants to highlight for us the inescapable fact that there are, indeed, paradoxes in his written Word. If one half of a paradox is hiding in Habakkuk and the other in Philemon, we can easily miss it or just choose to ignore it. But when they are together, as in these Proverbs verses, there simply is no way to dodge them.

Since we can't avoid this one, we will explore in the following chapter the paradox of answering fools and not answering fools.

Do answer them. Don't answer them. What an irresistible riddle!

ENCOUNTERING THE LORD OF PARADOX

To rephrase the famous words of Charles Dickens, a paradox is the best of things and the worst of things, and it's both of these at the same time. It is the best of ideas for those who want big answers that destroy their prejudices, and it is the worst of ideas for those who want small answers that confirm their prejudices.

Thumb through your Bible and you'll be overwhelmed by paradoxes. Resist your enemies *and* love them. Ignore hypocritical spiritual leaders *and* obey them.

Forget what's in your past *and* be careful to remember. Flee from evil *and* stand firm against it. Don't judge *and* judge rightly.

And that just begins to scratch the surface. We can exercise our own free will, but we are chosen by God. We are saved by faith, not by doing good deeds, but there is no faith if there are no works. We are to keep a reverential distance from God while at the same time barging right into his throne room.

Given the prevalence of biblical paradoxes, what are we supposed to believe? And more, *how* are we supposed to behave?

If the Bible's paradoxes were limited to apparent contradictions regarding our own behavior, at least we'd have to navigate in only one sea of confusion. But Scripture doesn't stop there. Even God's nature and his work in the world are riddled with apparent contradictions. God remembers our sins no more but will make us give an account for every idle word we utter. He is unchanging, but then again he can change in response to our prayers. He loathes the wicked, and he loves them so much that he sent his Son to die for these abhorrent people.

Jesus' teachings, and his person, are paradoxical as well. He is called the Prince of Peace, but he said most emphatically that he didn't come to bring peace. He tells us to be innocent as doves and yet to be shrewd and constantly on our guard. He exhorts us both to give without expectation of return and to give to gain friends for ourselves. He warns us that a wicked generation asks for signs, and then he gives us sign after sign. His thoughts are immeasurably above ours, and yet we have the mind of Christ. "Brilliant, untamed, tender, creative, merciful, slippery, loving, irreducible, paradoxically humble"[2]—this is Jesus!

If you read the Bible carefully and accept it as God's truth, then you can't avoid the reality of paradoxes. They are lurking everywhere, and on almost every conceivable issue that is important to our lives. I'm convinced that God cannot be understood apart from paradox. Skeptics have wrongly painted the paradoxes as contradictions and have tried to use seeming inconsistencies to call God's character into question. If they can prove that what God says is confusing and incoherent, they can then portray him as a confusing and incoherent deity.

However, paradox is far different from contradiction. As we explore biblical paradoxes we actually find a deeper, richer portrait of God emerging. The apparent contradictions, when rightly interpreted, unlock our understanding of God. He is paradoxical but never inconsistent or incoherent. When we face the Bible's paradoxes without flinching, we find a better way to relate to the God who reveals himself to us *through* mystery and paradox. As Thomas Mann reminded us, the opposite of a great truth is also a great truth. A paradox is an interweaving of two great and opposite truths.

THE PROBLEM OF PARADOXES

A good place to begin our quest is to define the problem. Understanding paradox will help us clarify the most important questions and then discover a multitude of life-enriching answers.

A simple dictionary definition describes paradox as "a seemingly contradictory statement that may nonetheless be true."[3]

The first point to understand is that a paradox is true. The whole thing. It is a challenging, mysterious marriage between two apparently incompatible ideas. It's true, but it keeps screaming at us, "I'm false and contradictory!" The combination of a true core with a false appearance is the essence of paradox. Let's first eliminate some things that are not paradoxes.

There are statements that are true and seem true. These are not paradoxes. When the Bible tells us that all humans will die, it is not only true, it rings true with everything we see in the world. We don't like it, but we can't deny it.

Then there are statements that are false and seem false to most of us. These, too, are not paradoxes; they are simply lies. "Those who hold different beliefs should be converted by force"; "Nonwhites are a lower creation than whites"; "Jews, gypsies, and certain other groups should be eradicated." Throughout history, those who insist that such lies are true—such as the crusaders of the Middle Ages, slaveholders in antebellum America, and Hitler's Nazi regime—end up being trampled by the inescapable lunacy of their positions. When a sufficient number of right-thinking individuals wake up to the truth, the nightmare of the lie disappears.

The Bible reports falsehoods that are clearly false, such as the deception that was pulled off by Joseph's brothers after they sold him into slavery. When they returned home without their brother, they produced a blood-stained garment, leading their father, Jacob, to believe that his son had been killed by a wild animal.[4] Such accounts in Scripture show us the consequences of lies and deception.

Finally, as we consider what a paradox is not, there are statements that are false but seem true, such as "malaria and yellow fever are caused by bad vapors and gases in the air" (accepted as truth for centuries) or "things in the world are so bad these must *definitely* be the last days" (a recurring "certainty" through the millenniums, with many incidences of erroneous dates set for Christ's return). These are not paradoxes but falsehoods and illusions, which show that our perception of reality is often impaired, perhaps severely. They can even be fatal illusions, as tens of thousands discovered while helping to build the Panama Canal without taking precautions against the mosquito, even though scientific papers had long identified this insect as the carrier of malaria.[5]

For those who set dates for the return of Christ, claiming this is the worst the world has ever been, a simple review of the fourteenth century would put things into perspective. That was the era of the Black Death and other unstoppable plagues, recurring famines, brigands controlling the highways, widespread serfdom and slavery, the Hundred Years' War, and a church hierarchy so corrupt that many in positions of power weren't even Christian. The world today is in the worst shape it's ever been? Far from it.

Sadly, some statements that masquerade as truth are dressed up in a facade of religious language—such as the recurring date-setting for the return of Christ. But with or without religious language, such assertions are falsehoods, not paradoxes.

A paradox is something altogether different. It is a complex statement that is true—all of it, both sides, no matter how mismatched they might seem. But because the truth is so big, or because we are so little, it just *seems* false and contradictory.

If we are unwilling to stretch ourselves by engaging biblical paradox, we'll end up being tiny in our beliefs about God, and because of that, tiny in our influence for the kingdom of God. We will spend part of the time confused and the rest of the time searching for something that will explain away the paradox. This tendency, all too common in religious circles, leads many to adopt unhealthy and extreme positions. Whole churches have been formed to maintain a focus on only half a paradox. If we aren't willing to embrace paradox—not just dabble in it or accept its existence, but *embrace* it—we will miss the opportunity to build a big life out of a full-size faith in a colossal God.

REAL AND APPARENT CONTRADICTIONS

We can't go very far in our pursuit of paradox without talking about contradictions. And as we do so, we encounter two types of contradictions: real and apparent. A paradox is an *apparent* contradiction, since it only *seems* that one half of the statement must be false. Our rational minds prefer to believe the absolute, universal validity of "if A, then not B." For example, if an animal is a cow, then it can't also be a horse. When we encounter opposing ideas, we often assume they can't be brought into resolution. But if we cling to this assumption, we'll miss a big part of who God is and how he operates in our world.

Because paradoxes in Scripture present themselves as apparent contradictions, it's harder for us to see the truth that dwells there. The two sides of the paradox grate on our minds, and the friction causes so much discomfort that we turn away. Or perhaps worse, we take one of the strands firmly in our grasp and ignore the other. This is more comfortable than wrestling with paradox—and more deadly, since it leads to unbiblical extremes.

As humans, we seem to be designed to search for order and harmony. This can be both an asset and a liability. It's an asset if we patiently continue to seek the whole truth. It's a glaring liability if we gloss over passages that seem to conflict and stop when we have found only a part of the truth. We stop because we don't want to think that hard, or because we want to hang on to the comfort we have in our current belief system. When we stop short of embracing biblical paradox, we cheat ourselves out of a deeper relationship with God. God reveals himself through paradox in part to remind us that he is far above simple formulas of logic.

As we explore the Bible's paradoxes in the chapters that follow, we will draw on the following important ideas.

Real Contradictions Exist

We shouldn't confuse paradox with actual contradictions. To contradict means "to assert or express the opposite of [a statement]; to deny the statement of; to be contrary to; be inconsistent with."[6] A real contradiction presents two ideas in fundamental conflict—two opposing ideas that can't be brought into resolution. They simply clash. We can say, "God is just" or "God is unjust," but we can't say both with any credibility. God is either just or he is unjust, but he can't be both.

Hypocrisy is perhaps the most common form of real contradiction. If we say that we love animals but we treat them with cruelty, we are contradicting what we say by what we do. We cannot be holy and deliberately sinning at the same time. We can *act* holy while we are sinning, but this is hypocrisy.

While real contradictions are impossible to reconcile, paradoxes are merely difficult to reconcile.

Contradictions Aren't Mysteries

People have developed many real contradictions. These man-made contradictions often are presented as "mysteries" so they can be sold as the truth. In the most harmful variety, these contradictions merge Bible concepts with added bits and pieces for effect. Since a human-manufactured contradiction screams against our minds and our faith, those who invent it have to sell it as a mystery. "Relax," they soothe. "It's just bigger than you."

Here's an example. We're instructed in the Bible to testify about our faith in God, to evangelize by proclaiming the gospel so that people can hear the truth and believe. And we're told in the Bible that any who choose not to believe will also be choosing (automatically) a very tough afterlife apart from God. These are both true statements.

The contradiction that many have created out of these concepts is this: If we fail to evangelize a certain individual, it will be our fault if he or she goes to hell. The unbiblical contradiction? It's each person's responsibility to make the right choice regarding God, but somehow it's *our* responsibility if someone else happens to make the wrong choice.

This contradiction is often used to push people into supporting new ministry initiatives or giving more money to their churches. The contradiction of dual responsibility for a person's commitment to God can lead to great pride if we take credit for "leading others to Christ" and also to great guilt if we fail in this venture.

But how can anyone's eternal future depend on another frail human being? How could a just God send a lost soul to hell because a church member decided to sleep in on Saturday morning rather than going door-to-door in the neighborhood to distribute gospel tracts? A person's eternal fate is based on his or her own decisions about God, not on whether a certain Christian remembers to share the gospel on a certain day. If we won't proclaim the love of God, he will send someone else. If necessary, he'll intervene directly.[7]

We're responsible for our disobedience, but other people are responsible for their own souls. We're responsible if we fail to act on the prompting of the Holy Spirit to go to them with the gospel, but they're responsible if they choose not to come to God. We'll miss the blessing, but they will still have full opportunity to decide.

It is a human-made contradiction that says the burden of salvation is on each individual and somehow also on everyone else. There is no mystery involved; it's simply a guilt trip designed to strong-arm churchgoers into volunteering more time or getting behind the pastor's new church-growth strategy. God is certainly big enough to get his message out, even if many of his children are lazy about doing their part.[8]

Such religious contradictions can seem legitimate, but they are manufactured and false. When our minds are repelled by these concocted contradictions, we need to say, "This isn't a mystery. It's nonsense." These ideas aren't bigger than we are; they're dumber than we are.

The Bible Contains Apparent Contradictions

The text of Scripture does indeed include plenty of apparent contradictions. They deliver confusion to the listless and ammunition to the atheists. Some are so glaring and fierce that they practically demand we shun them. Let's face it: Some of these are hard. They can be frustrating. If we're not careful, they can even threaten to derail our faith.

The only answer is to stare them in the face. "We have the mind of Christ."[9] If we ask the Holy Spirit to show us the way, he will do it. I think, perhaps, that he will even enjoy it.

The Bible Has No Real Contradictions

Since the Holy Spirit cannot contradict himself, we can be confident that the Bible has no real contradictions. God is complicated but consistent. Coherence is there, but we have to look for it.

"The point of each part only becomes fully clear when seen in relation to the rest," wrote J. I. Packer. "[This means] not setting text against text or supposing apparent contradictions to be real ones, but seeking rather to let one passage throw light on another, in the certainty that there is in Scripture a perfect agreement between part and part, which careful study will be able to bring out."[10]

The key to interpreting biblical paradoxes is careful study. God's treasure chest isn't opened for anyone who won't take the time to find the key.

Biblical Paradoxes Strengthen Our Faith

Why are biblical paradoxes so unsettling? Is it because they are so bold in their seemingly conflicting assertions, threatening to cast doubt on the reliability of Scripture and of God himself? Or is it because we're afraid of what we might find—that some of these are not apparent contradictions after all, but *real* contradictions that show God to be an unstable deity who can't seem to make up his mind? Or, even more unsettling, will these paradoxes tell us something about God that we don't want to know? Perhaps we'll find that he is not truly a God of love and mercy. Or is it simply that we want things uncomplicated, easy to understand, and supportive of our own pet desires and prejudices?

Distressing or not, the many paradoxes in Scripture cannot be ignored if we are to be complete in our faith. If we don't examine and understand them, they will linger in the back of our minds, haunting our faith. "If a man wishes to avoid the disturbing effect of paradoxes," wrote Elton Trueblood, "the best advice is for him to leave the Christian faith alone."[11]

If we don't face the reasons that make us avoid paradoxes, we'll never have the clarity or the courage to examine them for the truth they hold.

Paradoxes Address Both Faith and Reason

Perhaps the main reason we struggle with paradox is in itself a paradox, namely the paradox of faith and reason. We may struggle because paradoxes seem so intellectually dense, and we want to be people of faith, not intellect. Or perhaps the opposite is true. We want to be thinking Christians, yet there is so much in paradoxes that must be taken in faith and simply believed.

But the two are not mutually exclusive. We don't study to take the place of faith, but rather to strengthen our faith. We want to know more so we can believe more. And we want to trust more, so we can question and verify more. This is not a faithless intellectual quest but a search for understanding that builds our faith. The Christian life requires both. We need to use and delight in both our faith and our reason.

Scripture teaches that faith is being "sure of what we hope for and certain of what we do not see."[12] These paradoxes are high walls. We can scale them, but only when we take faith in one hand and reason in the other.

WHY DOES GOD MAKE IT SO HARD?

Why isn't God more straightforward in his revelation? Why doesn't his Word follow a simple outline so that we all can easily understand it? Part of the answer may be a bit unsettling: We saw earlier that "it is the glory of God to conceal a matter; to search out a matter is the glory of kings."[13]

Our God is a God of mystery and intrigue. He loves to create mysteries for us to search out and enjoy. He hides things from us so that we can *find* them. And God's tendency to conceal things isn't just a periodic hobby. Concealing things is God's *glory.* There is good reason for him to reveal himself gradually:

He is so magnificent and extraordinary that if we discovered him in his fullness all at once it would probably stop our hearts.

Thankfully, God does make some things "plain" to us,[14] but it adds to his renown to cloak much of the truth.

Jesus drills this point home and then adds another twist:

The disciples came to him and asked, "Why do you speak to the people in parables?"

He replied, "The knowledge of the secrets of the kingdom of heaven has been given to you, but not to them.... This is why I speak to them in parables:

'Though seeing they do not see;
    though hearing they do not hear or understand.'

In them is fulfilled the prophecy of Isaiah:

'You will be ever hearing but never understanding;
    you will be ever seeing but never perceiving.
For this people's heart has become calloused;
    they hardly hear with their ears,
    and they have closed their eyes.
Otherwise they might see with their eyes,
    hear with their ears,
    understand with their hearts
and turn, and I would heal them.'"[15]

This is one incredible passage. What was Jesus really telling his disciples, and what is he telling us? That he uses parables to *conceal* the truth. He hides things in stories so that people will have to listen with their spirits and not just with their logic. And here's the frightening twist: He works very hard to keep the truth forever away from those who choose to be hard of hearing and hard of heart. If we don't want to hear it in the way he lays it out, we'll never hear it at all.

Children love stories, and they're crazy about mysteries. Parables are stories that often contain a mystery. When Jesus tells us that we have to become like little children, he doesn't just mean that we need childlike faith and innocence; he means that we need to come at life and truth like little children, looking for the "stories" and unraveling the mystery that lies inside them. We need a passion for the mystery.

Professor Howard Gardner, in his book *Leading Minds,* tells us that inside every adult is a child who loves to hear stories and responds to them in a way unlike anything else.[16] That's the spirit that we have to bring to the exploration of paradoxes in Scripture.

Saint Augustine, a leading theologian of the early church, speculated that God allows casual hearers to misunderstand him "to conquer pride by work and to combat disdain in our minds…. Those things which are easily discovered seem frequently to become worthless."[17] We value most the knowledge we must struggle to acquire.

And here is perhaps the most direct answer to why God doesn't put the truth in a simple outline form. It's because the truth isn't simple. God's magnificence and wisdom are infinite, so great that they can't be expressed in neat, snappy sound bites. If you want a simple, easy-to-explain god, then you'll have to look in books other than the Bible.

To be sure, a paradox is a mountain. But as someone has asked, is it greater to move molehills a mile or mountains an inch?

BLACK-AND-WHITE THINKING

One more issue we have to consider is the matter of being "black and white" in our thinking. That expression has been used as both a point of pride and as a point of condemnation. "She is absolutely black and white" can mean she has chosen her principles and firmly stands on them, or it can mean she is rigid and dogmatic and recognizes none of the complexities or ambiguities of life.

But let's take a different slant on this issue. Let's start with a few questions:

- Is Jesus God or man?
- Did Jews or Gentiles kill Jesus?
- Which part of Scripture, the Old or the New Testament, emphasizes the importance of God's law?
- Which part of Scripture, the Old or the New Testament, emphasizes the importance of salvation by faith in God's grace?

Take a moment to consider your answers.

The short but complicated answer to each of these questions is *both.* Jesus is both God and man. This is orthodox Christian doctrine. But the difficulty in understanding this teaching has driven many people to pick one over the other. Entire heresies and whole new religions have been built on one side or the other of this incarnational paradox.

As to the second question, Jews (Sadducees and Pharisees and teachers of the law) *and* Gentiles (Romans) killed Jesus. The Messiah didn't arrive in Judea until after the Gentiles did. God structured the event so that both "divisions" of humankind, both Jews and Gentiles, share responsibility. In fact, it was not only both of those groups that killed Jesus—it was you and I as well.

When it comes to teachings on law and grace, both Testaments of the Bible emphasize both teachings. We don't see the books of Scripture that were recorded prior to Jesus' ministry on earth stressing God's law and judgment alone, with Scripture that follows Jesus' years on earth introducing us to grace. Both parts of Scripture do both.[18]

As we examine biblical paradox, we find that God is both/and—both sides of the paradox are true. The alternative interpretation is either/or—the conviction that either this idea or that idea is true, but not both. This view does not leave us with half a truth; it leaves us with a lie. God is not just *or* loving. He is both just *and* loving. When studying this both/and nature of paradox, we discover not confusion but more truth than we had previously grasped.

What is often called black-and-white thinking is really black-*or*-white thinking. We are called to resist black-*or*-white thinking so we can embrace the paradox of true black-*and*-white thinking. We are called to take *both* sides of the truth and hang on for dear life.

Learning to think in black-and-white terms does not mean we settle for a neutral, meaningless gray or that we compromise our beliefs. It means we keep both sides of the paradox clearly in view, even as we try to find the new truth that resides in the middle—the via media, the middle way. We don't overlook the black, and we don't let go of the white, and because of that we end up with the whole black and the whole white—and something more as well. Holding both strands in balance to find the greater truth is the core principle of halakic reasoning.

As you explore major paradoxes in Scripture, you'll come to a much more practical faith. You will be able to relate to a God who is an actual person, like you in many ways, because he made you to be like him. Your prayer life will change, your confidence in your faith will grow, and your effectiveness for the kingdom will be magnified. You will become clearer on how to judge people and situations and how to deal with evil and those who do evil. You will run your race with greater purpose because you will have gone inside the core of reality. You will understand a whole lot more and wonder a whole lot less. As Helen Keller observed, life is either the greatest of adventures or it is nothing at all.

At the same time, you will almost certainly come to a loftier view of God. You will wonder a whole lot more, and, yes, you'll understand a whole lot less than you thought you did before. You'll see that God is more astounding, more transcendent, and more breathtaking than you ever imagined. You will be drawn into a more remarkable sense of mystery as you discover that "the supreme paradox of all thought is the attempt to discover something that thought cannot think."[19]

OUR DESTINATION

The Bible can sometimes come across as a choir that has no harmony. We hear all the voices, but they don't mesh. We try to follow the score, but it seems to wander and circle around. It exasperates us.

When we face the troubling paradoxes of Scripture, we can take the easy route of focusing on one of the two sides and ignoring the other. We can pursue this course by selective Bible reading and choosing books that support what we already believe. We can try to reduce God to manageable size and pretend that there is no mystery left, that God is fully explainable.

Or we can take paradox for what it is, a collection of interlocking pieces of a celestial puzzle. We can spend the rest of our lives striving to learn and know and grow, and never get all the way there. But think how much deeper our faith will grow as a result of the journey! This is the only choice that gives us deep hope and clear direction.

Paradoxes are inherent in the nature of God and in the world he has created. They can, at some very deep level, be understood. But at the same time, they are so complex and astounding that we can never fully explain them. So let's start asking different types of questions about God—questions that will lead to a new type of answer, a both/and answer. This is the answer that doesn't settle all debates, but it does reveal how the pieces of the puzzle could fit together.

As you struggle with the paradoxes of Scripture, find one that hits you where you are right now, and go after it—fearlessly. In our study together, we will discover together that God is understandable, beyond our wildest hopes. We will also discover that God is stunningly unfathomable, beyond our wildest dreams.

FOR FURTHER THOUGHT AND DISCUSSION

1. What do you think God is trying to get across to us with the paradox found in Proverbs about answering and not answering fools?

2. How would you define a paradox? How is it different from a contradiction?

3. How do you feel about the idea of God concealing truth? Does it frustrate you and make you angry, or does it capture your interest and fire your curiosity? Why?

4. What do you think about the need for true black-*and*-white thinking? Where do you stand on the issue of the both/and approach to paradox?

Two

The Spiritual Pursuit
of the Both/And

How to Grab on to Both Sides of a Paradox

Christianity got over the difficulty of combining furious opposites by keeping them both, and keeping them both furious.

G. K. Chesterton

Now, there are two very decided and distinct sides to this subject, and, like all other subjects, it cannot be fully understood unless both of these sides are kept constantly in view.

Hannah Whitall Smith

Jon and Andy are good friends, but yesterday a simple discussion about the Bible suddenly turned into a heated debate over whether the Scriptures are accurate or just a jumble of myths and mistakes.

"The Bible is full of contradictions," Andy charged. "I've heard all kinds of explanations about why God said one thing in the Old Testament and then changed his story in the New Testament. The truth is that you Christians want to believe the Bible is true, so you rationalize it in any way you can. But I just can't buy it. If God was really behind this thing, he'd figure out a way to keep his story straight."

Jon did his best to argue for the reliability of the Bible, but a day later his friend's comments are still eating at him. The more he thinks about it, the more he fears that the Bible really is shot through with contradictions. Christ tells his followers to love their enemies, but God commands David to wipe them out. And then there are all the differences among Christian denominations. If the Bible has a clear, consistent message, why do different churches teach so many conflicting beliefs?

Finally, he decides to pray. *Lord, I know there's an answer, because I don't believe that you would really contradict yourself. But what's the answer, and where do I find it?*

We live in a mostly both/and world. Many of the great discoveries of science have been made by people who refused to accept a cut-and-dried explanation for reality. Writer Alan Lightman has observed that "like the great Danish theorist Neils Bohr, Einstein loved to provoke his imagination with…paradoxes."[1]

If a relationship with God doesn't provoke our imagination, what could? The rabbis, going back thousands of years, recognized the importance of paradoxes in understanding God's nature and his work in the world. In fact, they developed the approach of halakic reasoning to find the truth that is hidden in biblical paradoxes. This method of biblical interpretation rejects the premise that the Bible primarily presents an either/or view of life. Instead, the rabbinical tradition of halakic thinking helps us understand the spiritual reality of both/and, where we see compatibility and connection instead of conflict and confusion.

There are, of course, some either/or truths in the Bible. "You cannot serve both God and Money" would be a clear example of this.[2] In other words, you serve one master only, either God or material wealth. But Scripture does not contain nearly as many A or B choices as we might believe.

PRACTICING HALAKIC REASONING

Paradoxes are evident throughout the Bible, and the halakic approach to understanding Scripture opens our eyes and our hearts to the challenging, life-changing truth found in these paradoxes. Halakic reasoning is "the juxtaposition of two apparently contradictory statements from Scripture in order to draw a...conclusion regarding regulations for conduct."[3] While exploring the mystery and majesty of God, we learn whole new ways of thinking and acting and living. The process opens up endless possibilities of discovery, conclusion, revision, and expansion of our earlier ideas.

In this book, we'll look at ten of the Bible's most troublesome paradoxes. We're going to confront them head-on, and we're going to explore them in their full, confounding glory. We will embrace these apparent contradictions and come out with a deeper faith and a more complete understanding of God.

Using the rabbinical principle of halakic reasoning and interpretation, we'll see that in every biblical paradox *both* strands of the apparent contradiction are true. We'll also discover how the two strands complement, reinforce, and enhance each other. We'll see that without its opposing force, one of the strands alone would obscure the full truth about God and his work. The failure to incorporate halakic thought in some form will lead to one-sided, imbalanced teaching—and to one-sided, imbalanced Christians and churches.

As we look at the ten paradoxes in the following chapters, we'll learn to use the tools that mine the treasure of Scripture. Once you have practiced halakic reasoning, not only will your own faith be strengthened, but you will be prepared to answer those who denigrate the Bible because it is "full of contradictions." Your joyful answer will be, "I know exactly what you're saying. I have some personal favorites, and I'm wondering which ones have caught your attention."

THE LESSONS OF HALAKICS

Although Jesus' use of halakic reasoning will be our model, this approach has been used by teachers through the centuries. In fact, great leaders in every field have come to see the power of halakic reasoning, even if they didn't know what it was called.

Science

Neils Bohr, the theoretical physicist referred to earlier, built his whole scientific method around the halakic principle, which he called *complementarity*. Is light a wave or a particle? Bohr answered yes.

Richard Rhodes writes, "The solution, Bohr went on, is to accept the different and mutually exclusive results as equally valid and stand them side by side to build up a composite picture of the atomic domain. *Nur die Fülle führt zur Klarheit:* only wholeness leads to clarity."[4] Halakic reasoning, like complementarity, is founded on the concept that only wholeness leads to clarity.

Statesmanship

Winston Churchill, whom many consider the greatest political leader of the twentieth century, constantly thought in halakic terms. Was he for war, or was he for peace? The answer is yes.

"There was 'no contradiction,' Churchill said, between the policy of building up the [defensive] strength of the free world against 'potential armed Soviet aggression' and trying at the same time 'to create conditions under which Russia may dwell easily and peacefully side by side with us all,' " the British leader's biographer observed. "His appeal ended: 'Peace is our aim, and strength is the only way of getting it.... Indeed, it is only by having it both ways at once that we shall have a chance of getting anything at all.' "[5]

In this book, we will be operating on Churchill's principle that only by having both sides at once will we have any chance of getting anything at all. That is the halakic principle.

Philosophy

It's difficult to imagine meaningful philosophical discourse without the existence of apparent contradictions and the attempt to reconcile them. Are human beings mortal or immortal? The answer, of course, is yes.

"Serious things cannot be understood without laughable things," wrote Plato, "nor opposites at all without opposites."[6] Indeed, he taught that only by exploring opposites could we hope to find truth in synthesis.

If we understand only one side of a paradox, we don't really understand anything.

THREE BIBLICAL PARADOXES

Now that we understand something about paradox, both in Scripture and in human endeavors, let's apply halakic reasoning to three confounding paradoxes found in the Bible. These examples will demonstrate the application of the halakic approach.

Answer and Don't Answer Fools

A good place to start is the book of Proverbs, where we find in consecutive verses an obvious contradiction—or is it? Earlier, we looked at the following confusing advice:

> When arguing with fools, don't answer their foolish arguments, or
> you will become as foolish as they are.
>   When arguing with fools, be sure to answer their foolish arguments, or they will become wise in their own estimation.[7]

Let's restate this in the form of a halakic argument: We're commanded not to answer fools. We're commanded to answer fools. How can we *avoid* answering fools when God insists that we answer them? Conversely, how can we be careful to answer fools when we are commanded *not* to answer them?

On one side of this paradox, if we ignore the clear instruction against answering the foolish arguments of a fool, we'll end up becoming as foolish as the fool himself.[8] This resonates with our experience. No matter what we say in response to fools, they can come up with an unending supply of further stupid arguments, each of which moves us to frustration, anger, and the temptation to respond with our own illogical responses.

On the other side, we are clearly told to answer the foolish arguments of fools. The result of ignoring this directive is that the fools end up becoming wise in their estimate of themselves.[9] Again, this resonates with our experience. If we sit silently and let fools spew their nonsense, they will see our silence as affirmation of their arguments, or at least as an indication that we are unable to come up with anything to counter their foolishness.

So what do we do? We can't answer, but we must answer. This confounding paradox forces us into unfamiliar and uncomfortable territory.

Possible Answers

At least one possible answer is this: We must answer fools at some minimum level to keep them from becoming wise in their own estimation, but we must stop answering them long before we've been sucked into their web of foolishness. So it is in part a matter of degree—we will offer something but not too much, enough to stop them but not so much that it turns us into fools. Perhaps we can see that the best solution is also a matter of timing.

But there is another possible answer. Perhaps it's important *how* we answer the fool. We have to answer with words and tone and body language that prevent him from becoming brilliant in his own eyes, while at the same time we don't answer in a way that makes us as foolish as he is. We see that a response of "That's dumb" (even if it is) will move us into the fool's realm. The fool simply responds, "Well *you're* dumb!" and on it goes. However, we also see that a response of "I see what you're saying" will only confirm the fool in his absurd opinions.

So we choose our words with great care. Perhaps the fool says, "There's no use trying to persuade me. I know I'm right, and anybody who thinks differently is just being hardheaded." We respond with a brief comment that changes the nature of the conversation and takes the focus off the fool: "Erasmus would have had an interesting twist on that statement" or "What effect did that attitude have in the Thirty Years' War?"

Another possible conclusion to this paradox is that we shouldn't answer with words at all, so we can make sure we don't end up looking like the fool. Maybe our answer should be in facial expressions and body language so the fool and others can see that we don't agree, but they have no words from us that they can then attack. "In any answer the wise man gives he must protect his own interest against the fool."[10]

And maybe there's more. Think about the *purpose* of answering. To obey the double command in Proverbs 26, we will always avoid answering a fool in an attempt to win an argument, because there's no way to win. If it's a question of who's right or who knows more or who can debate the best, we bite our tongues. But we will *always* answer a fool to keep him from becoming a genius in his own mind. If it's a question of a fool playing God or influencing immature believers or confusing honest seekers, then we answer with both barrels blazing.

And even then, we don't provoke the fool to unnecessary argument. We don't say, "Here are five reasons why you are wrong," but rather, "Are you aware of the five arguments theologians have put forward that dispute your ideas?" or "How does your position align with the teachings of the early church fathers?" We try to expose the foolishness, which is a necessity according to our second proverb.

These are just a few of the possible halakic conclusions to be drawn from this apparent contradiction. Imagine what we could do if we were to line up all of the verses in the Bible on both sides of this paradox! We could fill several more pages with our halakic conclusions.

David's Son Is Also His Lord

Here's another example of halakic argumentation, a paradox that Jesus introduced to a group of Pharisees:

> While the Pharisees were gathered together, Jesus asked them, "What do you think about the Christ? Whose son is he?"
>
> "The Son of David," they replied.
>
> He said to them, "How is it then that David, speaking by the Spirit, calls him 'Lord'? For he says,

'The Lord said to my Lord:
    "Sit at my right hand
until I put your enemies
    under your feet." '

If then David calls him 'Lord,' how can he be his son?" No one
could say a word in reply, and from that day on no one dared to ask
him any more questions.[11]

The large crowd listened to him with delight.[12]

What was Jesus up to as he asked these questions? He was trying to get his
listeners—both the well-educated and the uneducated—to think outside the
box. It was a box that they, not God, had constructed. He was using the rabbinical principle of halakic argument to get them to face up to the apparent
contradiction of certain biblical passages that they should have known well. He
was pointing out that the Pharisees' way of looking at and interpreting the Bible
was one-sided and incomplete. Their approach could not explain the Bible's
fullness.

The Messiah, the Anointed One, is the Son of David. That part is true and
Jesus didn't dispute it. But David called this coming King *Lord*. This part is also
true, and it's also from the Bible. These two true and apparently contradictory
ideas were framed by Jesus in a halakic argument or question. In essence, he
said to the Pharisees: "The Christ is David's son, and yet David calls the Christ
Lord." Now the halakic question: "If David calls him 'Lord,' how can he be
his son?"

There were two reactions to this halakic question. Although the Pharisees—
the Bible scholars—were stunned into silence, the crowd, made up of simple
people who had no "investment" in the Pharisees' model but who loved stories
and mysteries and word plays, got it and enjoyed it thoroughly. Jesus was having great fun with the complexity of the Bible by showing them that it cannot
to be reduced to formulas.

Possible Answers

For the listeners, this meant that David and Jesus are two ends of an ancestral paradox. David was truly the "father" of Jesus, and Jesus did not deny being the "Son of David." But Jesus was saying that the Son is greater than the father, deserves homage from the father, and holds the father's fate in his hands. He was also saying that if David, the greatest king of Israel, can call the Messiah "Lord," it should not be beneath the Pharisees to do the same. Most of the listeners— Pharisee or peasant—had probably never thought about this astounding loop before Jesus asked his question. That is the power of halakic reasoning.

The Sabbath Day Debate

Here is one more example of halakic reasoning that was applied by Jesus:

> At that time Jesus went through the grainfields on the Sabbath. His disciples were hungry and began to pick some heads of grain and eat them. When the Pharisees saw this, they said to him, "Look! Your disciples are doing what is unlawful on the Sabbath."
>
> He answered, "Haven't you heard what David did when he and his companions were hungry? He entered the house of God, and he and his companions ate the consecrated bread—which was not lawful for them to do, but only for the priests. Or haven't you read in the Law that on the Sabbath the priests in the temple desecrate the day and yet are innocent? I tell you that one greater than the temple is here. If you had known what these words mean, 'I desire mercy, not sacrifice,' you would not have condemned the innocent. For the Son of Man is Lord of the Sabbath."[13]

Religious leaders were scrutinizing and criticizing Jesus' disciples. However, the disciples' only "offense" was picking some grain and eating it because they were hungry. But this was no minor offense to the Pharisees, who believed nothing should be done on the Sabbath (except, evidently, condemning others).

We have another apparent contradiction: You can't violate the Sabbath, and it's all right to violate the Sabbath. To state this as a halakic argument: We are told to keep the Sabbath holy. We are told that we can violate the Sabbath. How can the Sabbath be kept holy if it is all right for us to violate the Sabbath?

In answer, Jesus launched into a biblical story about David going into the temple and eating the holy, dedicated "showbread." The parallels were undeniable, and many of the Pharisees must have seen it: David and his friends, and Jesus and his friends, were hungry and took action—eating—that was apparently unlawful.

Possible Answers

What point was Jesus making about the consecrated bread? Perhaps that it was not as holy as a human being. That it was actually there to nourish people. That very soon he would make a new statement about another type of consecrated bread: "This is my body given for you."[14] "Take and eat; this is my body."[15] There is a thread that runs from the consecrated bread in the temple, through the heads of grain, to Christian communion—eating the Bread of Life.

Jesus followed this up with another example of the paradox, where he pointed out that the priests had to "desecrate the day" to do their work on the Sabbath, but they were still innocent. His point was clear: His disciples may have been "desecrating the day," but it was to do God's work, and they, too, were innocent.

What does his commentary on the priests and the temple service prove? Perhaps that the priests with their rituals were not there to be served but rather to serve the people. That the real hierarchy is the priests serving the people.[16] That service to people is more important than rules.

He didn't stop there. "While I'm on the subject of the temple," he seems to have been saying, "let me tell you that I am greater than the temple. The priests, like my disciples, are serving me." He was telling his listeners that "the Son of Man is Lord even of the Sabbath,"[17] so to serve him on the Sabbath is to keep the Sabbath.

He was so strong on this upside-down kingdom idea that he told them they had missed the whole point of a passage in the Prophets: "I desire mercy, not sacrifice."[18] The temple was all about sacrifice—thousands of animals were slaughtered there every year. But the point of the sacrifice was to show openness to God's mercy. Sacrifice is merely a means to God's desired end: mercy.

In a verse included in one of the other gospels, Jesus gave one of the halakic conclusions: "The Sabbath was made for man, not man for the Sabbath."[19] The Sabbath isn't some god or idol to be slavishly followed, and it's not a burden to be carried. The Sabbath is a tool to help people live successful and satisfying lives. Even more than a tool, the Sabbath is a gift. Everyone needs rest.

Jesus' comments give food for thought to those who would make up rules and regulations for the Sabbath, for how people should rest and meditate and do good.

THE HALAKIC APPROACH

What did Jesus demonstrate in his discussion with the Pharisees? He showed that Scripture interprets Scripture, and that one passage can and does modify others. We can't fully understand the Bible if we separate one part from another, especially if we separate apparently opposite parts. If we don't embrace both parts and find the whole God, in effect we've created our own god.

Halakic reasoning is not about averaging things out or seeking a compromise. It's about finding a greater truth in the tension of two opposites. In the chapters that follow, we will not attempt to soften either side of a paradox. We want each side to shout its unyielding truth.

Halakic reasoning requires extra work and careful thinking. The good news is that you don't need an advanced degree or an advanced brain to advance in understanding. "Highly creative people don't necessarily excel in raw brainpower," wrote author G. Paschal Zachary. "They tend to question accepted views and to consider contradictory ones."[20] If you are willing to question accepted views and consider contradictory ones, you are ready to use halakic reasoning.

Let's look briefly at what halakic reasoning will require:

Committing

You need to be willing to spend some time with this. Make this study your companion for the next few months. Committing means you'll have to do a bit of work to think and to challenge your own assumptions.

Digging

You can't do halakic reasoning without some raw material. That means you have to know the Scriptures that strongly support each side of a paradox. I know you'll think of other verses that address or shed additional light on specific paradoxes. Jot them in the margin. Don't let them get away. This can be great fun to do with a friend or a study group.

Extracting

It really is useful to know what scriptures mean. If you see a verse used in this book to support one side or the other in a paradox, and you don't see the connection right away, don't just throw it out. We have to be careful not to delete too quickly. Try to see what it really means and why it was included. For example, "the wild and often contradictory poetry of the *Psalms* is still mostly censored out of Christian worship."[21] We have to be inclusive, not exclusive.

Wrestling

We have to wrestle with these paradoxes. Sometimes, for example, we might find that the halakic conclusion is a matter of timing. In other words, it is a both/and but only shows evidence of that over time. Should we weep over sins or rejoice over our forgiveness? Yes. The weeping has to come first to make room for the rejoicing. There is no "cheap" repentance that comes without sadness, just as there is no "cheap" forgiveness that comes without happiness.

Ecclesiastes tells us, "There is a time for everything, and a season for every activity under heaven."[22] Sometimes, to understand halakic reasoning, we need to know there is a season for each of the two sides. With that understanding, we can look for the intended time for one activity and then the time for the other. Wrestling with paradox means you'll have to do a bit of analysis.

Blending

We will face the paradox at its extremes. We won't avoid these extremes but will rather embrace them and merge them. It is in the merging that the power of the extremes is used to build up our faith rather than destroy it.

Halakic reasoning is a meditative approach. I offer some halakic conclusions in this book, but your own contemplation will allow you to see more. The approach offered in this book—facing paradoxes squarely and fully and then finding the truths in the tension—is guaranteed to trigger thought and expand your sense of God. Go back and forth between the two sides, over and over, and mine each paradox for the halakic conclusions that are buried there.

THE PARTS OF A HALAKIC ARGUMENT

Halakic arguments are always made up of the same components, which include:

- *a truth.* We lay out a biblical truth as fully as we can. We make a list of every Scripture that seems to support that core truth.
- *an opposing truth.* We lay out another truth that is the apparent opposite of the first truth. Again, we make a list of all the Scriptures that lend weight to that core truth.
- *a purpose.* We commit to fully facing and understanding each truth and its ramifications. It can be helpful to ask, "Do I have any preconceived notions about either of these truths? Do I have any built-in opposition to changing my perspective?"
- *a willingness.* We choose to press the two truths against each other as hard as we can. We ask, "How can this verse be true if this other verse is also true?" and "Doesn't this verse seem to cancel out that one?" Earlier we asked the question, Is light a particle or a wave? One historian has observed that "humanity would continue to vacillate [on this question] until twentieth-century physicists vanquished the paradox by accepting it."[23] We have to go far enough to vanquish the fear in a paradox by accepting it.
- *a tension.* We look for the tension, and *rejoice* in the tension, between the two sides of the paradox. We want to leverage each side against the other. The practical way to focus this step is to frame the tension as a halakic argument or question.

- *a set of possible answers.* We answer the question as fully as we can to drain the halakic of as much of the new, fresh truth as possible. We go back and forth between the two lists, since we are sure that out of the interplay of the both/and truths we will get more truth. Throughout human history, new concepts have generally been grasped by picking up on the very deep but surprising connections that grow together out of two very different fields of thought. It's not just both/and; it's both/and *plus.* We see both sides fully plus the offspring that grows out of their union. We go beyond picking a side to marrying the sides.

THE FORMAT OF THE HALAKIC ARGUMENT

We will use the same format in each chapter, incorporating the halakic reasoning discussed previously. A consistent format will create a mental pattern that will help us when we are faced with other paradoxes. The format looks like this:

1. We will present the halakic question.
2. We will discuss some of the problems caused by the paradox, especially focusing on those that arise from adhering to one side over the other.
3. We will look at a significant number of verses that support the first side and then the second side of the halakic question. At this point, we will have the entire, seemingly contradictory matter on the table.
4. We will study the halakic question to discern a number of deeper both/and truths.

Will we get it all? Not likely. But using halakic reasoning to make paradox more understandable will produce growth in insight and knowledge, a difference in kind and not just in degree.

Take just a moment to picture for yourself what we will be doing. Put your arms straight out in front of you. Raise one and lower the other—this is the imbalance of favoring one side over the other. Now reverse their positions, and you can sense the swing to opposites that is so easy to do. Now level them again. Form two fists—this represents your embracing of each of the two sides of the paradox.

Then crash your fists together and open your fists upward, intermingling your fingers—that is the halakic, to merge the two and see what grows. Balance, embrace, collide, observe—the solution to paradox.

WHERE THIS LEAVES US

We are about to embark on a journey through ten of the Bible's major paradoxes. This will fall far short of exhausting the list, but it should give you the tools to face the challenge of other paradoxes as you come upon them. (For a longer list of tantalizing paradoxes to study, see chapter 13.) We will see that, when we come to the fork in each road, we can take both paths.

The great American educator Louis Agassiz believed that "what the student needed above all was the chance to learn to think for himself. So he ought to pursue the line of investigation that interested him most."[24] As you consider the paradoxes in the ten chapters that follow, feel free to read them in the order that interests you most. As you read, think for yourself. Think of other verses that apply on either side of each paradox. Listen to the Holy Spirit. Pray the prayer of the psalmist, "Open my eyes that I may see wonderful things in your law."[25] Draw your own halakic conclusions, even if just tentatively.

And as you dive into paradox, get ready to encounter a God who is greater and more wonderful than you ever imagined.

FOR FURTHER THOUGHT AND DISCUSSION

1. How would you describe halakic argumentation? What do you think about applying this approach to paradoxes in the Bible?
2. As you review the parts of halakic arguments, which do you think will be the most challenging for you? Why? What will you do to meet this challenge?
3. Review the ten paradoxes in the table of contents (chapters 3-12). Which are the most interesting for you? What appeals to you about these? Why?

PART II

Ten Paradoxes
That Enrich Our
FAITH

Three

The All-Knowing God
Who Forgets

WHY THIS PARADOX IS ESSENTIAL TO OUR FORGIVENESS

The LORD has sworn by the Pride of Jacob: "I will never forget anything they have done."

AMOS 8:7

For I will forgive their wickedness and will remember their sins no more.

JEREMIAH 31:34

Try to put yourself in this scenario: A coworker, who for the past few weeks has been asking questions about God, pulls you aside with a distressed look on her face.

"I've been thinking about what you said the other day—that God knows everything that I've done and that he loves me anyway," she says. "It's a nice idea, but I've lived a really wild life, and I don't see how God could just forgive me for it. It seems like he'd hold it against me or at least expect me to do something big in return."

"But that's the best part. He doesn't require you to fix things before he'll forgive you," you tell your colleague. "In fact, once he forgives you, he doesn't even remember what you did."

"But I thought you said he knows everything. How can he know everything and forget all the things I've done? That doesn't make any sense."

She makes a good point. How do you answer this one?

"Well," you begin, "maybe we're not meant to understand it. We just need to accept it."

"I see," she says, with a puzzled look. Then, as she walks away, it sounds like she mumbles something like, "I don't understand this stuff at all…"

The woman asking these questions isn't the only person who's confused about God and his ways. How can any of us explain the all-knowing nature of God in light of his love and forgiveness?

One of the great struggles of human relationships is to forgive and then really forget. Forgiving can be extraordinarily difficult, as we all know. But it can seem like a child's game compared with the monumental challenge of forgetting. Now think about this dynamic as it applies to God. He is omniscient; he knows everything that can be known: past, present, and future. So how can it be possible for him to forget anything—much less human sin, which is an affront to everything he stands for?

God's omniscience raises other big questions. For instance, if he can look into the future and see every instance of every person on the planet doing evil things, why doesn't he stop them? If he knows in advance that one of us is about to make a really foolish decision, why doesn't he step in and wave a red flag? And perhaps most critical to our relationship with him, if he always knows about all the evil we have ever done and ever will do, how can he have an intimate connection with us? He is holy and all-knowing; we are sinful and chronically limited. How can God avoid being disgusted with his miserable children whenever we try to talk to him?

These questions lead to one of the most powerful and freeing of all the paradoxes of the Bible: Our all-knowing God also forgets.

Always Remembering and Sometimes Forgetting

God says that he knows all things. He also tells us that he forgets or that in some cases he doesn't know. How can God be all-knowing and still not know, or forget, what he once knew? This isn't some play on words. The Bible tells us that both sides of this paradox are true! God knows all things. And God forgets or sometimes does not know.

Since our relationship with God is crucial to our well-being, this paradox has serious ramifications. Does he really know everything before it happens? If so, how can he ever have a real relationship, one that's full of give-and-take, with people like us? And does he really remember everything we ever did, no matter how small and no matter how bad it was? If so, how can we ever approach him with freedom and confidence?[1] He's perfect, and we're full of sin.

On the other hand, is it possible that there are some things that God really *doesn't* know ahead of time? If so, how can we experience any safety or security if the future is random, if even God will be surprised by it? And if God really can forget what he once knew, might he forget to love us or to render justice to the guilty?

We have a problem no matter which side we cling to. The either/or approach to this paradox leaves us with a bad choice and a big hole in our relationship with God. This is not just theological hairsplitting. Understanding this paradox is crucial to having a full relationship with God.

Let's look at the either/or choice that seems to confront us and consider the results. What are we left with if we cling to just one side of this paradox?

God Knows All Things

If we pick side A and say simply that God knows all things (the traditional doctrine of *omniscience*[2]), we could end up with catastrophic results. Every time we meet with God now, or every time we see him in heaven (and eternity is a very long time), we'll be aware that he still knows all the horrible details about the rotten lives we've led. It's hard to see how a holy God wouldn't be offended every time he thinks about these sins, and it's even harder to see how he would want us to hang around with him. Such a state of all-knowing would spoil our relationship with him.

But there is more. This "knowing all things" side of the paradox would mean that we could never elicit an emotional response from God, because he already knows everything in advance. An omniscient God simply couldn't be surprised and made happy by us, or frustrated and made angry by us. According to this view, any "emotions" attributed to God in the Bible are mere anthropomorphisms (which means we are trying to understand or describe God by attributing human descriptors to him). But, according to this view, these descriptors don't apply. He already knew what we were going to do and, as a result, can't feel emotions based on our decisions or actions.

This view is actually less than an anthropomorphism. Instead of saying that God is like us, we are saying God isn't like us, that he is *less* than us. We can choose to forget things and be surprised or delighted or disappointed by how things turn out. But not God. By exercising the simple human ability to forget things, we believe we can do something that God just can't do.

Even more sadly, this view crushes any true relationship we would hope to have with God. Since relationships involve a two-way dynamic, with give and take, action and reaction, we can't be involved in a real relationship with God. But how can this be, since he loves us and claims to be our best Friend? In a real relationship, one party initiates, the other reacts, the first one responds, and on it goes. How do we do this with a Being who already knows everything we will say or do and therefore feels no emotion in response to our words and behavior?

At the end of this path, God becomes a victim of his all-knowing nature. He doesn't want to think about certain things, but he can't help himself. He's omniscient, so he *has* to know these things. What else can he do?

God Is Able to Forget

We might suspect that clinging to the other side of the paradox will satisfy our concerns. But, in fact, we don't do any better if we pick side B and say simply that God forgets or doesn't know some things. If we adopt this view, we end up picturing God as a kindly old grandfather. He's doing the best he can, but he can't really stay on top of everything. We can imagine that God is a "boys will be boys" kind of God who is blissfully unaware of all the harm that people are doing to themselves and to one another.

Or we might land on another false conclusion. We can believe that God forgives by forgetting, as we are often told to "forgive and forget" when others offend us, even if the offender doesn't repent. Many people believe God is like this, forgetting and overlooking, simply loving everyone and taking everyone (or at least most people) to heaven as he practices "unconditional love."[3]

This idea can color our own behavior toward others. We can condition ourselves to "forgive" someone without first remembering the offense, confronting the sinner, and clearing the air. We can overlook the truth that forgiveness is a transaction rather than a unilateral decision, a relational rather than a solitary act.[4]

Perhaps worst of all, we can convince ourselves that God won't make us face the consequences of our actions. He won't make us reap what we sow, even though Scripture makes that principle clear.[5] God is just way too nice for that. Come to think of it, this God is just like us, lacking the backbone to confront us and hold us accountable for our misdeeds.

What Scripture Says

Since our initial foray into option A or B hasn't gained us much beyond additional confusion, let's examine several passages from the Bible on each side of this paradox. We'll find that each option is fully supported by the Bible.

The God Who Knows All Things

The Bible is relentless in presenting God as a Being with vast knowledge that is far beyond anything we can even imagine. We are told, simply, "the LORD is a God who knows."[6] And he has always known what he was going to do, because he's the one "who does these things that have been known for ages."[7] What we see happening now has been known by God since eternity. God never asks himself, as we ask ourselves, "Now why did I do that?"

And it's not just knowing; it's also understanding. God totally understands what he fully knows. We are told in absolute terms that "his understanding has no limit."[8] He never has to wrestle with trying to figure anything out, including the thorniest paradoxes. He is the ultimate storehouse of knowledge, because in him "are hidden all the treasures of wisdom and knowledge."[9]

Just to emphasize the transcendence of what God knows, we find that no one can teach him anything. "Who has understood the mind of the LORD," asks the prophet Isaiah, "or instructed him as his counselor? Whom did the LORD consult to enlighten him, and who taught him the right way? Who was it that taught him knowledge or showed him the path of understanding?"[10] The obvious answer is "no one!" God isn't the receiver of knowledge—he is the *source* of it.

There is no escaping God's irresistible ability to know. The psalmist asks, "Would not God have discovered it, since he knows the secrets of the heart?"[11] In the purest sense of the words, there are no secrets since God truly is all-knowing.

Why can't we escape his knowledge? Because he wants to know us and he has the way to know, "for the LORD searches every heart and understands every motive behind the thoughts."[12] Not just our thoughts, but even the *motives* behind our thoughts. Much of the time, we don't know the real motives behind our own thoughts. And trying to hide anything is useless. "'Can anyone hide in secret places so that I cannot see him?' declares the LORD. 'Do not I fill heaven and earth?' declares the LORD."[13] Wherever we go, he's already there.

And God is really good at seeing us both in our glory and our shame. He can see our entire past, our complete present, and our whole future—before any of it happens. "O LORD, you have searched me and you know me. You know when I sit and when I rise; you perceive my thoughts from afar. You discern my going out and my lying down; you are familiar with all my ways. *Before* a word is on my tongue you know it completely, O LORD."[14] We can give up trying to have a truly private life, since "a man's ways are in full view of the LORD, and he examines all his paths."[15] In the school of life, this is the most serious final exam.

And there's more. God knows a whole lot more than we can even imagine. "His understanding no one can fathom."[16] We'll never know what God knows. We'll never even know *how much* God knows. He tells us about some of what he comprehends—"He reveals deep and hidden things; he knows what lies in darkness, and light dwells with him"[17]—and that is the *only* reason we can know these things.

We read as well that Jesus holds all of God's knowledge. He tells us: "All things have been committed to me by my Father."[18] To the closest followers of Jesus this was evident. "Now we can see that you know all things," they said.[19]

We wish it weren't so, but God knows all the wrongdoing in our lives, no matter how hard we try to hide it. "You have set our iniquities before you, our secret sins in the light of your presence."[20] The psalmist prays, "Forgive my *hidden* faults."[21] Since God knows much more about us than we can ever know about ourselves, we find that it's important to confess even the sins we have committed unintentionally and unknowingly.

Since we either don't believe that God is all-knowing, or we prefer to ignore it, we often attempt to hide our sins. That's a mistake. "Woe to those who go to great depths to hide their plans from the LORD, who do their work in darkness and think, 'Who sees us? Who will know?'"[22] Our illusion that God doesn't see is a pathetic display of our own ignorance and arrogance.

He knows the details, the quantity, and the quality of our sins. "For I know how many are your offenses and how great your sins."[23] He doesn't miss anything: "*Everything* is uncovered and laid bare before the eyes of him to whom we must give account."[24] And what God knows, he doesn't forget. "The LORD has sworn by the Pride of Jacob: 'I will *never* forget anything they have done.'"[25] Never, like eternity, is a very long time.

Jesus really makes us squirm on this point. "I tell you, on the day of judgment people will render an account for every careless word they speak."[26] We can't erase anything, "For God is greater than our hearts, and he knows everything."[27] We are told, in a simple and terrifying summary, that "God will remember their wickedness.[28]

The bottom line? It's a clear truth of the Bible, a truth that led to the creation of the doctrine of omniscience, that God has no external limitations on his knowledge. If it happened, it didn't slip past him. If it is going to happen, it's already on his radar screen. And as we'll see again in chapter 5, the paradox of the changeless God who changes, God is not a Being who is limited (as we are) by internally crippling limitations.

There is nothing outside him or within him that prevents him from knowing. We can be sure that God *knows*.[29]

The God Who Forgets Some Things

The Bible is just as relentless in presenting God as a Being who has an amazing ability to forget what he once knew. And he can also choose not to know about things that offend him.

This forgetting aspect of God contains some really good news for us. We are told, "God has even forgotten some of your sin."[30]

But it gets better. God tells us, magnanimously, "I, even I, am he who blots out your transgressions, for my own sake, and remembers your sins no more."[31] He put his finger on the delete key, and those transgressions are gone. And if not for us, at least for himself he chooses not to remember the long trail of sins.

We have to do our part to give up the sin. But "If we confess our sins, he is faithful and just and will forgive us our sins and purify us from all unrighteousness."[32] To purify, in biblical terms, doesn't mean to just "set it aside." It means "burn it up and make it go away."[33]

There is more in store for us, however, than just forgiveness (as fabulous as that is). He says, "For I will forgive their wickedness and will remember their sins no more."[34] God isn't going to pull it out of an archive later on and use it to shame us. He declares without question or hesitation that "*all* their past sins will be forgotten."[35] The result? "If anyone is in Christ, he is a new creation; the old has gone, the new has come!"[36] Gloriously, what went before—with its sin and shame—has gone.

God's ability to forget becomes our ticket to a totally clean slate. We are told adamantly that "*None* of the sins he has committed will be remembered against him."[37] A thick encyclopedia of sins has been replaced by a single sheet that reads, "This page intentionally left blank." He takes the action that makes it so: "As far as the east is from the west, so far has he removed our transgressions from us."[38]

In addition to God's willingness to forget our sin, he can also choose not to know about evil. The prophet Habakkuk says to God, "Your eyes are too pure to look on evil."[39] God just can't make himself look at it until it reaches a level that demands his intervention: "Then the LORD said, 'The outcry against Sodom and Gomorrah is so great and their sin so grievous that *I will go down and see* if what they have done is as bad as the outcry that has reached me. If not, I will know.'"[40] Like a parent who hears a child outdoors screaming, God comes down to check things out to see what the trouble is—and to see what needs to be done. But he doesn't need to be in the middle of everything.

He can, apparently, choose not to know even about things that will turn out well. "*Now* I know that you fear God," the Lord said to Abraham after stopping the sacrifice of his son Isaac, "because you have not withheld from me your son, your only son."[41] Moses told the Israelites, "Remember how the LORD your God led you all the way in the desert these forty years, to humble you and to test you *in order to know what was in your heart,* whether or not you would keep his commands."[42] God perhaps chooses not to think about the outcome so he can be truly delighted with our love and commitment: "The LORD your God is testing you to find out whether you love him with all your heart and with all your soul."[43]

In one of the most astounding statements in a book full of astounding statements, Jesus—God in the flesh—tells us that he is content to have another member of the Trinity, the Father, know things that he doesn't know: "No one knows about that day or hour, not even the angels in heaven, nor the Son, but only the Father."[44] This in spite of the fact that we earlier learned from Scripture that Jesus knew everything.

God has some internally imposed limitations on his knowledge—limitations chosen by him. This is a clear truth of Scripture: If it has happened, God can choose to forget about it. If it is going to happen, he can choose not to think about the details if doing so will spoil his relationship with us or cause him to "look on evil." Although God is without external limitations or internal disabilities, apparently he can choose to limit himself. He intentionally doesn't know some things, and he can choose to forget others.[45]

THE DEEPER MEANING OF BOTH/AND

There is no question in Scripture that God knows everything. But God also forgets some things. And in some instances, he chooses not to know. When Scripture says that God knows, it means he knows; and when it says he forgets, it means he forgets. There's no way to dodge it. So what are the other both/and truths that we might find in this paradox?

God Can Know, and God Can Limit His Knowledge

We see that God has access to all knowledge. He has no limitations imposed on him from outside forces or from internal disabilities. But God is not a victim of his knowledge, somehow forced to know what he doesn't want to know or to remember what he wants to forget.

God can choose to limit his knowledge. It is a limitation, to be sure; but it's a voluntary, self-imposed one. It takes a lot of power to keep an all-knowing God from knowing, and it shouldn't surprise us that only God has that much power. No one can stop God from knowing—except God.

Just as God uses his knowledge to limit his power (he could have created our solar system with fifty or a hundred planets, but by his knowledge he limited himself to just a few), so he can use his power to limit his knowledge. We discover in this halakic conclusion that his knowledge and power are his attributes and tools, not his masters. God is in control, not the rules of logic or systematic theology.

We are delighted to discover that God can choose not to know for the sake of our relationship with him. Why does he use his power to choose not to know? So he can be involved in a mutual and genuine relationship with us. When parents see their child wrapping a present for them, and they could look to see what the gift is if they want to but choose to look away instead, they are practicing this aspect of God's choosing.

This is why God can and will in some sense "leave" us. He can put space between us and choose to look the other way for a time so that we can freely choose and act, and he can evaluate what we've done when he "comes back." King Hezekiah experienced this: "But when envoys were sent by the rulers of Babylon to ask [Hezekiah] about the miraculous sign that had occurred in the land, God left him to test him and to know everything that was in his heart."[46]

God Can Choose to Forget

We see that God can go beyond "not knowing" and can choose to forget things he already knew, for the sake of his relationship with us. If a memory would impair his communion with us, he is so powerful that he can push it aside. Why would he do this? Because God is the great Remover of Stains. He turns scarlet into snow white and crimson into wool.[47] When we remove a stain from an article of clothing, we don't continue to "see" or to think about the stain every time we wear the clothing. It's gone. So it is with God and the sin he has forgiven.

And he keeps erasing the blackboard to give us an ongoing clean slate. Spiritual enemies keep writing on the board—and for some reason, *we* keep writing on the board—and God comes in right behind us and wipes it away. Unlike Jacob Marley in *A Christmas Carol,* we have no massive and lengthening chain clamped tightly and unbreakably around our legs.

So God offers us the most magnificent transaction: If we repent, he forgets. We do have to really repent and let him do the cleaning up. "Although you wash yourself with soda and use an abundance of soap," he says, looking at our futile efforts to live a good life, "the stain of your guilt is still before me."[48] The sequence is clear. God doesn't just forgive us and then hope we'll change. It is first a change of direction (repentance) on our part, next he forgives, and then he forgets.

But how can he forget? Because he is God. He has the power, and he chooses to use it on our behalf. With us, memories of sin and failure can come back. With God, when it's gone it stays gone, because he is more powerful than we are. Why would he do this? Because he is "compassionate and gracious, slow to anger, abounding in love."[49] As far as our ongoing relationship with God is concerned, there is no better news than this, that he has an eraser that he is glad to use.

God Chooses to Forget When We Repent

But what about the Day of Judgment? That will be a pretty tough day, a detailed audit that no corporate tomfoolery could ever get around. "And I saw the dead, great and small, standing before the throne, and books were opened. Another book was opened, which is the book of life. The dead were judged according to what they had done as recorded in the books."[50] We'd better have a good defense attorney, because this is a capital case, and we are facing a death sentence.

The hard truth about judgment is that God does make us give account for every idle word, but according to this halakic conclusion, he does this only if we haven't first asked him to forgive those idle words. He couldn't possibly ask us to account for things he has already chosen to forgive and forget. So the only words he could ask us to explain are the ones that we didn't ask him to forget. The rest are gone.

There is no stronger encouragement for Christians to keep the "open" list of sins short, even empty. We can and should pray that God will wipe out our low moments: "Do not remember our sins forever," prayed Isaiah.[51] Yes, Lord, do not remember our sins forever.

God gives us a picture of this idea of sin disappearing over the horizon in the example of the scapegoat. The scapegoat carried the sins of the Israelites far away from them, never to be seen again.[52] As we saw earlier, God changes even the appearance of the transgressions: "Though your sins are like scarlet, they shall be as white as snow; though they are red as crimson, they shall be like wool."[53]

We Can Follow God's Example

We can learn to follow God's example, not holding grudges when the problem that caused them has been cleared up. God lets things go (after they've been repented of), and so should we. God doesn't say, "Remember when you…," and neither should we. When we hear voices reminding us of an erased past, they are coming from a source other than God.

Maybe part of our problem with believing that God could really forget is that we don't think we would do that if we were God. If we knew some horrible thing about a person, we'd make a point of not forgetting it. But, thankfully, God doesn't share our petty enjoyment in recalling another person's failures.

In our own lives, we can choose, like Paul, to join God in "forgetting what is behind."[54] We can forget our sin and guilt. We can stop talking about the details of our sins, since that is no longer "us" or a part of our story. We can remember God's goodness in forgiving us and helping us with the consequences, but we let the sin and guilt and shame go once and for all. We're careful to remember the traps so we can avoid them, but not so we can live our lives in regret. Our "testimony" becomes simply, "I can't remember that garbage anymore."

When we are reminded about past forgiven sins, we can be sure it is not God who is reminding us. It could be the Evil One, other people, or our own sinful nature, but it can't be God—because he just doesn't remember.

We Can Imitate God in Choosing Not to Know Evil

Another lesson we learn from this paradox is that God chooses to avoid looking at evil. He uses his power to keep from being tainted by it. He simply doesn't want to "know" about it or be aware of its details ("Your eyes are too pure to look on evil"[55]). This is why he had to go down to Sodom and Gomorrah to "see if what they have done is as bad as the outcry that has reached me."[56] Is it really a surprise that a holy God would choose not to think about evil and corruption?

This is, at least in part, an answer to the question, How can God see all of this evil and not intervene? The answer is that he doesn't see it. The human exercise of free will, and the evil that free will may cause, can only exist because a holy God chooses not to look at it—for a time. When people finally do enough evil to make him look on what he hates to look at, he reacts with an outrage that only his purity can compel.

And here is a lesson for us. We should choose to be like God and not know about the details of evil. We should "in regard to evil be infants."[57] We should want to be commended like those who "have not learned Satan's so-called deep secrets."[58] Studying the details of satanic cult practices, the beliefs of bizarre religious groups, or the blow-by-blow horrors of a vicious crime is not suitable for people who want to be "like God in true righteousness and holiness."[59] If we want to be like God, we do not look curiously or unnecessarily into these things. We let them go.

God is good, so he chooses not to know evil. And we see that God is love, so he chooses to forget our sin. How can it get any better than this?

WHERE THIS LEAVES US

We are told that "God is love."[60] But we are never told that "God is knowledge" or that "God is power."

God can subordinate knowledge and power to each other, and he can subordinate both of them to love. This halakic argument teaches us that this is exactly what he does. Knowledge and power are attributes of his nature, but they are fully under his control. He is able to use these tools to further his "core," which is love.

God can see it all, know it all, and understand it all. But he can also look the other way. He can wait to find out, and he can choose to forget. The main reason he does these things seems to point in one direction: his unrelenting love for us.

We do want God to remember us, but only in a certain way. We should pray with the psalmist, "Remember not the sins of my youth and my rebellious ways; according to your *love* remember me, for you are good, O LORD."[61]

Even after a careful examination of this paradox, we can't be sure that we have found all the halakic conclusions. Our analysis, however true, is not the whole truth on this subject, and our conclusions are not the last word. We have discovered some of the answers, but not all of them. You can, perhaps, discover more.

This much is certain, however: We have an awesome God. He has the ability to know everything, the love and holiness to cause him to forget, and the power to make it so.

FOR FURTHER THOUGHT AND DISCUSSION

1. What was the most startling insight you gained from this paradox? What made it so startling?

2. What are you going to change in your relationship with God or your prayer life as a result of this halakic study? How will your confession of sin be affected?

3. What are you going to change in your relationship with other people— the things you'll be willing to overlook, what you choose to forget?

4. What other truths or insights have occurred to you concerning God's all-knowing yet sometimes-forgetting character?

Four

The God of Judgment
Who Gives Us a Break

<small>M</small>ERCY AND JUDGMENT CAN'T EXIST IN ISOLATION

For God will bring every deed into judgment, including every hidden thing, whether it is good or evil.

ECCLESIASTES 12:14

He does not treat us as our sins deserve or repay us according to our iniquities.

PSALM 103:10

The sixth-grade Bible class was studying Moses and the Israelites. The lesson flowed smoothly until one boy raised his hand.

"I don't get it," he exclaimed. "I thought God was loving and kind and forgiving. But the God we've been talking about seems mean and strict. He keeps punishing the Israelites for messing up. Is that what God is *really* like?"

"Yes," the teacher responded. "God punishes people for their sins. But he is also a loving and merciful God who forgives us when we ask him to."

"I'm confused," said a girl in the back. "Which one is he—merciful or judgmental? He can't be both, can he?"

The teacher took a deep breath and looked at the roomful of young faces. The curriculum guide didn't supply an answer to this question. So what's a teacher to do?

And just as important, what are *we* to do?

Once again we encounter a seemingly contradictory portrait of God. In one passage of Scripture he is raining down judgment for disobedience. Then a few pages later, he responds to a plea for mercy and lets someone off the hook. We're thankful for the merciful side of God, since we've all been in situations where we counted on him to give us a break.

But at the same time, there is something about God's merciful side that troubles us. What if "mercy" means he's wishy-washy, deciding to just let evil-doers off scot-free? Or how about all the times we're harmed by evil, including the generalized evil of our fallen world? Does God's mercy mean that the bad guys can freely victimize the innocent and then go merrily about their lives without paying for their injustice?

On a personal level, we all want to call upon God's mercy when the need arises. But with the bigger picture in view, we sure hope the wrongdoers have to pay and pay big. What might this paradox teach us about judgment and mercy?

JUDGING US AND GIVING US A BREAK

If you've read a parenting book or attended a seminar on family life, you've heard about "tough love." A parent who wants the very best for her child will tighten the screws when the child heads off in a destructive direction. Likewise, we're all familiar with tender love. You don't see many paintings of mothers spanking their children. Instead, you see depictions of mothers with rapturous eyes gently caressing their angelic offspring. And if we think about it, most of us have experienced both sides of a parent's love.

Scripture teaches us that God is our heavenly Father, and that God is love.[1]

If an earthly parent can embody both tender love and tough love, why wouldn't God also parent us with a similar range of nurture and discipline? But how can God bring every deed into judgment if he does not repay us according to our sins? If he inhabits both extremes of this continuum, doesn't that introduce a conflict in his character?

Entire theological systems have been built around each of the two sides of the judgment/mercy paradox, and whole lives have strayed as people have adhered to one side or the other, adopting an unbalanced extreme.

God Condemns and Judges Sin

If God is determined to render judgment and nothing can dissuade him, then who can possibly measure up to his standards? We're all doomed no matter what we do or what we believe. If even our very best works are like "filthy rags,"[2] doesn't that mean that everything we do is subject to judgment?

If we focus on the idea that God is going to bring every deed into judgment, we'll endure sleepless nights and face days filled with anxiety. We will never feel worthy of anything but judgment and condemnation. We might find ourselves groveling before God, hoping against hope that somehow our pitiful begging will eventually soften his heart.

We don't even measure up to our own standards, so there is no hope that we'll even get close to the requirements put in place by a holy God. And that just takes into account the sins we allow ourselves to indulge in. What about the abundance of temptation that constantly beckons, trying to crowd into our lives? We have a sinful nature that doesn't get reformed when we become Christians, so we're constantly at risk. It's an internal terrorist, doing its best to create havoc and turn us into "instruments of wickedness."[3]

A focus on God's judgment will also cloud our view of others. Someone gets sick? Must be a sin problem. A friend loses his job? We always suspected God would punish this guy, but we didn't realize judgment would come in the form of unemployment. Two rowdy teenagers lose their lives in an auto accident? Must be the hand of God. What else can we, or they, expect from a God who is bent on vengeance?[4]

Clinging to the "judgment" side of the paradox leads to hypocrisy as we condemn people even for minor failures while temporarily turning a blind eye to our own misdeeds. Many people feel anointed to be the critical mouthpiece for a raging God. They fail to see their own pride—a sin that provokes God's judgment—at the root of their condemning attitude.

Churches that follow this path end up hard and intolerant under the guise of "standing up for God and the Bible." Certain sins, either through overt preaching or tacit understanding, become the "unforgivable sins." Smoking, alcohol, gambling, divorce, homosexuality, and pregnancy outside marriage have long been such targets. And even the more pluralistic or "inclusive" churches get in on the act by judging those who judge others, thus becoming intolerant of intolerant people.

God Shows Mercy to Evildoers

If we go to the other extreme, selecting side B of the paradox, we end up with a merciful God but no fixed principles. Nothing is heinous enough to provoke God to judgment.

Clinging exclusively to God's mercy, we end up glossing over the "law" part of the Bible. All that commandment stuff and the stringent regulations and punishments—gone! We can find false security in believing that God no longer judges people or punishes sin. We can tell others that we're living in an "age of grace" that covers all our failures.

At this extreme, people feel free to lead sloppy lives, to do whatever is expedient or comfortable, with little regard for what God desires. After all, God is merciful, and we know in advance that he's going to forgive us. We can offend God but still be sure, even while we're sinning, of a painless outcome. Paul anticipated this view when he said, "Shall we sin because we are not under law but under grace?"[5] His answer was a strong "No!" But if we swing to the mercy side of the paradox, it's hard to avoid such presumption. When you hear people say lightly, "We're under grace, not law," you might very well be in the neighborhood of the mercy extreme.

This view colors not only our view of God but also our view of other people.

No matter what a person does or says, who are we to judge? It doesn't matter if people destroy others, it doesn't matter if they don't repent, it doesn't matter that they will repeat their evil since they got away with it the first time—it only matters that we show mercy to the destroyer. Churches with this focus push acceptance in lieu of crucial biblical requirements such as repentance, confession, and an acknowledgment that God's judgment does indeed hang over sinners.

The all-mercy view misrepresents the character and nature of God and also raises troubling questions, even for those who desire an all-accepting God. For instance, how could God, even if he is full of mercy, not pour out judgment on people who are so wicked that they shouldn't be allowed to walk on planet Earth, much less enjoy the pleasures of heaven? Recent history is crowded with examples: Adolf Hitler, Joseph Stalin, Mao Zedong, Pol Pot, Idi Amin, Osama bin Laden, and Saddam Hussein, to name just a few. And then you read the words of Paul, a man who killed people simply because they were Christians. He pronounced himself the worst sinner ever, and yet he experienced God's mercy.[6] Is there really no degree of sin that can move God to withhold his mercy?

WHAT SCRIPTURE SAYS

The Bible provides plenty of support for each side of this paradox. And our own temperaments—whether we are naturally rules-oriented or laissez-faire—also colors our perceptions. Let's see what the halakic argument looks like.

The God of Judgment

Think maybe God won't notice a few things? Better think again. We're told, "You may be sure that your sin will find you out."[7] Nothing will be swept under the carpet, because there *is* no carpet.[8]

No one is going to escape God's judgment. "For we must all appear before the judgment seat of Christ, that each one may receive what is due him for the things done while in the body, whether good or bad."[9] For most of us, it could take a long segment of eternity to receive our due for an endless list of sins.[10] Wrath is cumulative and can be preserved for a very long time.[11]

You might think you're safe from judgment because you've joined a church, been baptized, or made a profession of faith. But simply knowing the truth is not sufficient to deflect God's judgment: "We must pay more careful attention, therefore, to what we have heard, so that we do not drift away. For if the message spoken by angels was binding, and every violation and disobedience received its just punishment, how shall we escape if we *ignore* such a great salvation?"[12] Knowing the truth seems to raise the bar, not lower it.

Knowing the truth and then suppressing it is a bad plan. "If we deliberately keep on sinning after we have received the knowledge of the truth, no sacrifice for sins is left, but *only* a fearful expectation of judgment and of raging fire that will consume the enemies of God."[13] If we have the truth and choose sin, we have in effect chosen to face God's ferocious judgment and his raging fire.

How about the argument that what you're doing is no worse than what other people, even some Christians, are doing? Scripture shows that even if we're just picking up bad habits from the people around us, we're in for judgment. "I will execute judgment on you at the borders of Israel. Then you will know that I am the LORD.... For you have not followed my decrees or kept my laws but have conformed to the standards of the nations around you."[14]

Neither do we earn an exemption just because we are God's people. "For it is time for judgment to begin with the family of God; and if it begins with us, what will the outcome be for those who do not obey the gospel of God?"[15] Judgment doesn't start with those who thumb their noses at God. It starts with those who claim a relationship with God.[16]

But surely there is leniency shown toward those who don't know any better? No. "In the past God overlooked such ignorance, but now he commands all people everywhere to repent. For he has set a day when he will judge the world with justice by the man he has appointed."[17] Saying, "But I didn't know!" doesn't hold water. It may be true that you don't know, but you *can* know. Claims of "not guilty by reason of ignorance" will be ignored.

God has to judge because God is just.[18] If we claim to know and understand God at all, we have to acknowledge that he not only exercises justice, he *delights* in it.[19]

Judgment is a textured web of decisions and actions directed at our world. We find that God brings judgment in this life on:

- *individuals,* since "There is no one righteous, not even one."[20] No one gets a free pass.
- *families,* even families who have faith in God. Two believers, Ananias and Sapphira, were struck dead after giving money to the church. They sinned when they said they were donating the whole amount they had gotten from selling a piece of property, when in reality they were only giving a part of it.[21] They received death for charitable giving, since it was wrapped in a lie.
- *entire nations,* when they misuse and abuse the power God has allocated to them. "The kings of the earth take their stand and the rulers gather together against the LORD and against his Anointed One.… The One enthroned in heaven laughs; the Lord scoffs at them. Then he rebukes them in his anger and terrifies them in his wrath."[22] No nation wants to hear *that* laughter.
- *churches,* since God's people are not immune to judgment. "Hear the word of the LORD, all you…who come through these gates to worship the LORD.… Reform your ways and your actions, and I will let you live in this place."[23]

And he doesn't stop there. In the afterlife, God judges:

- *believers,* whose work on earth will be judged in the next life. Our "work will be shown for what it is.… It will be revealed with fire, and the fire will test the quality of each man's work.… If it is burned up, he will suffer loss; he himself will be saved, but only as one escaping through the flames."[24]
- *unbelievers,* who will stand before the throne of Jesus Christ. "And I saw the dead, great and small, standing before the throne, and books were opened.… The dead were judged according to what they had done as recorded in the books.… Each person was judged according to what he had done.… If anyone's name was not found written in the book of life, he was thrown into the lake of fire."[25] Many have mistakenly assumed that death would put an end to their problems.

The Bible is full of frightening statements about punishment and impending doom. Oddly, God's glory is seen, in part, in the punishment he dishes out.[26] This reminds us that God judges the world and inflicts punishment so that people will know he is God.[27] "I will inflict punishment on Moab. Then they will know that I am the LORD."[28]

At other times, God punishes people to persuade them to turn from a harmful path. The book of Judges demonstrates this repeatedly.[29] So does the story of King Nebuchadnezzar, who lost his mind and lived among wild animals before the judgment finally connected with him and he was restored. "I...raised my eyes toward heaven, and my sanity was restored," he said.[30]

Sometimes punishment comes as a consequence of sin, even if the person has already repented of the sin. King David's first son with Bathsheba died even after David repented of his adulterous liaison.[31]

And then there is God's final judgment. We read of his overwhelming, unstoppable judgment in the Bible's descriptions of the end of the world. "And God has also commanded that the heavens and the earth will be consumed by fire on the day of judgment, when ungodly people will perish.... The heavens will pass away with a terrible noise, and everything in them will disappear in fire, and the earth and everything on it will be exposed to judgment."[32]

You dismiss God's role as Ultimate Judge at your own peril.[33]

The God Who Gives Us a Break

All of us have known at least a few people we consider to be exceedingly kind. God puts all of them to shame. God goes out of his way to offer kindness to all, even to the ones who are least deserving of kindness. "He does not treat us as our sins deserve or repay us according to our iniquities."[34] He's got every reason to be angry with us, to hate us, to punish us, but he doesn't do it. In God's world, "Mercy triumphs over judgment!"[35] Just when we think there is no hope, just when we're sure we deserve to be crushed, God comes into the game and scores the final goal—mercy.

Even when we haven't done the slightest thing to warrant his mercy, he still offers it. "But because of his great love for us, God, who is rich in mercy, made us alive with Christ even when we were dead in transgressions—it is by grace you have been saved."[36] God in his mercy gives life to the dead.

No one would have the hope of salvation outside of God's mercy. "He saved us, not because of righteous things we had done, but because of his mercy," Paul reminded Titus.[37] God's mercy is our only hope, and fortunately it's all we need. Many have tried to buy their way into God's favor by offering their time, talents, energy, and financial resources. But God draws up only one formula: Sacrifice doesn't get the job done, but mercy satisfies a desire that lies deep in his heart.[38]

Mercy is also a place of refuge and protection.[39] "Have mercy on me, O God, have mercy on me, for in you my soul takes refuge."[40] If we hide out in God, we apparently have every right to claim his mercy.[41] Even when we're at death's door, even when we can't see the light, mercy makes the difference.[42] Mercy is the great escape.

In Scripture, we see God's mercy from the beginning. It didn't start with the death and resurrection of Jesus. Mercy started with God. His mercy is "from of old."[43] God hears our cry for mercy and answers it with mercy.[44] How could this not produce love for God?[45] When we need mercy, God expects to hear from us.[46] And we can expect to hear from him.

God's mercy isn't a random feeling; it's a choice that God makes. "Then Moses said, 'Now show me your glory.' And the LORD said, 'I will cause all my goodness to pass in front of you, and I will proclaim my name, the LORD, in your presence. I will have mercy on whom I will have mercy, and I will have compassion on whom I will have compassion.'"[47] This is one of the most intimate interactions between God and a human recorded in Scripture.

But the interaction raises a significant question: "To whom does God choose to show mercy?" Some have interpreted God's statement to Moses as an indication that he arbitrarily eliminates many from the possibility of receiving his mercy, but we read elsewhere that "his mercy goes on from generation to generation, to *all* who fear him."[48] God set up the ground rules for determining who will receive his mercy. Fearing him is one. Loving him is another.[49] The requirements for receiving God's mercy are simply to fear him and to love him. There is nothing arbitrary about it at all.

Even when we haven't repented of our sin, God's mercy may maintain a presence in our lives. "For many years you were patient with them. By your Spirit you admonished them through your prophets. Yet they paid no attention, so you handed them over to the neighboring peoples. But in your great mercy you did not put an end to them or abandon them, for you are a gracious and merciful God."[50] God demonstrated his mercy to ancient Israel even when they insisted on rebelling against him.

God's patience and mercy toward the wayward often upsets those who are trying to follow him. How often have people asked, "How can God be good if he lets all the bad people continue to do bad things?" Even the prophet Jeremiah struggled with this question: "You are always righteous, O LORD, when I bring a case before you. Yet I would speak with you about your justice: Why does the way of the wicked prosper? Why do all the faithless live at ease?"[51] God's mercy is so effusive that it can appear to be the most unfair thing we've ever observed.

If we give it some thought, we realize that's the case. God's mercy *is* a violation of justice. Always. Mercy means he's letting people off the hook who don't deserve a break, people who actually deserve judgment and punishment. In reality, *none* of us deserves mercy. That's the wonder of it.

The prophet Micah was so taken by this kind God that he overflowed with different ways of saying it. "Who is a God like you, who pardons sin and forgives the transgression of the remnant of his inheritance? You do not stay angry forever but delight to show mercy. You will again have compassion on us; you will tread our sins underfoot and hurl all our iniquities into the depths of the sea. You will be true to Jacob, and show mercy to Abraham, as you pledged on oath to our fathers in days long ago."[52] God gets angry, but he doesn't stay that way. As soon as we turn, he shows compassion and annihilates our sins. Mercy causes him to save us and to show us his kindness and love.[53]

As we examine this paradox in Scripture, we are also surprised to find that mercy is not the opposite of the law. Jesus explained: "Woe to you, teachers of the law and Pharisees, you hypocrites!… You have neglected the more important matters of the *law*—justice, mercy and faithfulness."[54] As Jesus pointed out, mercy is in fact a crucial feature of the law.

Given our propensity to sin, it's comforting to know that God's mercy never ends.[55] This is why Peter could admonish those who were eager for God to wipe out the "bad guys": "The Lord isn't really being slow about his promise to return, as some people think. No, he is being patient…. He does not want anyone to perish, so he is giving more time for everyone to repent…. The Lord is waiting so that people have time to be saved."[56] What people often perceive to be a shortage of justice is, in reality, an abundance of mercy.

Finally, at the end of our journey, mercy is the passport we must be holding if we hope to get into the eternal land of heaven.[57] And no matter how great our failure, we can be issued that passport.

It's astonishing but true: When we fail, God still lets us pass the course.[58]

THE DEEPER MEANING OF BOTH/AND

God is the final Judge who holds sinners accountable—the One who punishes the wicked. God is the source of all mercy, the One whose mercy never fails, who extends mercy to all who ask. Given the starkness of this paradox, what are the both/and truths that we might find?

The first conclusion is that God judges everyone and everything down to the smallest error, and also that God is willing to overlook anything up to the most horrendous crimes. These truths seem incompatible, but Scripture tells us they are both true.

God's judgments can disappear. He somehow "forgives all your sins…. He will not always accuse, nor will he harbor his anger forever;…as far as the east is from the west, so far has he removed our transgressions from us."[59] Mercy is the solution to our very ugly problem.

But how can God be willing to judge everything and at the same time be willing to show mercy for everything? There must somehow be a connection between judgment and mercy.

Judgment and Mercy Appear in Sequence

Could it be that one of these comes before the other? Perhaps a person's sin has to be addressed before God's judgment can end and his mercy can kick in. "None of those condemned things shall be found in your hands, so that the LORD will turn from his fierce anger; he will show you mercy, have compassion on you, and increase your numbers, as he promised on oath to your fore-fathers."[60] In this passage, we note that the key to receiving God's mercy is that we can't cling to anything that obstructs his mercy. We have to confess our sins, turn away from them, let go of them. If we don't, our lips may be asking for mercy, but our hands are asking for judgment.

A lot of "turning" is involved in this business of judgment and mercy. We have to turn away from God's judgment and turn toward him—to *repent*, a word that means "to change directions"—in order to access his mercy. "Repent, all of you who ignore me," God says, "*or* I will tear you apart, and no one will help you."[61] Although judgment causes God to turn away from us, mercy causes him to turn back. "Turn to me and have mercy on me, as you always do to those who love your name,"[62] pleaded the psalmist. "Turn to me and have mercy on me."[63]

Mercy is a two-way street. The mercy is granted by God, but it is prompted by our recognition of his righteous judgment and by our repentance from the thoughts and actions that bring that judgment on our heads. Forgiveness is a transaction—a conversation, a reconciliation—between God and us.

There might be a second way this sequence is important. Perhaps we need to access God's mercy before his judgment fully kicks in. God sends his mercy in part to preserve us from judgment. "Rend your heart, and not your garments. Return to the LORD your God, for he is gracious and compassionate, slow to anger and abounding in love, and he relents from sending calamity."[64] His judgment is right behind his mercy, waiting to descend on us if we don't position ourselves for his mercy.

Mercy Toward Others Is a Prerequisite for Receiving Mercy

Jesus lays out a sequence of justice and mercy as the pattern for human relationships. "If your brother sins, rebuke him, and if he repents, forgive him."[65]

We are not told to forgive regardless of the other person's heart attitude. Only "*if* he repents" in response to our rebuke should we forgive. We should always be ready to forgive and ask God to keep our hearts pliable and not bitter in the meantime, but forgiveness—mercy—is a two-way transaction. Too many have abridged this verse to read, "If your brother sins…forgive him," leaving out two critical words: *rebuke* and *repent.*

Once our brother or sister repents, we must offer mercy if we want to receive God's mercy. James, a leader of the early church, made this connection clear. "Judgment without mercy will be shown to anyone who has not been merciful."[66] We can't expect to get mercy if we won't give it.[67]

What about those who are not our brothers and sisters in the faith? Well, God isn't surprised when sinful people sin. They don't have much of an alternative. As one pastor said, "We shouldn't be surprised when lost people act lost."[68] But before those who don't know God can comprehend his mercy, they must first have a sense of his judgment. Mercy has little impact if an individual doesn't first recognize the extent of his problem, and if he doesn't understand the fearsome judgment he is inviting into his life.

We May Receive Mercy But Still Face Consequences

In one of the oddest stories in the Bible, King David took a census, an action that God had opposed. David immediately felt guilty and admitted his error, saying, "I have sinned greatly and shouldn't have taken the census. Please forgive me for doing this foolish thing."[69] God had the prophet Gad bring a message to David. We might expect this message to have mentioned mercy and forgiveness. Instead, God gave David a menu of three really tough choices: three years of famine, three months of pursuit by his enemies, or three days of plague on the land. In a massive understatement, David said, "This is a desperate situation!"[70]

David let God's mercy be his guide and picked the plague. "Let us fall into the hands of the LORD," David reasoned, "for his mercy is great."[71] A death angel wiped out seventy thousand people in three days, until the Lord poured out his mercy. Because judgment is part of God's equation, a core part of his character, we find that mercy does not mean "no consequences."[72]

Still, God does not shut down his mercy during times of punishment. "If they violate my decrees and fail to keep my commands, I will punish their sin with the rod, their iniquity with flogging; but I will not take my love from him, nor will I ever betray my faithfulness."[73] His love and mercy remain, always, even during periods of judgment. We may leave the boundaries of his love and its conditional benefits, but the love endures, unfailing.

In Light of God's Judgment, Mercy Prompts Gratitude

We see from our halakic reasoning that mercy is not a small thing, because *judgment* is not a small thing. The sins that are forgiven and the judgment that is avoided should drive us straight into the arms of our loving God. "A person who is forgiven little," said Jesus, "shows only little love."[74] But *anyone* who is forgiven—even those of us with a high regard for our own goodness—is in truth forgiven much, and we should love much in response.

Judgment and Mercy Work Simultaneously

Even as mercy and judgment are sequential, as we saw earlier, mercy and justice also work at the same time. For the unrepentant there is judgment, while the contrite receive God's mercy. "The Lord knows how to rescue the devout from trial and to keep the unrighteous under punishment for the day of judgment."[75] Judgment and mercy are operating at the same time, often in the same situations. If we turn toward God, he will in his great mercy rescue us and bring judgment on his—and our—enemies. If we turn away from him, he will punish our sins while holding us for judgment day, unless we turn back toward him.

We see this dual action—mercy on those who turn toward him and judgment on those who turn away—again and again in the Bible. "Therefore, say to the Israelites: 'I am the LORD, and I will bring you out from under the yoke of the Egyptians. I will free you from being slaves to them, and I will redeem you with an outstretched arm and with mighty acts of judgment.'"[76] We find that judgment isn't always a bad thing. In fact, we're thankful for God's judgment when it falls on evil people who are harming us!

Eventually, this mix of judgment and mercy produces justice. "Yet your countrymen say, 'The way of the Lord is not just.' But it is their way that is not just. If a righteous man turns from his righteousness and does evil, he will die for it. And if a wicked man turns away from his wickedness and does what is just and right, he will live by doing so. Yet, O house of Israel, you say, 'The way of the Lord is not just.' But I will judge each of you according to his own ways."[77] Judgment is retributive justice, a balancing of the scales, a matter of reaping what we sow. But when judgment is mixed with mercy, it becomes *restorative* justice. We know that the judgment is there to bring us retribution, and we look for the mercy that will bring us restoration.

Judgment and Mercy Are Both Parts of Justice

We find that the common understanding of God's justice as retribution and punishment is an incomplete picture. It's easy to confuse justice with judgment. The biblical view of justice is that it is more than retribution. It's treating people fairly, especially honoring the rights of those who have less power than we have. God judges with justice. God rules with justice. There is frequent mention of justice being a part of God's kingdom, which implies that justice can't just be linked to sin.

Justice requires both judgment and mercy. "This is what the LORD Almighty says: 'Administer true justice; show mercy and compassion to one another. Do not oppress the widow or the fatherless, the alien or the poor. In your hearts do not think evil of each other.' "[78] Administering true justice and showing mercy aren't opposites. To administer true justice means to show mercy toward those who are needy—a very large group indeed.

Jesus lived out the meaning of justice and mercy. "Here is my servant whom I uphold, my chosen one in whom I delight; I will put my Spirit on him and he will bring justice to the nations. He will not shout or cry out, or raise his voice in the streets. A bruised reed he will not break, and a smoldering wick he will not snuff out. In faithfulness he will bring forth justice; he will not falter or be discouraged till he establishes justice on earth."[79] Judgment and mercy are collaborators, working together to bring justice into the world. God does good and fights evil—at the same time.

The Cross Is the Bridge Between Judgment and Mercy

In the final analysis, we find that we need a bridge between God's judgment and mercy in our lives. This paradox finds its bridge, its resolution, in the cross of Christ. How can a perfect and holy God relent from punishing sin? Because of Christ, who accepted judgment in our place so he could offer us mercy. "Therefore, there is now no condemnation for those who are in Christ Jesus," we are told to our delight.[80]

We discover that "God presented him as a sacrifice of atonement, through faith in his blood. He did this to demonstrate his justice, because in his forbearance he had left the sins committed beforehand unpunished—he did it to demonstrate his justice at the present time, so as to be just and the one who justifies those who have faith in Jesus."[81] If a typical Christian is asked, "What did God demonstrate on the cross?" he or she will say, "His love." Few would say, "His justice." But justice is indeed demonstrated in the sacrifice of Christ.

Every deed does in fact come under judgment. But the question is, On whom does the judgment fall? On us—or on Jesus? Is the cross an instrument of judgment, or is the cross also an instrument of mercy? Yes, indeed.

WHERE THIS LEAVES US

We saw in the previous chapter that God reserves the right and has the power to limit himself. He can easily remember our sins, but he chooses not to. He invokes this self-limitation again when he uses his mercy to limit his judgment. He doesn't condemn all of us to eternal punishment, which is actually what we all deserve. He also uses his judgment to limit his mercy. Those who do not repent of their sins, who choose not to appeal to God's mercy for forgiveness, are barred from heaven.

Both of these self-limitations are necessary if God is to be God. His mercy informs his judgment, just as his judgment informs his mercy. Justice is both/and to the fullest extent. Everyone can get a break—but not everyone will.

God is good and his love is unfailing, but he also allows, even causes, some bad things to happen when our sin has earned his judgment. In part, he uses the pain of punishment to lead us to repentance and to seek his mercy so we can escape further judgment.[82] He is also patient in his mercy, waiting for us to see our sin for what it is.[83] At some point, however, he judges the sinful life.

In the midst of it all, his goodness drives him to be gracious and to show us compassion, and his power is great enough to show us his mercy in the midst of bad times, whether deserved or undeserved. "The LORD longs to be gracious to you; he rises to show you compassion. For the LORD is a God of justice. Blessed are all who wait for him!"[84] We need God's judgment to drive us to mercy—and then, incomprehensibly, his mercy dissolves the judgment.

We hear much talk today about "unconditional love." But there is no such thing in the Bible or in the real world. There is conditional love—love that will not be a mere doormat, love that is real and mature. This is a love that takes account of God's judgment. And there is unfailing love—love that will not insist on its own way, love that persists in the face of ingratitude and icy coldness, love that is stubborn and childlike. This is the love that takes account of God's mercy.

All of God's love is both conditional and unfailing, a love that holds judgment and mercy in perfect balance.[85]

FOR FURTHER THOUGHT AND DISCUSSION

1. If you only had three minutes to tell someone about the judgment of God, what would you say?
2. Are you glad God is a God of judgment? Why or why not?
3. Why does God grant us mercy? What causes him to do it?
4. If we focused solely on God's mercy, what kind of life, and what kind of church, would we have? What if we focused solely on his judgment?
5. If you knew someone who was trapped in a sin, what would you tell him or her about God's judgment? What would you share about God's mercy?
6. What other insights have you gained concerning mercy and judgment?

The Changeless God Who Changes

WHY AUTHENTIC RELATIONSHIP REQUIRES GIVE-AND-TAKE

I the LORD do not change.

MALACHI 3:6

My heart is changed within me.

HOSEA 11:8

Andrea was having lunch with a friend when she mentioned that she was praying for the friend's mother, who was battling cancer.

"Don't bother," the friend said.

"Why not?" Andrea asked, shocked at her apathy.

"I don't mean to sound rude," the friend explained. "It's just that last Sunday my pastor talked about how God is unchangeable. He said God has already decided everything. So I can't see how prayer will make a difference if God has already decided what's going to happen with my mom."

"The fact that God doesn't change doesn't mean that our prayers don't affect his decisions," Andrea suggested.

"It's so confusing. It's hard enough trying to understand why God would allow my mother to get cancer, but now I can't even feel comfort in praying for her," the friend admitted with tears in her eyes. "I just need some answers."

So do I, Andrea thought.

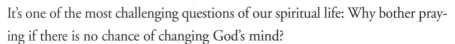

It's one of the most challenging questions of our spiritual life: Why bother praying if there is no chance of changing God's mind?

We're torn because we want two things from God that appear to be contradictory. On the one hand, we want a God who provides us with security and stability and consistency—an *unchanging* God. On the other hand, we'd really like a God who engages us in genuine relationship involving real give-and-take. In our heart of hearts, we long for a relational God who responds to specific circumstances and needs in our lives. In other words, we're looking for a *changing* God.

We sense that in searching for a God who provides us with the permanence that we need, we might end up with a God who has no capacity for taking a personal interest in us. On the other hand, if we find a God who engages us in the day-to-day relationship we need, he just might be a little too changeable to inspire much confidence.

We want both sides of God—a changeless God who changes—even if we don't see how that could be possible.

CHANGE WITHOUT CHANGE

The changing God who doesn't change is a paradox that goes to the core of our relationship with God. Some may argue that we should continue to plead with a God who, in fact, never changes. But the math just doesn't work out. We sense in our souls that if prayer has no chance to make a difference, then it's not really prayer. Why waste our time praying against a stacked deck?

Here then is our halakic question: God says that he is the Lord who does not change. The biblical record also shows that God does change, deciding in some instances not to do things he had already decided he would do, and deciding at other times to do things he had said he would not do. How can God be an unchanging God if over and over again he changes his mind?

God Doesn't Change

If God is truly changeless, what's the point of praying or taking decisive action? If God has already determined the outcome, and if there is no chance that he'll change, then aren't we just acting out a mindless charade? And isn't God just fooling us when he seems to answer our prayers, when in fact he decided long before that he would do what we just happened to ask for?

If we choose side A of this paradox, taking the approach that God cannot change (the doctrine of *immutability*), we end up with some tough results. The dominant theological position for most of the last two thousand years has been that God is completely and inarguably immutable. According to this view, God is unchangeable in both his character (his essence and ethics) and in his life (his relationships and emotions).

This idea came in part from trying to answer an either/or question. As they considered the question, "Does God change?" believers generally picked the answer that made God appear to be the most awesome, the most unlike us: God *can't* change. An either/or answer, however, prevents us from considering that God might be both unchanging and changeable.

The core of the immutability teaching has been that any changeability would imply a change from one state or condition to another. God would have to change from a lesser to a greater condition, or from an imperfect to a more perfect state. Or the opposite—God would have to change from a perfect state to something less. "If God were changeable," wrote a prominent nineteenth-century theologian, "he could not be the most perfect being."[1]

This rigid definition of change, which insists that all change in God must necessarily cause a change in his being or essence, has an interesting side effect. It actually strips God of much of his power. Why? Because even if he wanted to change, he couldn't—because he is God. Being God ends up being the most rigid, limiting, inflexible existence in the universe.

This view fails to account for the many types and forms of change. As a human being, I can change my mind without changing my principles. Can't God do the same? Could he have the power to change in details of action or decision without experiencing the slightest change in his perfect character?

People who hold an absolute view of immutability say that God might *seem* to change, but it isn't a real change. It's simply the working out of what he had determined from eternity. He had already decided in advance to do something that, because we're so limited in knowledge and understanding, appears to be a change. Again, this makes God the least free being of all, powerless to change an action or decision.

Taken to the extreme, this is a deistic position. God is the "watchmaker" who creates the universe and then winds it like a clock. Once the clock is ticking and the hands are moving, he walks away. But the people who advance the immutability teaching generally don't think of themselves as deists. They seek a God who decides once and doesn't change his decree (the deistic view), but also a God who somehow manages to be involved in the ebb and flow of life after making all the decisions in advance.

But how can this work? The God who decides all and sets all in motion is a nonrelational, even nonpersonal God. He isn't really a person since he does not or cannot relate to us as a person. Even a great pastor and writer like A. W. Tozer could state that "all change must be on our part."[2] But this idea of rigidity on the part of God, according to theologian Isaak Dorner, "stands in starkest conflict with the concept of divine personality."[3]

In terms of our daily lives, what is the result of the "no change" view? God becomes a static and nonemotional being, without any real life. If that's who God is, how can any of our prayers make a difference? A wrong view of God in this area easily leads to a wrong view of our own lives. We can end up not seeing ourselves as true participants with God in the ongoing process of reconciliation. What difference can we possibly make to advance the kingdom of God?

The strict immutability teaching fails to recognize the possibility that by creating free beings—you and me—God has voluntarily chosen both to extend and to limit his power. He extends his power, since free beings who are like him can creatively change the flow of history within God's ultimate plan. And he limits his power, since he allows free beings to do things he would not do, to do things he doesn't want them to do, to mess things up that will require him to change his mind or plans in response.

There is another view, that God is above time and comprehends it fully in his foreknowledge (or "simultaneous knowledge," where everything is perceived at once). We're left with a God who is in full awareness (and in some views, full control) of the situation, but who does what it takes to make things *look* like we are having a real friendship with him. In other words, he is faking.

This view can cause us to manipulate the Bible. Too many stories illustrate that God changes his mind in response to human choices and actions. He even changes in response to human *negotiation* (for example, with Abraham over Sodom and Gomorrah, with Moses over the fate of the Israelites, with Hezekiah over his fatal illness, and with Mary over the wine shortage at Cana).[4] This view makes a sham out of biblical stories that show God's reaction being conditioned upon and responsive toward our human choices.

This idea of immutability is closely tied in with the concept of *impassibility*, the idea that God is incapable of emotion or passion. "The question [of] how far the attribution of an emotional nature to God could be reconciled with the concept of his unchangeableness," said one theologian, "has never been thoroughly treated by either the Christian or non-Christian philosophy of religion."[5] The problem is, the two can't be reconciled. God cannot be emotional and unchangeable at the same time. He can't be truly surprised and disappointed and angry if he had time to prepare for these things from...forever. The doctrines of impassibility (no emotion) and immutability (no change) rise or fall together.

The bottom line? The idea of a changeless God denies God's self-chosen roles as Father, Brother, Counselor, Guide, and Friend, and replaces them with the cold, impersonal role of Sovereign. This belief can deaden what could otherwise be a vibrant Christianity.

God Can Change
What happens, though, when we side with the "God changes" camp? If our either/or choice is that God is a being who changes, then does he change continually?

If so, how can we know anything about him, since he might have changed since we last learned about his character? And how should we relate to him after he changes? Is it possible that he might become less loving or less forgiving or less interested in our well-being?

To land entirely on the B side of the paradox doesn't leave us feeling any better than the rigid A-side view, the doctrine of absolute immutability. If we say that God is a changing God, rolling through time just as we are but on a higher level, our security in his constant love and care for us can evaporate.

We might conclude that God's promises and commitments could very well change, depending on what he "learns" as he goes along. Perhaps even his love for us could change or falter. Maybe there really *is* no unfailing love. Maybe he'll come to the conclusion that we truly are a lost cause.

In an effort to allow for God's intimate relationship with people, several solutions have been proposed. One is *process theology,* which assumes that God is bound up with us in the adventure of history, but that he operates within the same limitations we face. He doesn't fully know or control the future. God, like us, is a fellow participant in the process of life and time.

This leaves God looking a lot like just a bigger version of us. He has good intentions. He means well. But we hope that he learns what he needs to know in time to keep the universe from falling apart. If he isn't a really quick study, the gaps in his knowledge could kill us.[6]

Others have proposed *openness theology,* an "openness of God" approach, which also assumes that God is involved in time and history and unable to know or fully control the future. In contrast with process theology, this view of God acknowledges that he is "perfect," in the sense that he is already fully good. Once he knows the facts, he'll make honest and caring decisions. In other words, he has solid operating principles, but he is still learning what is going to happen in the universe.[7]

Both of these views run counter to the biblical teachings of God's omniscience and omnipotence. They leave us with a God who doesn't and can't know everything and a God whose power is limited by time. What if something bad sneaks past him? What if he isn't "big" enough to make things happen when he learns the facts and decides how he'll respond?

The problem is the "smaller" God that emerges from these two theologies. God is indeed more relational (in fact, much more "human"), but he is less trustworthy because he is less "God." How could God create the entire universe and keep it going in decent fashion when he can't even know what you and I are going to do this afternoon?

If we side entirely with the idea of a changing God, we have a God who is personal and relational, but who is also inconsistent and lacking control. If we side exclusively with the immutable God view, we end up with a God who is entirely consistent and in control, but who is impersonal and can't relate to us. Neither of the one-sided views gives us a true, whole God.

What Scripture Says

Because of halakic reasoning, we at once see this conflict as a paradox, and we know that with God *both* strands are true. He is uncompromisingly unchanging and readily changeable, and he expects us to tightly embrace both sides of the mystery.

The God Who Never Changes

Let's examine what the Bible says about God's not changing. The clearest declaration from God on the subject is this: "I the LORD do not change."[8] The things he creates might change, but he does not. "In the beginning you laid the foundations of the earth," the psalmist writes, "and the heavens are the work of your hands. They will perish, but you remain; they will all wear out like a garment. Like clothing you will change them and they will be discarded. *But you remain the same,* and your years will never end."[9] Creation changes but God simply "remains the same."

He makes plans and, unlike us, he does not change his plans. "The LORD Almighty has sworn, 'Surely, as I have planned, so it will be, and as I have purposed, so it will stand.'"[10] And his plans have no expiration date. "The plans of the LORD stand firm *forever,* the purposes of his heart through all generations."[11] Forever is a long time. "The LORD has sworn and will not change his mind," we are told categorically.[12] God is not someone who revises his plans.

And no one else has the power or authority to make God change his plans. "No plan of yours can be thwarted," we are told.[13]

God doesn't stop at making unchanging *plans;* he also makes unchanging *promises.* He has given us "a faith and knowledge resting on the hope of eternal life, which God, who does not lie, promised before the beginning of time."[14] Certainly sounds like it was decided once, for all time. His unchanging promises cause his people to say, "Not one word has failed of all the good promises he gave through his servant Moses."[15] When God says it, we can be sure that not even a small detail will change.

Just to make sure there is no doubt, God *swears* that his words will not be changed. "By myself I have sworn, my mouth has uttered in all integrity a word that will not be revoked."[16] He swears he won't change because he wants to make sure we understand that once he says something it is a certainty. "So when God wanted to give the heirs of his promise an even clearer demonstration of the immutability of his purpose, he intervened with an oath."[17]

There's some really great news in this unchanging world of God: His love for us is unalterable. " 'Though the mountains be shaken and the hills be removed, yet my unfailing love for you will not be shaken nor my covenant of peace be removed,' says the LORD, who has compassion on you."[18] We've got his love and his peace. Forever.

When God promises punishment, he often refuses to change his mind. We're told that God does not relent from sending punishment.[19] "I have spoken and will not relent, I have decided and will not turn back," he says in chilling fashion.[20]

Not only is God unchanging, but when we read about his Son, we hit bedrock. "Jesus Christ is the same yesterday and today and forever."[21] The way he was at Creation is the way he was at Calvary. The way he was at the Resurrection is the way he is right now. And the way he is this second is the way he will be at the Last Judgment and the wedding banquet of the Lamb.

God doesn't change. We can count on that.[22]

The God Who Readily Changes

And without question, the Bible teaches us that God is changeable. After pledging destruction on Israel, he says, "My heart is changed within me; all my compassion is aroused. I will not carry out my fierce anger, nor will I turn and devastate Ephraim."[23] In addition to changing a firm decision, we can feel in this passage the vast churning and changing of God's emotions.

He also changes in response to our prayers and pleadings. We're told that "he took note of their distress *when* he heard their cry; for their sake he remembered his covenant and out of his great love he relented."[24] Here God's judgment and punishment were planned, and then they got cancelled.

In a remarkable passage, King Hezekiah received a personal prophecy—a word directly from God. It came through the great prophet Isaiah, who spoke these words for God: "This is what the LORD says: 'Put your house in order, because you are going to die; you will not recover.'"[25] Sounds like predestination, no exceptions allowed. If *Isaiah* shows up at your door and says you're gone, then you're gone. Period.

But Hezekiah, who apparently didn't know that God doesn't change, prayed fervently. He asked God to change, to cancel what he just said, to let him live. The result? Isaiah didn't even make it back home from visiting Hezekiah. He was immediately sent back to say, on behalf of God: "I have heard your prayer and seen your tears; I will heal you."[26]

In this instance, we either have two gods, or we have one God who has just changed his mind.

The pleadings for God to relent, to change, to make a shift don't even have to be for our own benefit. Abraham had an extensive negotiation with God over the cities of Sodom and Gomorrah *after* God had decided to wipe them out.[27] It is one of the most remarkable conversations in the Bible—Abraham haggling with God over the fate of the wicked cities. Our choice is simple: Either God was having a real give-and-take discussion with his friend Abraham, or God was just toying with the patriarch, making Abraham *think* he was striking a deal with the Lord. God either allowed Abraham to influence his decision, or he put on a pretty good show.

Even regular folks can make decisions that affect God's plans. Our repentance—making a decision to change our ways—prompts God to change from a planned action or judgment. "If at any time I announce that a nation or kingdom is to be uprooted, torn down and destroyed, and *if that nation I warned repents* of its evil, *then* I will relent and not inflict on it the disaster I had planned."[28] God doesn't announce that nations *might* be in trouble, but rather that they *will* be demolished. But with a simple change of heart by those who are about to be obliterated, God's whole plan for annihilation goes out the window.

If we repent, he relents. His change is based on our change. "Now reform your ways and your actions and obey the LORD your God. Then the LORD will relent and not bring the disaster he has pronounced against you."[29] If we change, he changes. This happens so often that Jonah says simply, "You are…a God who relents from sending calamity."[30]

But this works both ways. God can have a party planned for us, and we can spoil it. "If at another time I announce that a nation or kingdom is to be built up and planted, and if it does evil in my sight and does not obey me, then I will *reconsider* the good I had *intended* to do for it."[31] He announces: "Good things are going to happen to you!" But if we let prosperity go to our heads, if we take God for granted, if we go our own way, God will pull the plug. He reconsiders the good he was going to do.

As we saw with his forgetting, his changing is prompted by love. "Rend your heart and not your garments," the prophet Joel admonished. "Return to the LORD your God, for he is gracious and compassionate, slow to anger and abounding in love, and he relents from sending calamity. Who knows? He may turn and have pity."[32] We've always got a chance because God is a God who changes.

There's no denying it. God changes, and the astounding truth is that his changing is often in response to our changing.[33]

THE DEEPER MEANING OF BOTH/AND

If we ponder the truth of the unchanging God who changes, what comes to light regarding God's character and his work among us? First is the undeniable and astonishing truth that God is both unchanging and changing. But how can he be two opposite things? For both to be true—and we have seen the biblical record that supports that both are indeed true—there must be some things about God that are unchanging and some other things about God that are changeable.

God's Character, Purposes, Ethics, and Love Do Not Change

God is clearly unchanging in this regard: His character and his purposes are constant. It is in this sense that Jesus is the same "yesterday and today and forever."[34]

God's ethics don't vary. What he hated at Creation, he still hates. The same things still disgust him. And what he loved at Creation, he still loves. The same things still please and delight and thrill him. Sin is still and always the problem, and Christ is still and always the only solution.

God is also unchanging in his unfailing love for us. He is never going to drop the ball. To borrow a line from an action movie of a few years ago: "I may *take* you down, but I'll never *let* you down."[35] As we saw in the previous chapter, God may have to knock us off our high horses, but he'll always be there to pick us up after we come to our senses and ask for help.

Our Give-and-Take Relationship with God

The Bible drives us toward the idea that there is reciprocity and ongoing change in our relationship with God. Reciprocity is the fluid, genuine interchange between two thinking, feeling beings. Reciprocity means that you do something, and I respond. I do something, and you respond. Our relationship grows, and our lives are deeply interwoven.

Scripture provides too many examples for us to simply discard this idea. God is in an authentic relationship with us. And it *must* be reciprocal to be authentic, a fact that collides with common misunderstandings about God's immutability. "The whole Bible is a record of God's changing relational interactions with man [that] in no way threaten or compromise God's essential immutability," writes theologian Bruce Miller. "God never lacks the power, wisdom or knowledge which might cause him to later regret a decision, but…He changes his actions in response to changing human conditions."[36] Many scriptures, as we have seen, demonstrate this truth.[37]

Reciprocity is first found in the Godhead itself, which (as Dallas Willard reminds us) is a community of divine persons joined by a common core.[38] The Trinity is the ultimate both/and combination of unity and diversity. The Father asks the Son to become a human being, an ultimate act of reciprocity, and the Son agrees. The Son lives in regular communion with the Father, a union so deep that in facing the crisis of impending death the Son pleads with the Father to call the project off. The Father holds firm, and the Son renews his commitment to the point of his final cry for reciprocity: "My God, my God, why have you forsaken me?"[39]

God's decision to have reciprocity—real relationship—with beings outside of himself took place in Creation. He was complete within the Trinity. Creation added nothing to his essence (it didn't make him any more "God") or to his ethics (it didn't make him any more perfect). Instead, Creation was driven by his relational nature, already alive and well in the Godhead itself, and by the passion he felt for sharing his love with others—like someone who decides to have a child. He didn't *need* it for relationship; he already had relationship within himself: Father, Son, and Holy Spirit. But it seems that he *wanted* to extend his love to a wider field for the benefit of both himself and his creation.

Our Authentic Relationship with God

We can see that God goes to extraordinary lengths to achieve understanding and empathy, to be affected by us and impassioned by our needs. This is seen in the Son of God becoming human, to redeem us and make atonement to the Father, but also in some way to share in our humanity: "Because he himself suffered when he was tempted, he is able to help those who are being tempted."[40] Jesus didn't pretend to be tempted; he *was* tempted. He knows how to help people living in a fallen world because he was a person living in a fallen world.

The deepest form of relationship is built around love, which cannot exist without freedom. This implies that a sovereign God has freely chosen to create beings who are free to accept or reject him, beings who can make decisions that are beneficial or destructive, wise or foolish. Further, he has chosen to relate to these beings in an authentic way. Rather than responding with a fixed decision made from eternity, he responds as the relationship itself grows and demands.

Our Changing Relationship with God

God's love is unchangeable—or in biblical terms, *unfailing*. His desire for fellowship with all human beings does not change, and neither does his offer of redemption and relationship. He tells us clearly, "Ask and it *will* be given to you; seek and you *will* find; knock and the door *will* be opened to you."[41] If there is a failure in relationship, it is ours, not his.

But we also see that his love has boundaries and that we can choose to leave it rather than remain in it.[42] Although his love is unfailing, it isn't "unconditional." Instead, it is responsive to our asking, seeking, and knocking. The fulfillment of God's desire for us (and his offer to us) depends on our response to his overtures. If we resist, we close ourselves off from access to his unfailing love.[43] If we respond with our hearts, he saves us, adopts us, and showers us with communion and blessings. We change, and then a miraculous thing happens: God changes his response to us and opens the way to his unchanging, unfailing love.

We have seen in the Scriptures that God will change his course of action based upon our decisions and course of action. But God can't and won't change his principles. Any change in decision or course of action doesn't alter his changeless character. We see even more that the changes we find God making are in fact *guided* by his changeless character.

As Professor Alan Padgett writes, "Changes in God, remember, are a result of his decision to create a changing world and to be really related to it.… God can change in what he does, without changing who he is."[44] Just as we can change our lunch plans without changing our character, so God can change.

God's willingness to change his decisions and courses of action means that he has *more* power, not less. He has the ability to allow free beings to freely decide, then to freely react in an ongoing interchange—but without affecting his long-term plans and goals. It is a great leader indeed who can maximize the degree of his followers' involvement and allow them to modify his decisions and actions while still accomplishing his mission.

Our Creative Partnership with God

Our relationship with God is creative. When we go out to dinner with someone, we have no script. The conversation is created by the situation, the context, the issues on each of our minds, and the interplay of words and thoughts and emotions. We create conversation, and in turn the conversation helps create our relationship. It is hard to imagine that the God who created this energy and emotion wouldn't want to enjoy participating in it.

His creativity, in fact, continues throughout time and the ages to come. Even as you are reading this, he is creating new life, both physical and spiritual. And he intends to keep doing it. In a future time, he will create a "new heaven and new earth."[45] In an astonishing statement of mutuality in this creative process, he tells us that "we will also reign with him," which implies our participation in an evolving future.[46] We are a living, breathing extension of God's creative core, and our creative freedom is evidence of his power.[47]

The idea of joining God in ongoing creation is not just for the future. We are made in the image and likeness of a creative Being, so we must possess some element of that creativity. He wants us to work with him here and now to create and to cause real change.

Our Both/And Relationship with God

Although change can be scary to most of us, it's a normal part of a creation that our Creator said was "good."[48] According to philosophy professor William Hasker, the idea that God should experience the universe timelessly "relies heavily on the doctrine of divine simplicity. [This has] been very deeply influenced by the perception that change as such is inferior to permanence…[but] a workable universe…needs both [change and permanence] in full measure."[49] We need a God who is both changeless and changing, and we need a universe that is the same way—full of things we can count on and full of things that surprise us.

Halakic reasoning and interpretation push us toward another astounding idea: Could God somehow and at once be both outside of time *and* inside of time? Amazingly, God seems to be both above time and in it (in theological terms, he is both transcendent and immanent). In the beginning, God was already there.[50] But his many intrusions into history show that he can choose to be in time as fully as we are. God himself gives us the both/and: "I live in a high and holy place, *but also* with him who is contrite and lowly in spirit."[51] He is there, and he is here. He is in eternity, and he is in the room with you right now.

We see that the knowledge available to God includes both simultaneous knowledge *and* foreknowledge: He can see everything at one time, and he can see what is coming down the road long before it arrives. He is outside of time, in possession of simultaneous knowledge, and he is in control of his eternal plan. But he is also inside of time; he is a living being who shares an evolving and mutually creative relationship with us while being able to see the end of a situation before it arrives.

This split in types of knowledge is seen in God's response to Abraham's pleas that he spare the evil cities of Sodom and Gomorrah. God is outside of time: He hears the outcry that rises out of the mists of time. And then he is wondrously inside of time: He comes down to see what's going on, to live in "real time." He comes down from his "high and holy place" to immerse himself in time. "It follows," argues philosophy professor Nicholas Wolterstorff, "given that all human actions are temporal, that those actions of God which are 'response' actions are temporal as well."[52]

God's Changes Always Align with His Unchanging Character

God is love not only in an abstract sense, but in the full sense of an intimate, loving Being.[53] God's other "powers and attributes do not in the last analysis exist for themselves," wrote theologian Isaak Dorner, "as if they were for themselves absolutely necessary; they exist for absolute love."[54] Unlike all the false gods of history, our God isn't a great God because he knows things or can do things. He is a great God because he is love.

God is love in his essence and nature but also in his free actions. His life and energy and vibrant love are no less eternal than his changeless being. God is free to do anything—as long as whatever he does is aligned with who he is.[55]

God structured his creation and his relationship with his creation on the same principles that have existed within him from eternity. There is freedom to love and be loved. And he brings his knowledge and power to bear on making these relationships of love free and genuine. Because he is God, he can structure life to meet the test of authentic relationship, a relationship that is free to change.

WHERE THIS LEAVES US

The study of the unchanging God who changes suggests a breathtaking view of God and his relationships. It suggests that God, for the sake of relationship, brings all that he is to bear in his dealings with human beings. He brings his changeless nature, or rather the changeless attributes of his nature, into play with and for us. And he also brings his relational orientation and immense emotions and passions—his ability to change and respond to us—into play with and for us.

All of this is an extension of the principle that "God is love."[56] He is unchangeable in his character and changeable in his living relationships, all of which is good news for us.[57]

We find in this halakic conclusion a much bigger God, a God who is greater because he *isn't* unchangeable. "It is not inherently 'greater' to be inflexible," writes Dallas Willard. "This unfortunate idea is reinforced from 'the highest intellectual sources' by classical ideas of 'perfection,' which stressed the necessity of absolute inalterability in God. But in a domain of persons...it is far greater to be flexible and yet able to achieve the good goals one has set."[58]

This halakic truth maximizes God's freedom in relationship without diminishing his omniscience. And it actually enhances his omnipotence, because it allows his massive power to inform and direct his other attributes, *including* his omniscience.

This means that when we pray to God, he is really listening and really interested in what we have to say, be it praise or petition or simply conversation. While we are speaking, he doesn't tap his fingers in boredom, finish our sentences for us, or find something more interesting to do. He really listens, and he really lets our prayers influence him.

He rejoices, with genuine delight, when we think good thoughts or make good decisions or repent of bad ways. And we can laugh with joy like a child with a present to give when we "surprise" a God so loving and great that he lets himself be surprised.

Because he is the changeless *and* changing God, we have both the security and the unending joy of true relationship.

For Further Thought and Discussion

1. What would you say to someone who believes it's useless to pray to God because he won't change his decisions or actions in response to our prayers?

2. What is good about the ways in which God never changes? What is good about his reserving the freedom to change in some ways?

3. How does the idea that God really can change his decisions, his responses to us, and his courses of action alter your understanding of your relationship with him?

4. How do other verses in the Bible relate to the paradox of the unchanging God who changes?

5. Think of some ways in which you can change your mind or response without changing your principles or goals. Do you agree that God could do the same?

Six

The God Who Loathes and Loves the Wicked

WHY A RIGHTEOUS GOD WOULD EMBRACE THE UNRIGHTEOUS

You hate all who do wrong.

PSALM 5:5

For God so loved the world that he gave his one and only Son.

JOHN 3:16

Eduardo agreed to lead the youth group discussion as a favor to a friend. Now he wishes he'd had other plans.

"I hate the guy. He's a real jerk!" exclaims a teenage boy sitting across the table.

Eduardo searches his mind for a good response but doesn't come up with anything that will satisfy the angry teenager.

"God doesn't want us to hate anyone," he begins. "You should try to love this boy the way Christ does, even if he makes fun of your faith."

"But we just read in Psalms about David hating the wicked. And last week the Bible study pointed out that God hates those who are wicked," the teen counters. "This kid is definitely wicked. He hates the church and he doesn't believe in God. What's the point of trying to be nice to him?"

"God loves everyone and offers salvation even to the wicked," Eduardo explains. "Even the worst criminal in the world has a chance to be saved. You can't just hate someone because you think there is no hope for him."

"Well," the boy says, "either God hates the wicked or he loves them. Which is it?"

The rest of the youth group is getting restless, so Eduardo offers to continue the conversation later. But as he goes on with the study, he can't help but wonder what he'll tell the teenager. After all, the angry young man just made a very good point.

We recoil at all the evil in the world. Often it seems that the worst element of humanity is gaining the upper hand, making innocent people suffer as evildoers push forward their sinister agendas. Surely God must hate this even more than we do, considering his holiness and his standard of absolute righteousness.

So what did Jesus mean when he said we should love our enemies? How can we love a dictator who massacres thousands of his own people or a drug dealer who destroys the lives of untold numbers of young people? It seems that God's love raises as many questions as it answers, that love is not as simple as it seems.

LOVING AND LOATHING

We can bring a lot of theological and personal baggage to this paradox. We hear sermons on God's unfailing, sacrificial love, and we hear other sermons on God's holiness and justice and his hatred of the wicked and their unrighteous acts. Here is the paradox: How can God hate the wicked and love the wicked at the same time? Aren't hate and love mutually exclusive?

There is a parallel paradox for our own lives. Scripture teaches that we are to love even our enemies and bless those who abuse us.[1] But there are other verses that demand opposition to evildoers.[2] How can *we* hate the wicked and love the wicked at the same time?

This is one of the hardest concepts to grasp and practice well in the Christian life. Only by approaching it as a paradox do we stand a chance of getting it right.

God Hates the Wicked

Can God create people and end up hating them? How could a good God be ready and willing to destroy his own creation? How does the idea that "God is love" fit into this equation?[3]

If we choose side A of this paradox and say simply that God hates wicked people, we end up with a hard and unforgiving God. And we develop in our own lives a harsh attitude toward others. God ends up looking like the Great Hammer in the Sky just waiting for a chance to nail somebody. Just look at all those scriptures where he tells leaders and prophets and armies to wipe out entire groups of people, right down to the children! His standards are high and absolute, and people don't even come close to meeting them.

If that is the complete picture, then we'll struggle with trying to have a relationship with this God who very probably can't stand us. Who wants to relate to a deity who is so unyielding? And what kind of God would create someone just so he can work up a good, strong hatred toward the person and then destroy him? That's just the opposite of a loving Father or Friend or Guardian.

If we see God as the supreme hater, it's easy to blame him for everything bad that happens. If someone commits a murder, it must be God bringing judgment on the victim. If someone loses a job, it must be punishment for some misdeed. If someone is afflicted with a terminal illness, look no further than a disapproving God sending the lightning bolt of cancer. If we find biblical warrant for such an angry God, we'll also find great satisfaction when the bad person gets it. After all, he deserved it. He hated God, so he reaped God's judgment.

This view very naturally leads to selective acts of compassion. We only help the innocent and the truly needy people, since we don't want to get in the way of God's wrath having its full impact on a deserving sinner. In fact, why take the chance of helping someone who might be the target of God's wrath? If we alleviate that person's hunger or poverty or suffering, we could be in the wrong. It's probably better just to back off entirely, since *no one* is good enough to avoid making God angry.

This idea can produce hard-edged sermons, churches, and Christians. When we look around us, all we see are brazen sinners! Why, they reek of immorality and rottenness. When the Great Exterminator gets around to them, they'll wish they had changed their ways sooner. Pledging allegiance to the A side of this paradox will likely produce Christians who won't lift a finger to help guide those who are spiritually misled or to help those who are losing their grip on their souls.

God Loves the Wicked

Things don't get much easier when we examine the B side of the paradox. How can we understand the God who insists on loving the most despicable evildoers imaginable? But, if God really is love, as the Bible proclaims, doesn't he have to love us no matter *what* we do? Why worry about righteous living? Let's party!

Choosing the B side, however, does much more than give us license to throw off moral limits on our own behavior. It also strips God and his followers of any power to overcome evil. In place of the power over evil, it delivers a blanket tolerance of wickedness. "The only thing necessary for the triumph of evil," said British statesman Edmund Burke, "is for good men to do nothing."[4] If we see love as the extent of our responsibility toward others, then we'll do nothing that is effective in stopping wrongdoing in this world. Evil will indeed triumph.

We can find ourselves believing that God overlooks sin or that he forgives sin even in the absence of repentance and confession. We can adopt the cliché that God "hates the sin and loves the sinner," an inaccurate idea that treats sin like a separate substance completely isolated from the person who uses it to victimize others. And if we're completely honest, we'll admit that we are much more likely in practice to love the sin and hate the sinner. Why else do people feed on media reports of scandal and corruption while clucking their tongues at the scoundrels who are so brazen in their sin?

And if love is God's sole response to human sin, what are we to do with Nero, Attila the Hun, Genghis Khan, Ivan the Terrible, or the genocidal maniacs bleeding Africa today? Make room for them around the campfire? How about slave traders and rapists and serial killers and people who traffic in child pornography or kill nearly born children? Should we lovingly embrace them without holding them accountable for their violence against others?

But then there are the biblical passages about God's judgment. Admittedly, he wiped out entire cities, entire nations. You'd think God could at least be consistent when it comes to loving the wicked. Is he just being forgetful when he unleashes judgment? Are we wrong when we hope God *isn't* a lover of the wicked, when we secretly want to hate the evildoers with as much passion as we can muster? If they commit violence, don't they deserve our hatred?

Still, there are all those verses about love. So if we have to love the wicked, perhaps the best course is to offer "cheap grace"—just tell the sinner to believe in Jesus and everything will work out. And then there is the extreme application of "unconditional love," the belief that God will accept everyone into heaven. After all, a loving God could never really send anyone to hell, could he? We can blithely say, "We're all God's children," ignoring the fact that we only become a child of God when he decides to adopt us.

Churches that align themselves with the B side of the paradox demand very little of their members. Just come around once in a while, contribute some money and time when you can, and claim to be a Christian. We can easily create a pseudo-Christianity that is easier to market; a collective, religious self-esteem movement that is completely disconnected from confessed sin, genuine repentance, or God's work of redemption.

WHAT SCRIPTURE SAYS

It may not make us happy to think about a God who loves awful people. And it may not make us happy to think about a God who loathes anyone. But we're about to meet him.

The God Who Loathes the Wicked
If you do wrong, God hates you. "You hate *all* who do wrong," the psalmist says.[5] The full meaning of this hits us when we realize that *everyone* has done

wrong. Does that mean that God hates you and me? Unfortunately, this verse doesn't carve out an exception for anyone.

The psalmist goes on to pronounce, "Bloodthirsty and deceitful men the LORD *abhors*."[6] Now we're moving into the big leagues. How many of us have ever been deceitful? Okay, tough question. But at least we haven't been bloodthirsty! Actually, we have. "The tongue has the power of life and death," the Teacher tells us.[7] Verbal abuse is indeed a violent act.[8]

We're told, simply and chillingly, that "the wicked and those who love violence [God's] soul hates."[9] Again, in case we think we're pure enough to rise above this, the apostle Paul reminds us that "*all* have sinned and fall short of the glory of God."[10] Maybe we believe we're safe because we haven't committed any big-time, "mortal" sins. Surely God can abide a few minor sins? We need to think again. It doesn't take some over-the-edge perversion to arouse his wrath. "The Lord detests all the proud of heart."[11] Just thinking that you're better than you really are doesn't get you disliked by God—it gets you *detested* by God. And although pride is one of the "deadly" sins, at core all sins are deadly.[12]

But it's not enough that God hates the wicked. The Bible demands that *we* hate the wicked. "Do I not hate those who hate you, O LORD, and abhor those who rise up against you?" King David asked.[13] He expected God to appreciate his hatred for God's enemies, and this is not just an "Old Testament" expectation. Jesus added his support in Revelation when he commended the Christians of Ephesus: "I know you don't tolerate evil people."[14] Our age reveres the idea of tolerance for everyone. But God reserves his praise for those who are *intolerant* of wicked people, who know that tolerance of difference and tolerance of evil are two very different things.

It doesn't stop there. God doesn't just hate the wicked—he even hates the things they think about. "The LORD detests the thoughts of the wicked."[15] Wicked people can't think a thought that in any way connects with God. His people fall in line with God's view: "I hate double-minded men,"[16] says the psalmist with conviction. The words of the wicked don't score any higher. God sees the liar's lips moving, and he detests them.[17]

Then there is hatred toward types of people. Of the "six things the LORD hates," according to the Teacher, at least two are categories of people: "a false witness who pours out lies and a man who stirs up dissension among brothers."[18] Surely a false witness includes gossips and slanderers as well as those who testify with lies in a court of law. And how easy it is to stir up dissension, even in the church!

God hates people who do crooked, unethical things. "For the LORD your God detests anyone who…deals dishonestly."[19] This includes people who rob stores and those who pilfer from the company till, but what about people who say nothing when they are undercharged for a purchase?

Perverse people come under special scorn. "The LORD hates people with twisted hearts."[20] After listing a number of specific offenses, God says, "Anyone who does these things is detestable to the LORD, and because of these detestable practices the LORD your God will drive out those nations before you."[21]

God's loathing takes into account cumulative wickedness. "Because of *all* their wickedness…I hated them there," he explains.[22] He watches and waits and hates the wicked for their fatal illusion that they can make their own rules and still escape the loathing of God.[23]

Rejection of Jesus earns disaster. "If anyone does not love the Lord—a *curse* be on him,"[24] the apostle Paul declared. And here, the curse doesn't come from doing wicked things or even actively hating Jesus: It comes from *not loving* him.

If we are wrong, being powerful won't save us. "But even if we or an angel from heaven should preach a gospel other than the one we preached to you," wrote Paul, "let him be eternally condemned! As we have already said, so now I say again: If anybody is preaching to you a gospel other than what you accepted, let him be eternally condemned!"[25] Paul repeated his point to make sure we understand.

"Should you help the wicked and love those who hate the LORD?"[26] we are asked, with the unspoken answer being a thunderous *NO!* We could conclude from this that we should, for example, never bail an unrepentant person out of jail or work for a boss who is known for cutthroat business practices. And we are never to love people who hate God.

If wicked people show up at the door, we're to close and lock it. "If anyone comes to you and does not bring this teaching [about the truth of Christ]," wrote the apostle John, "do not take him into your house or welcome him."[27] Why not? Because "anyone who welcomes him *shares in his wicked work*."[28] Just being hospitable to a wicked person makes us accomplices to evil.

When we hear about the slimy things that people think up and do, we're supposed to hate them. "I look on the faithless with loathing."[29] With that in mind, should we even attend a public meeting with people who think Christianity is a bad joke? No. "I abhor the assembly of evildoers and refuse to sit with the wicked," says the psalmist.[30] This might give one pause before accepting an invitation!

This idea of separating ourselves from wrongdoers reaches into the church fellowship as well. We are supposed to "warn a divisive person once, and then warn him a second time. After that, have nothing to do with him."[31] No "hello" in the hallway, no sending little notes of encouragement, no lunches to try to talk some sense into the troublemaking brother or sister. Just simply "have *nothing* to do with him."

Then there are verses about God's people rejoicing when the rotten person gets her just deserts. "The righteous will be glad when they are avenged, when they bathe their feet in the blood of the wicked."[32] The response God expects from his people when they see the wicked destroyed is gladness.

There can be no question. God loathes the wicked intensely.[33] And he expects us to be like him.

The God Who Loves the Wicked

Even a cursory reading of the Bible reveals that God is love. And not only is he love, but he has an intense love for sinners.

"Do I take any pleasure in the death of the wicked?" he asks, expecting a no.[34] When bad people die, it would appear that there is no happiness in heaven. "Rather," he goes on, "am I not pleased when they turn from their [wicked] ways and live?"[35] God is always hoping, always waiting for the moment when the wicked will turn toward him and live.

God loves the wicked so much, in fact, that in many ways he treats them just like decent folks. "He causes his sun to rise on the evil and the good," we're reminded, "and sends rain on the righteous and the unrighteous."[36] You don't deserve good things from God? Too bad—you're going to receive them anyway! Theologians have long called this disturbing habit of God "common grace." The wicked get good things simply because they are here and God is God. He keeps sending good things to bad people, hoping they will finally figure out who the Gift-giver is.[37]

One of the biggest complaints about Jesus? "But the Pharisees and the teachers of the law muttered, 'This man welcomes sinners and eats with them.'"[38] He didn't just devote a few moments to sinners, smiling and waving to them from across the room. He went out of his way to welcome them. He *ate* with them! He made such a habit of this that he said, sounding frustrated and sarcastic, "The Son of Man came eating and drinking, and they say, 'Here is a glutton and a drunkard, a friend of tax collectors and "sinners."'"[39] He didn't stop loving sinners just because his religious opponents accused him of unrighteous priorities. Instead, he pointed out that loving, welcoming, and eating with wicked people doesn't make you like the sinners—it makes you like our loving, merciful God.

But with Jesus this went far beyond just a willingness to spend time with sinners. In his own exasperating way, he seemed to *prefer* the company of the wicked to the company of that era's religious stalwarts.[40] Jesus said with no ambiguity: "It is not the healthy who need a doctor, but the sick."[41] He *loves* the sick, the sinners, the lost. That's why he came to earth in the first place, he tells the Pharisees with a piercing dismissal: "But go and learn what this means: 'I desire mercy, not sacrifice.' For I have not come to call the righteous, but sinners."[42]

Some of Jesus' best friends were very wicked people:

- *Mary Magdalene,* a close companion of Jesus, had been possessed by seven demons, which Jesus had to cast out of her.[43] Before she met Jesus, she was not that century's version of Mother Teresa.
- Jesus stayed in the home of *Zacchaeus,* a chief tax collector, an experienced bad guy of the time.[44] Tax collectors made their living by charging people a lot more than what was due to the authorities and pocketing the difference.

- Jesus befriended a down-and-out *Samaritan woman,* a woman so low that even *she* couldn't believe he would "lower" himself by speaking to her.[45] She was a foreigner, an unbeliever, sexually immoral, and she belonged to a people considered a "mongrel" race by the devout Jews of that era. But when Jesus stopped to rest on a hot, dusty journey, she was exactly the kind of person with whom he wanted to spend time.

God is constantly thinking about the wicked and about how to get them to come back to him. He sent his prophet Jonah to Nineveh, one of the most wicked, brutal cities on the face of the earth. It was full of people so rotten that Jonah didn't want to go. Jonah detested sinners, and he knew how much God loves wicked people.

God said to him, "But Nineveh has more than a hundred and twenty thousand people who cannot tell their right hand from their left, and many cattle as well. Should I not be concerned about that great city?"[46] God is concerned, always, about the condition of the wicked. He knows how little they know and how much they need help.

Nobody, ultimately, falls off God's radar screen of love. When Jesus was crucified between two felons, "those crucified with him also heaped insults on him."[47] Bad idea, given their situation and proximity to eternity. And yet, a very short time before they all died, one of the criminals changed *completely* and pleaded with Jesus to "remember me when you come into your kingdom."[48] Jesus didn't berate the man for waiting until the last minute. And he didn't remind this criminal of his earlier heartless taunts. Quite the opposite. Jesus said simply: "I tell you the truth, today you will be with me in paradise."[49]

"For God loved the world"—not planet Earth but people—"in this way: He gave His One and Only Son, so that *everyone* who believes in Him will not perish but have eternal life."[50] God loves miserable, rotten, lost, sinful people. Jesus, after all, did not die for good people.[51] Jesus' words echo through the centuries: "Father, forgive them, for they do not know what they are doing."[52]

Jesus once said, "Greater love has no one than this, that he lay down his life for his friends."[53] But in his own actions he went much further. He laid down his life for his *enemies.* His love is greater even than the greatest love.

Jesus commands us to imitate him. "But I tell you who hear me: Love your enemies, do good to those who hate you, bless those who curse you, pray for those who mistreat you."[54] A tall order, indeed. Our natural response is to go to the other side of the paradox and pray these people into the ground.

"Hatred stirs up dissension," we're warned, "but love covers over all wrongs."[55] Wickedness won't win, so we don't have to fear it. When we can face ridicule and abuse from others without malice toward them, we have arrived at a place where we can love the wicked—and offer them a chance to change.

There is no room for hating a fellow believer, even a stumbling one. "Anyone who claims to be in the light but hates his brother is still in the darkness."[56] Our brothers and sisters may actually *be* in the darkness, but if we hate them for it, we join them there.

Just as we were told elsewhere in Scripture to take tough action against the wicked, now we're told to do just the opposite: "Do not repay evil with evil or insult with insult, but with blessing."[57] Why? Because God loves the wicked, and he gives us specific directions about smothering wickedness with love. "If your enemy is hungry, give him food to eat; if he is thirsty, give him water to drink."[58] Mother Teresa echoed this call: "I invite all those who appreciate our work," she wrote, "to look around them and be willing to love those who have no love and offer them their services."[59]

Stephen, a spiritual giant of the early church, echoed Jesus' prayer for the wicked people who were stoning him to death. "He fell on his knees and cried out, 'Lord, do not hold this sin against them.'"[60] That's what loving the wicked is all about: blessing them, pleading for them, offering them a better way.

There is no question that God loves the wicked, and so should we.[61]

THE DEEPER MEANING OF BOTH/AND

So what are the both/and truths we see in this paradox? For one, it's clear that God does, in fact, loathe *and* love the wicked. And it's not that he loathes sinners in a certain period of history—say the Old Testament—and then switches to love with the New Testament. He loathes and loves the wicked *at the same time.*

We Are Sinful but Made in God's Image

Many have said that people are basically good, and many others have said that people are inherently bad. But both statements are true: We are basically good *and* inherently bad. We are good in the sense that God made each of us in his own image and likeness.[62] When God looks at us, he sees some reflection of himself, and he loves the family likeness. Meanwhile, we are truly bad: We "are accustomed to doing evil"[63]; we are "skilled in doing evil"[64]; we "invent ways of doing evil."[65] This is the aspect of our being that God loathes.

God has two different ways of dealing with people. He is both kind and stern. "Consider therefore the kindness and sternness of God," Paul proclaimed, "sternness to those who fell, but kindness to you."[66] And God is comfortable with both courses of action. "Just as it pleased the LORD to make you prosper and increase in number, *so it will please him to ruin and destroy you.*"[67] This is an astonishing idea, that God is just as pleased to destroy human beings as he is to bless them.

Any thoughtful person can see immediately that our sin is what puts the barrier—an inescapable judgment, a fierce enmity—between us and God. This halakic forces us to give up the notion that God loves the sinner and hates the sin. We see that God makes no such distinction, at least with truly wicked people. When we spit in God's face, he takes it personally. He blames *us.* People and nations can come to the point where they are past hope, where they deserve and will receive God's loathing.

But it isn't God who dooms them. "An evil man is snared by his own sin," we're taught.[68] We see that sin is personal. It belongs to individual people and groups of people and ultimately can't be separated from the sinner—except when help is sought from heaven.

We had earned God's loathing; we were in a very bad way. He had every reason to think stern thoughts about us—and he did. And then, because he values the people he created, he gave up his own life to have us for his children.

Even the Wicked Receive God's Love

"Nothing prevents one and the same thing being loved under one aspect, while it is hated under another," wrote medieval theologian Thomas Aquinas. "God loves sinners…for they have existence, and have it from Him. In so far as they are sinners…they are hated by Him."[69]

Is it a good thing that God loves the wicked? It's the best thing, since we find that *we* are the wicked. The prophet Isaiah confirms our guilt: "For everyone is ungodly and wicked."[70] In talking about Jesus, Peter told a large crowd that God "sent [Jesus] first to you to bless you by turning *each* of you from your wicked ways."[71]

Amazingly, God offers kindness to the wicked in the hope that they will repent. God asks wicked people, "Do you show contempt for the riches of his kindness, tolerance and patience, not realizing that God's kindness leads you toward repentance?"[72] "Don't misunderstand me," God seems to be saying. "Don't mistake my kindness and patience for approval of your thoughts or actions. Accept me while I still give you breath."

Eventually, as we have seen, he stops sending the life-giving breath. God lets sin reach its "full measure,"[73] an interesting biblical concept that perhaps hints at the tipping point between loathing and loving. God doesn't react to the first sin, or even to many sins, with an irreversible loathing. He doesn't act with finality; he doesn't expose his full loathing until sin reaches that tipping point.

We see that our willingness to be forgiven is the key. If we keep our hearts hardened against all of God's overtures, we leave him no option but to loathe us. We find that wicked people aren't condemned because they are wicked, but rather because they are not willing to accept God's love. He is always close to humble, repentant sinners, but "the proud he knows from afar."[74] If we think we can save ourselves, if we have that level of absurd arrogance, he simply lets us try.

There does seem to be hope for all of the wicked, no matter their sins. One of the best cases in point is the apostle Paul, the transformed Christian-killer. Still, there is a point of no return. "I assure you," said Jesus, "that any sin can be forgiven, including blasphemy; but anyone who blasphemes against the Holy Spirit will never be forgiven. It is an eternal sin."[75]

What does it mean to blaspheme the Holy Spirit? Jesus said that when he sends "the Spirit of truth who goes out from the Father, he will testify about me."[76] So if we deny the Spirit's testimony, if we hold firmly that he is lying and that Jesus is not the Christ, we are blaspheming the Holy Spirit. This does not mean that we have once said, "I don't believe in God" or "I don't believe in the Holy Spirit." It's a matter of persisting in this rejection of the One about whom the Holy Spirit is talking. Refusal to believe the only One who can save us is self-destructive. We can be unwilling to accept God's mercy—to our own ruin.

Those who steadfastly refuse God's open, welcoming arms find themselves in the worst of company. "Who is the liar? It is the man who denies that Jesus is the Christ. Such a man is the antichrist—he denies the Father and the Son."[77]

While we are free to refuse the only One who can save us, the fact is, God doesn't want *any* to perish. He loathes wickedness, but he is amazingly patient before he finally wipes out the wicked. "He is patient with you, not wanting anyone to perish, but *everyone* to come to repentance."[78]

We find that God can look fully into the face of evil people and still somehow reach out to offer his embrace. "O Jerusalem, Jerusalem," Jesus lamented, "you who kill the prophets and stone those sent to you, how often I have longed to gather your children together, as a hen gathers her chicks under her wings, but you were not willing!"[79] He thinks about the murderers, he knows about their many sins, and still he wishes he could gather them under his wings.

One thing we see about this God of ours is that he takes special delight in saving the really rotten people. Paul called himself a "blasphemer and a persecutor and a violent man,"[80] then said (after declaring himself to be the worst person ever), "But for that very reason I was shown mercy so that in me, the worst of sinners, Christ Jesus might display his *unlimited patience* as an example for those who would believe on him and receive eternal life."[81] Incredibly, Paul is saying there is no question he was the worst and, incredibly, that this is *exactly* why God rejoiced in saving him—to prove once and for all that the unfailing love of God is always out there, ready to be poured out and win the day.

While he remains disgusted over what we've become, God continues to drench us in mercy and love—and hope for what we might become. "It is never too late to be what you might have been," wrote novelist George Eliot.[82]

God's Definition of Hate

For most of us, hate grows from anger at those who have hurt or insulted us. The initial feeling of anger isn't held against us. We are designed to be treated with respect and dignity, and when we receive the opposite treatment, it's hard not to want to strike back in kind.

But in God's kingdom, hate is a certain relationship to people, forces, or influences that oppose God. In other words, we have such a great love for God that everything that stands against him is disgusting to us. We have to love the wicked but do it without allying ourselves with them.[83]

We show love very carefully to those still inside the walls of evil. We're given the paradoxical instruction to "snatch others from the fire and save them; to others show mercy, mixed with fear—hating even the clothing stained by corrupted flesh."[84] Should we try to show wicked people the light? Absolutely. But we snatch them from the fire quickly so we don't get burned. We have to take special precautions when trying to help people who are committing sins with which we ourselves have struggled (like drunkards helping drunkards). If we're too close to the problem, we can *become* the problem.

We're not to be overcome by their evil, but rather to "overcome evil with good."[85] We focus on the positive, even in the face of our enemies' hatred and taunting. We resist our enemies; we don't let them win, and we don't join them. And we wait for God to act on our behalf, even while we continue to love the enemy and bless him. If we love our enemies, God promises our "reward will be great, and [we] will be sons of the Most High, because he is kind to the ungrateful and wicked."[86]

We should be ready to offer kindness and hope to the wicked. "When I say to a wicked man, 'You will surely die,' and you do not warn him or speak out to dissuade him from his evil ways in order to save his life, that wicked man will die for his sin, and I will hold *you* accountable for his blood."[87] It isn't enough to be against evil or to condemn the wicked. God expects us to take positive action, to care about them, to *love* them. Kind actions can open doors, which is one of the reasons we're told to feed our enemies when they're hungry.

Although we are supposed to pray for and bless our enemies, we can't pray that God will force them to be saved. "There is a sin that leads to death," wrote the apostle John. "I am not saying that he should pray about that."[88] This is the sin of blaspheming the Holy Spirit—steadfastly rejecting the Christ about whom the Spirit testifies—that we discussed earlier.

For us, the crucial question is, How do we love *and* loathe the wicked? There is no formula. We will have to be guided by the Holy Spirit, to select in each case from the biblical menu of options, such as turning the other cheek, returning good for evil, blessing those who curse us, giving them food and drink, teaching or showing them the way, praying that God will bring people and circumstances into their lives that will cause them to consider their ways, avoiding them, refusing to show them hospitality, confronting them, warning them, stopping them, and overcoming their evil with good. We have to find the right and most effective ways to respond to the wicked, and we have to be ready to change our response over time—particularly when they make a change.

The Difference Between God's Enemies and Our Enemies

Could it be that we have to distinguish between different kinds of wicked people, different kinds of enemies? As we sift through the Scriptures, we begin to see that we're responsible to have a holy hate for *God's* enemies while loving our *own* enemies. We hate God's enemies for their stance against God, not because they've offended us. "Do I not hate those who hate *you*, O LORD?"[89] the psalmist asks. His hatred is not ignited by personal opposition or animosity. We might be living in such a way that we provoke another's hostility. But hating God is the one bad decision that is eventually fatal, and always to be loathed.

It seems that we should pray *against* the wicked and not just *for* them. What pushes the needle on the dial away from praying for and toward praying against? First, their consistent opposition to God and his kingdom should alter the tone of our prayers. Second, we should consider praying against the wicked when our love and best efforts push them toward more ingratitude and abusiveness rather than toward repentance. Third, our prayers should change when the wicked begin causing great harm to others, especially the innocent and defenseless. And finally, we should pray against the wicked if the Holy Spirit gives us a glimpse of their dark hearts and moves us to oppose them with faith and righteous indignation.

The Bible gives us the model and the words, and on this delicate matter we're much safer using scriptural language than trying to make up our own. The psalms are loaded with prayers against the wicked. Many of these psalms were called by the early church "imprecatory psalms" (*imprecatory* means "to invoke or call down [evil or curses], as upon a person"[90]). "Break the arm of the wicked and evil man"[91]; "let the wicked be put to shame"[92]; "may the wicked perish before God"[93]—all are examples of this kind of prayer.

"My God!" the psalmist explodes. "I've had it with them! Blow them away!... Knock the breath right out of them, so they're gasping for breath, gasping, 'GOD.' Bring them to the end of their rope, and leave them there dangling, helpless."[94] In the end, we apparently have no choice but to reject those who have rejected God.

And although it seems we are to pray for justice, we are instructed to leave all judgment to God. We leave our hands off the situation so that we will do nothing prematurely, nothing to impede the wicked person's path to God, and nothing to prevent God from issuing his judgment at the appropriate time. We make room for God to exercise wrath. "Do not take revenge, my friends, but leave room for God's wrath, for it is written: 'It is mine to avenge; I will repay,' says the Lord."[95]

Only God finally knows when people are past hope. Unlike us, he never moves too soon, and unlike us, he never waits too long. We know his timing and methods are perfect. We can rejoice that true justice is always carried out by God. We can rejoice also when we see our Father's victory over those who have long defied him.

Although God goes a long, long way with us, we can exhaust his patience and become a stench in his nostrils. "My Spirit will not contend with man forever," he says, sounding weary as well as frustrated.[96] Finally, when all is said and done, he wants the wicked to be gone. In a terrifying story, he says, "You will stand outside knocking and pleading, 'Sir, open the door for us.' But he will answer, 'I don't know you or where you come from.... Away from me, all you evildoers!"[97] In this final catharsis, the all-knowing God says he doesn't even *know* the wicked. They have been erased.

But God never wants it to be this way. His love keeps hanging in there, waiting, watching, hoping, acting, intervening. Unless *we* close the door forever, he never gives up, never forgets us, never stops scheming and plotting to entice us to find him.

We see that God isn't gentle with sin. But he is, indeed, gentle.

WHERE THIS LEAVES US

As we think about this unsettling paradox, we come to see that there is "a time to love and a time to hate."[98] We found in this halakic investigation that God does both: He loves the wicked, and he loathes the wicked. And if we want to be like God, we have to find a way to both love and loathe the wicked too.

FOR FURTHER THOUGHT AND DISCUSSION

1. How would you describe what it means to loathe the wicked?
2. How would you describe what it means to love the wicked?
3. How will this halakic study change your prayer life? How will it change your opinion of how you should treat others, especially those who spurn God?
4. What ideas discussed in this chapter bother you? Why? What will you need to do to incorporate these ideas into your life?
5. Is God calling you to view anyone differently? Who is this person? What will it take for you to make this change?

Seven

The Prince of Peace Who Bears a Sword

Two Paths of Peace, Two Paths of War

~~~

Peace I leave with you; my peace I give you.

John 14:27

Do you think I came to bring peace on earth? No, I tell you, but division.

Luke 12:51

Meredith and Anne teach in the same Christian school, but they haven't been getting along due to a difference in philosophy.

"Meredith's approach is so frustrating," Anne explained to her husband. "The way she uses trivial issues to judge the students' Christian commitment infuriates me. I know it's damaging their view of themselves and of God. But I'm not the school principal, so I don't really have the right to say anything."

She let out a defeated sigh. "I've prayed over this issue, but I just can't seem to find peace about it."

Her husband tried to offer some advice. "Maybe God wants you to take a stand for the students and challenge Meredith, and that's why you don't feel peace."

"But we're supposed to be Christlike, and I have very little patience with her," Anne admitted. "I'm afraid if I said anything, it wouldn't be said with love. Plus I sometimes wonder if maybe God approves of her approach, and I'm the one who's wrong."

Anne's husband pictured Jesus turning over the tables of the moneychangers. "Christ didn't always approach things peacefully," he reminded his wife. "Remember the scene he made in the temple?"

"I know," Anne said. "It's just that I've been taught that Christians are supposed to be peace-loving people. I know if I say something to Meredith, it's going to stir up trouble."

"Maybe instead of praying for peace, you should pray for strength," her husband said. "In this situation, it sounds like you're going to need it."

This paradox hits close to home for most of us. We think we're to be meek and mild mannered, and we do our best to live that way. But then something upsets our spiritual equilibrium, and we're faced with a choice: Do nothing and maintain a surface-level peace, or confront the situation and risk open conflict. Neither option appeals to us, and it seems unclear what a Christian's true responsibility is. But it does seem clear that maintaining the peace at all costs may not be the best course of action.

THE PEACEFUL SAVIOR WHO BRINGS CONFLICT

We like to think of Jesus as a gentle, quiet, loving person who came to unite and heal and forgive. But this image collides with a different biblical perspective on Jesus, the portrait of a firm, intense person who came to *divide* people.

Jesus is the Prince of Peace who said, "Peace I leave with you; my peace I give you."[1] And Jesus said, "Do not suppose that I have come to bring peace to the earth. I did not come to bring peace, but a sword."[2] How can Jesus be the Prince of Peace if he did not come to bring peace?

This paradox paves the way for a much bigger—and a much different—view of Jesus than most of us have ever considered.

The Peaceful Jesus

What if Jesus were concerned only about peace—to the exclusion of anything that might stir up trouble? Is there no situation that calls for God's people to be angry or confront wrongdoers? Is it ever appropriate for followers of Christ to initiate conflict?

We read in Isaiah that Jesus is the Prince of Peace,[3] a title for the Savior that makes us feel good. It's an image of Jesus that is nice and understanding, the type of person we feel would never be harsh or combative. The biblical stories about Jesus' touching lepers and visiting sinners and weeping over Jerusalem become our dominant image of him, because they show us the Jesus who makes us feel comfortable.

But with that picture of Jesus occupying our understanding of what he is like, we can easily disregard the biblical reality that Jesus is a strong and demanding personality. We read stories in Scripture where Jesus insults people, talks negatively about leaders in front of their followers, and makes whips—more than once—to drive people out of the temple.[4] What are we to do with a Prince of Peace who cracks a whip to clear scoundrels from a place of worship?

Thinking that peace is the central message, we might believe that peace will come to us, no matter how we are living, if we just "believe in Jesus." We will gravitate toward messages that say, "Become a Christian and you will have peace," in spite of passages that *promise* pain, persecution, and suffering to those who faithfully follow Christ.[5] Overlooking those passages, we can easily conclude that peace is unconditional, at least for Christians. When everything is going well, we assume that we are on the right path and simply receiving the peace that Jesus promised, regardless of the condition of our lives.

Embracing the Jesus who is peace and only peace can leave us feeling justified in inactivity and guilty about our challenging relationships. Churches that focus on this side of the paradox can easily end up as mushy, feel-good havens for people who are in denial about the God of swords and whips.

The "Tough" Jesus

At the other end of the paradox, we can end up with an emphasis on Jesus' "tough" nature. Those who have been harshly judged or abused might welcome a harsh Son of God who delivers judgment, thinking their own tormentors will get their just deserts. Or the image of a tough Jesus might repulse them, since such an image could remind them of their tormentors. We can wrongly minimize or ignore the reality that Jesus is a gentle and yielding personality.

If Jesus is the enforcer of God's wrath, we might become anxious and fearful because there really are no guarantees of peace. We can become despondent over the bad things that happen, the disappointments of life, and the sense that misery in our fallen world will never be alleviated.

A focus on the tough-minded Jesus might lead us to avoid attempts at reconciliation when relationships are estranged. "We had to part company with those people," we might say (and often over the pettiest of issues). We might feel justified in stirring up conflict with people, even (maybe especially) with fellow believers with whom we don't see eye to eye. After all, Jesus didn't go out of his way to keep people happy.

When we've walked this path long enough, we can end up believing that we have to postpone our hope of peace until the next life. Even though life on earth is constant torment, at least after we die we'll "rest in peace" at last.

Limiting our view of Jesus to the Son of God who brings a sword instead of peace can leave us feeling insecure, justified in fighting over insignificant points, and feeling guilty if we fail to challenge any wrong of which we're aware. Churches that focus on this side of the paradox can easily become hard, comply-or-else citadels for people who would gladly trade in their plowshares for swords.

WHAT SCRIPTURE SAYS

Our childhood images of Jesus leave us with a mental picture of a carpenter with strong callous hands who gently blesses little children. His strength is subordinate to his tranquil nature. The story about clearing the temple is underplayed, as if it were some sort of aberration. As we examine the biblical basis of this paradox, we can't help but see that Jesus is truly the Prince of Peace—but that he didn't come to make everybody feel good.

The Prince of Peace Who Gives Us Peace

If there is anything that Jesus was clear on, it's this: He came to bring peace.

"Peace I leave with you," he assured us, "my peace I give you."[6] He was speaking of the peace of God, the peace that is beyond understanding.[7] Jesus says peace is a gift, and he is the Giver.

"I have told you these things, so that in me you may have peace," he says.[8] This news of peace is so outstanding that the prophet says, "Shout, Daughter of Jerusalem! See, your king comes.... He will proclaim peace to the nations."[9] In a world that is never free of war, Jesus has a different message, a proclamation of peace.

Jesus is, in fact, the One by whom we obtain peace. We're told that "the punishment that brought us peace was upon him."[10] Whatever punishment and strife were due to us for our bad attitudes and rotten behavior, Jesus took them on himself and by that act earned us peace. And it is a past-tense proposition, the punishment that *brought* us peace. It's not a promise that is waiting to be fulfilled at some time in the future. Jesus set out to "reconcile to himself all things, whether things on earth or things in heaven, by making peace through his blood, shed on the cross."[11] Peace usually comes after a war, and the war that brought us back into communion with God was indeed a bloody one. We are told by Isaiah that the Redeemer brings healing to us by his wounding. He brings peace to his own through violence to himself.

Peace isn't something we have to wait for, something we get when we die. Peace is now. "I will make a covenant of peace with them," God promises.[12] We certainly have a part in the process: to commit our souls to Christ. But if we do, he brings a lot more to the partnership than we do. He brings us peace.

This peace isn't sent to us in a trickle. "I will extend peace to her like a river," God promises.[13] That's what we're looking for, a river of peace. We need refreshment, and that's what Jesus offers.

Peace is so much a part of Jesus' nature that Isaiah encouraged God's people, "For to us a child is born.... And he will be called...Prince of Peace."[14] Just as God is love, so is he peace.[15] "He will be their peace," the prophet Micah said.[16] Peace, it turns out, is a person.

"Now may the Lord of peace himself give you peace at *all* times and in *every* way," Paul said, blessing the Thessalonians.[17] God is able to give us peace every moment of our lives, for the rest of our lives. Spiritual peace? Mental peace? Emotional peace? Peace about decisions and career paths and relationships and service and ministries? Yes. God's peace touches on every area of life.

He can bring peace because "he himself is our peace."[18] And it doesn't matter where you are—how close to him or how far away—he preaches the same message: peace. It's there, if you want it.

We are physical beings who face danger just by getting up in the morning. We can be attacked by diseases, disabling accidents, and other physical disasters, all causing great distress. But if we look to the Prince of Peace for healing, we can find a peace that no doctor or pharmaceutical company can offer. "Daughter, your faith has healed you," he told one sick woman. "Go in peace and be freed from your suffering."[19]

Peace isn't limited to an internal calm in the midst of disaster. It also means protection from disaster. "I will grant peace," he says; "you will lie down and no one will make you afraid."[20] I once talked with an Ethiopian who had made his way from his home country to the United States. "Here," he said with emotion, "you can go to bed and not worry about someone coming and taking you away in the night." That's what the Prince of Peace offers us: "You will not fear the terror of night.... A thousand may fall at your side, ten thousand at your right hand, but it will not come near you," we are promised. "If you make the Most High your dwelling—even the LORD, who is my refuge—then no harm will befall you, no disaster will come near your tent."[21] If we trust in him, the wicked can't come in and get us, because "he grants peace to your borders."[22]

We see this Prince of Peace characterized in the Bible as a "lamb," as peaceful and gentle a creature as there is. No one is ever attacked by a lamb or abused by a lamb. Even when Jesus appeared in a resurrected body to his terrified disciples, he was still the Lamb. "Jesus came and stood among them and said, 'Peace be with you!'"[23]

Jesus' birth announcement was, "Glory to God in the highest, and on earth peace to men."[24] The Pax Romana—the Peace of Rome—was nothing compared with the peace of God. "LORD, you establish peace for us," Isaiah prayed.[25]

Who could question the powerful truth that Jesus is the Prince of Peace who gives us peace?[26]

The One Who Brings a Sword

If there is any point that Jesus was clear on, it was that he didn't come to bring peace. "Do not suppose that I have come to bring peace to the earth. I did *not* come to bring peace, but a sword."[27] He came to a people whose land was occupied and ruled by a Gentile conqueror. The Jews of Judea wanted to be delivered from their enemies so they could inhabit the land in peace. Surely peace was part of the Messiah's mission. But Jesus stated firmly, in the clearest of language, "I did not come to bring peace." *Don't even think it,* he is saying.

Instead of what everyone longed for, Jesus said he was bringing a *sword.* A sword is used to cut things in two. And that's exactly what Jesus intended to do. "For I have come to turn 'a man against his father, a daughter against her mother, a daughter-in-law against her mother-in-law—a man's enemies will be the members of his own household.'"[28] We expect pastors and priests and marriage counselors and friends to help bring peace to our relationships. Jesus gave himself a different role, a different job description. He came to break up relationships, to cut friendships in two, to divide people who are closely related, to create warfare inside of homes. His sword was for families, not for Romans.

He added, "From now on there will be five in one family divided against each other, three against two and two against three. They will be divided, father against son and son against father, mother against daughter and daughter against mother, mother-in-law against daughter-in-law and daughter-in-law against mother-in-law."[29] The hard fact is, the Prince of Peace turns people against each other.

And if this doesn't sound harsh enough, there's more. "I have come to bring fire on the earth, and how I wish it were already kindled!" Jesus said with passion. "Do you think I came to bring peace on earth? No, I tell you, but division."[30] The Prince of Peace came to bring division. We can conclude that if we have Jesus involved in our lives, we should expect—and we are going to get—division.

We see this One who doesn't bring peace characterized in the Bible as a lion, a ferocious predator. "For I will be like a lion.... I will tear them to pieces and go away; I will carry them off, with no one to rescue them."[31] When this "Lion of the tribe of Judah"[32]—Jesus—comes, those who resist him will stand helpless before him.

And don't think that Jesus is a Lion who holds back. "Woe to you, teachers of the law and Pharisees, you hypocrites!" Jesus said to their faces. "You travel over land and sea to win a single convert, and when he becomes one, you make him twice as much a son of hell as you are.... You blind fools!... You blind guides!... You are like whitewashed tombs, which look beautiful on the outside but on the inside are full of dead men's bones and everything unclean.... You snakes! You brood of vipers! How will you escape being condemned to hell?"[33] Most of us would wince at being called a hypocrite. What would you do if Jesus showed up at your door and called you a "son of hell," a "blind fool," a "whitewashed tomb," a "snake?"

"Now then," he said, "you Pharisees clean the outside of the cup and dish, but inside you are full of greed and wickedness. You foolish people!... Woe to you, because you are like unmarked graves, which men walk over without knowing it." The teachers of the law were there with the Pharisees, and one of them said to Jesus, "Teacher, when you say these things, you insult us also." They should have kept quiet. "Woe to you," he said to them, "because you build tombs for the prophets, and it was your forefathers who killed them."[34]

What about "serving" God, but in a bad way? For example, what did Jesus do with those who followed the tradition of making animals available for sale in the temple for ritual sacrifice? We are likely to think Jesus would give these people partial credit for trying. "In the temple courts [Jesus] found men selling cattle, sheep and doves, and others sitting at tables exchanging money. So he made a whip out of cords, and drove all from the temple area, both sheep and cattle; he scattered the coins of the money changers and overturned their tables. To those who sold doves he said, 'Get these out of here! How dare you turn my Father's house into a market!' "[35] It's hard to picture the face of this angry prophet—how many people have ever seen such a painting of Jesus? But Jesus was being just like his Father: "The LORD Almighty will lash them with a whip," we're told by the prophet Isaiah.[36]

And amazingly, this was not a one-time event. The temple-clearing described by the apostle John happened early in Jesus' public ministry, but he did it again two Passovers later. "Jesus entered the temple area and drove out all who were buying and selling there. He overturned the tables of the money changers and the benches of those selling doves. 'It is written,' he said to them, ' "My house will be called a house of prayer," but you are making it a "den of robbers." ' "[37] The gospel writer Mark added that Jesus "would not allow anyone to carry merchandise through the temple courts."[38] He drove them out, wrecked their trade-show booths, called them robbers. And then he stood there, alone, glaring at them, blocking their paths, an unstoppable and unrelenting foe. Whatever else this is, it is not a picture of peace.

As we read the accounts of the angry Jesus, we notice a reason that he doesn't bring peace: People ignored his earlier anger and actions and went right back to their old ways. They went back to business as usual, hoping Jesus wouldn't notice. It's easy to imagine, though, that people were always just a little nervous when Jesus came to the temple.

What would Jesus do? is a question we often hear. Well, what would Jesus do at many church and ministry events today? What would he do about the cheapening and commercialization of his message? Would he say, "I don't agree with the methods, but at least you're getting the word out?" Or would he make a whip and clear out the church, the arena, the concert hall, the bookstore, or the convention center? Perhaps we should be a little nervous whenever Jesus is around *our* meetings.

Peace gets preached a lot, because peace is a pleasant and comforting concept. "But [Jeremiah] said, 'Ah Sovereign LORD, the prophets keep telling them, "You will not see the sword or suffer famine. Indeed, I will give you lasting peace in this place."' Then the LORD said to me, 'The prophets are prophesying lies in my name.... Those same prophets will perish by sword and famine. And the people they are prophesying to will be thrown out into the streets of Jerusalem because of the famine and sword.'"[39] If we know something is wrong, in a situation or a nation, we shouldn't listen to sweet messages of peace. We can be sure that Jesus is coming and that famine and the sword are right behind him.

The prophet Ezekiel revealed the judgment that would come upon teachers who whitewashed the truth by assuring people that peace was the order of the day. "They lead my people astray, saying 'Peace,' when there is no peace, and because, when a flimsy wall is built, they cover it with whitewash.... The wall is gone and so are those who whitewashed it, those...who prophesied to Jerusalem and saw visions of peace for her when there was no peace."[40]

We'd like to think that following Jesus would assure peace in our dealings with others. But we're told clearly that everyone who follows him will encounter not peace but persecution.[41] In fact, we should be concerned when people are *not* persecuting us. "Woe to you when all men speak well of you," Jesus said.[42] When we're at peace with everyone, we somehow find ourselves at war with Jesus.

Those who speak falsely about peace will continue doing so to the end. "The day of the Lord will come like a thief in the night. While people are saying, 'Peace and safety,' destruction will come on them suddenly, as labor pains on a pregnant woman, and they will not escape."[43] When people are in great turmoil, they want a message of peace and safety and hope. But they won't get these things. They will receive destruction instead.

There can be no doubt. Jesus didn't come to bring peace.[44]

THE DEEPER MEANING OF BOTH/AND

Logic won't get us very far as we try to reconcile the idea of a Prince of Peace who bears a sword. As we look at the paradox, we see that Jesus gives peace and doesn't give peace. But how can he do both? How can he be the Prince of Peace and the Prince of Sword and Division at the same time?

Let's dive into this paradox to see what deeper meanings we find there.

There Are Two Paths

Jesus is a living example of the truth that "there is a time for war and a time for peace."[45] As we consider the ramifications of peace and war, it's possible to see this as two paths. One path is peace with God and war with evil, which are consistent with each other. The other path is peace with evil and war with God, again a consistent pairing.

Could it be that there are two kinds of peace—the genuine peace that comes from God, and the phony peace that comes from the world? Could there be a heavenly peace that comes from God when we live in right relationship with him? Could there also be a counterfeit peace that comes from people, a peace of deception that leads to war with God?[46]

Could there be a heavenly war that comes from standing up for God and trying to make a difference?[47] And a human war in which we try to justify ourselves but end up demolishing everything and everyone around us?

Peace Comes As a Result of Our Choices

Peace is not an automatic thing. We have to learn the "way of peace."

"The way of peace they do not know," Paul wrote to the Roman Christians.[48] Peace is a destination, and we have to follow the right path to get to it. "If you, even you, had only known...what would bring you peace," Jesus lamented, "but now it is hidden from your eyes."[49] And we have to do more than find the way of peace—we have to *love* the way of peace. "Therefore love truth and peace," said the prophet Zechariah.[50]

We learn that peace is offered to all by God and should be offered by God's people to others. But we also learn that if the receiver is not deserving, the peace should and will return to the sender, like a letter sent to a wrong address. When Jesus was instructing his followers about their missionary trips, he told them, "First say, 'Peace to this house.' If a man of peace is there, your peace will rest on him; if not, it will return to you."[51] God starts out with peace, and he expects us to do the same. "If the home is deserving, let your peace rest on it; if it is not, let your peace return to you."[52]

Peace Is Won Through War

Genuine peace is purchased at a great price. "The punishment that brought us peace was upon him," Isaiah taught, speaking of the future crucifixion of Jesus.[53] The hard work of reconciliation was achieved by Jesus' "making peace through his blood."[54] There is no cheap peace, as countless soldiers have learned firsthand.

We have a price to pay as well, for peace is also purchased by our own suffering. "No discipline seems pleasant at the time, but painful," the writer to the Hebrews said. "Later on, however, it produces a harvest of righteousness and peace *for those who have been trained by it.*"[55] There is, indeed, pain and suffering. But if we are trained by suffering, if we learn the lessons that God is allowing discipline to try to teach us, the peace will come in a bountiful harvest.

We Are Called to Work for Peace

It is our responsibility to work for peace in all our relationships. "If it is possible, as far as it depends on you, live at peace with everyone," we are told.[56] If we can live our lives in the kingdom of God with courage and conviction and integrity, and at the same time not stir up any minor or unnecessary division, we are living in the spirit of this Scripture. But if a relationship forces us to give a piece of our character away as the price for peace, the price is too high. In those instances, the peace no longer depends on us. Peace is no longer "possible."

We Must Avoid False Peace

We can achieve a false peace by selling out the Prince of Peace. King Ahaz "took away the Sabbath canopy that had been built at the temple and removed the royal entryway outside the temple of the LORD, in deference to the king of Assyria."[57] What are we willing to do to have peace with God's enemies? Who are the "Assyrians" of our lives, the ones who get us to take the things of God out of our lives because godly influences cause them discomfort? Family? Friends? Neighbors? Bosses? Coworkers? Fellow church members?

When faced with a choice between relational peace and loyalty to Christ, we have to side with Christ and separate from the person who pushes us to down-play our relationship with God. We have to let Jesus bring the sword and fire and division into these relationships. This must be in part what Jesus meant when he said, "If anyone comes to me and does not hate his father and mother, his wife and children, his brothers and sisters—yes, even his own life—he cannot be my disciple."[58]

We know from our own experience that it is always easier, and often seems safer, to take the path of false peace. We opt for false peace when we are only willing to condemn the evils of history—Nazism, communist dictatorships, slavery—but refuse to speak out against the evils that surround us among our own people, in our own nation, in our own time.

There Are Conditions for Peace

Like any victor in war, God sets the terms of peace. There are at least ten conditions to be met if we want the Prince of Peace—rather than the Sword-Wielding Prince—to rule us.

The baseline condition is that we must belong to him. "The LORD blesses *his people* with peace," the psalmist writes.[59] There is no peace unless we belong to the Prince of Peace. "Therefore, since we have been justified by faith," the apostle Paul wrote to the Romans, "we have peace with God through our Lord Jesus Christ."[60] Jesus did the work on the cross. If we believe it and make it our own, we will have the only true peace.

Second, we must "seek peace and pursue it."[61] Peace isn't offered to us on a silver platter, waiting to be picked up by whoever happens to come along. We have to want it and go after it and not stop until we get it. And we must be party to a binding arrangement. "Therefore tell him I am making my *covenant* of peace with him."[62] We have to get deeply involved in an irrevocable covenant with Jesus, a peace treaty with God.

Third, we must know the connection between righteousness and peace. "The fruit of righteousness will be peace," Isaiah wrote.[63] The psalmist tells us that "righteousness and peace kiss each other."[64] Since peace and righteousness are that intimately connected, we have to avoid peace-destroying sin if we want the Prince of Peace to visit us. "I will listen to what God the LORD will say; he promises peace to his people, his saints—but let them not return to folly."[65] If we "return to folly," we throw away our peace.

Fourth, we must walk consistently in God's ways. "Those who walk uprightly enter into peace," Isaiah said.[66] When we come to God by faith, he expects us to walk with him in faith. There is a side benefit to this. "When a man's ways are pleasing to the LORD, he makes even his enemies live at peace with him."[67] If we walk with God in faith, we are assured that God will work on our enemies around the clock until he takes the fight out of them.

Fifth, we must do good. There is "honor and peace for everyone who does good."[68] We don't get peace by trying to please ourselves but by doing good for others. It's another upside-down principle: We get personal peace by doing other-centered good. And there is no limit to the number of people who can get in on this honor and peace. It is for everyone...who does good.

Sixth, we must be meek. Ironically, there is no peace for the arrogant and braggarts and pushy people. "But the meek will inherit the land and enjoy great peace."[69] God delights in taking "the land" away from those who demand it and then giving it to those who have no earthly chance of getting it.

Seventh, we must be controlled by the Holy Spirit. Even those who know God and are in a covenant with him can be out of control, thinking the wrong things, wanting the wrong things, doing the wrong things. But "the mind controlled by the Spirit is life and peace."[70] We have to submit our minds to the Holy Spirit every day, or we will end up in spiritual turmoil.

Eighth, we must present our requests to God. "The peace of God, which transcends all understanding" comes from bringing our requests to God and expecting those requests to be fulfilled.[71] "Do not be anxious about anything," Paul wrote to the Philippian church, "but in everything, by prayer and petition, *with* thanksgiving, present your requests to God."[72] How can we thank God for something at the same time we are asking for it? Perhaps because we are asking by faith, because we are "sure of what we hope for and certain of what we do not see,"[73] because we believe we have the answer to our request as soon as we ask for it.

Ninth, we must keep trusting in God no matter what comes our way. "You will keep in perfect peace him whose mind is steadfast, because he trusts in you."[74] We have to be "steadfast," holding on to Jesus for dear life if we want "perfect peace." This is why Jesus could fall asleep in a small boat in the midst of a fierce storm: He was in perfect peace.[75] But he said he would give us his peace, so we can have this perfect peace too.

Tenth, we must love God's law. "Great peace have they who love your law, and nothing can make them stumble," wrote the psalmist.[76] "This is love for God," wrote the apostle John, "to obey his commands. And his commands are not burdensome."[77] Even the path to peace—his law—is peaceful. "This is what the LORD says—your Redeemer, the Holy One of Israel:... If only you had paid attention to my commands, your peace would have been like a river."[78]

The prophet Isaiah reminds us, "There is no peace...for the wicked."[79] God offers nothing but warfare to those who oppose him. But who, exactly, are the wicked? *We* are. And because we are wicked, because we have all sinned and fallen short of the glory of God, we will have no peace—unless we learn about the way of peace and accept it.[80]

We Can Imitate God by Extending Peace

In the Bible we read that we should always start our contact with another human being with an offer of peace. "Blessed are the peacemakers, for they will be called sons of God," Jesus taught.[81] We should "try to live in peace with everyone"[82] and "live in peace with each other."[83]

There is a time for God's people to stand against the enemies of God. There is a place for holy anger, there is a time for holy indignation, there are situations that demand a holy clearing of the temple. Jesus doesn't always bring peace, and if we are his people, we should not always bring peace either. We should offer no soothing words to wicked people, no false peace to unrepentant sinners, no whitewash to people building graffiti-filled walls.

But we have to remember that God first holds out the olive branch of peace. He does not attack when there is a chance someone will accept that branch from his hands. "When you march up to attack a city," he says, "make its people an offer of peace."[84] The peace we offer should be on God's terms, of course; it should be in line with the ten conditions we looked at earlier. But the offer of peace should always be made, even when conflict seems inevitable.

Why? For one simple reason: Although we are in an army, our commander is the Prince of Peace.

Where This Leaves Us

We see that Jesus will bring peace or war, gentleness or anger, depending both on how we relate to him and on what we do. "What do you prefer?" the apostle Paul asked the Corinthian church. "Shall I come to you with a whip, or in love and with a gentle spirit?"[85] This is the question the Prince of Peace asks of every person. Which do you prefer? Do you want the Prince who brings a sword? Or do you want the Prince of Peace, the one who will come into your life "in love and with a gentle spirit"?[86]

Even to the end of our days, even to the end of time, we should pursue the great peace of God. "So then, dear friends," wrote the apostle Peter, "since you are looking forward to this, make every effort to be found spotless, blameless, and *at peace with him*."[87] We are either at peace with him or at war with him. May we always be found at peace with him.

"This is how you are to bless the Israelites," God commanded Moses to teach Aaron, the first high priest. "Say to them, 'The LORD bless you and keep you; the LORD make his face shine upon you and be gracious to you; the LORD turn his face toward you and give you peace.'"[88]

May it be so for you.

For Further Thought and Discussion

1. After studying this paradox, when you hear the title "Prince of Peace," what thoughts come to mind?

2. What was the most startling thing you learned about the Prince who *doesn't* bring peace? How will this change the way you think about life? the way you relate to others? the way you relate to God?

3. Describe in your own words the two kinds of peace.

4. As you look back over the ten conditions for receiving peace, which one or two of the conditions will require the most personal attention?

5. What can you do in the next few months to create and build different ways of thinking or acting to prepare the conditions for peace in your life?

Eight

The God of Truth Who Sends Delusions

THE CONTRAST BETWEEN FACTS AND THE TRUTH

~~~

It is impossible for God to lie.

HEBREWS 6:18

God sends them a powerful delusion so that they will believe the lie.

2 THESSALONIANS 2:11

Two friends were discussing things children say to justify doing whatever they want.

"My son really had a good excuse yesterday," Jennifer began. "His junior high youth group has been studying some of the Old Testament stories, and he concluded that it's okay to lie sometimes, because people like Rahab and David did it without getting punished for it."

"He sounds like a smart kid," her friend Maria said. "What did you tell him?"

"Well, I explained that usually God won't tolerate lies or liars. I said that those were very specific and unique cases and that David and Rahab had both sinned when they lied. But God chose to overlook it because it helped God's people."

"I understand what you're getting at," Maria said, "but do you really think God can overlook sin? After all, he is holy and sinless and just. And then you have verses that show how God blessed David and Rahab after they told those lies. Maybe we're missing something."

"I know. It's all so confusing," Jennifer answered. "Plus if I admit that at certain times it's all right to lie, then what am I going to say to my son who is just looking for an excuse to tell the occasional lie? I wish the Bible were clearer on all this so I could explain it better to my son—and to myself, for that matter."

A king and a prostitute lied, and God blessed both of them. What's more, both of these "liars" were included in the genealogy of Jesus. And Rahab is listed in the "Faith Hall of Fame" in Hebrews 11. So what gives?

Does God have a double standard when it comes to telling lies, excusing some who bend the truth while holding others accountable? Or does it have to do with a few very specific times in history when someone lied and God decided to look the other way? And what are we supposed to do with other stories in Scripture that portray God's actually sending delusions? Are there indeed legitimate exceptions to the no-lying rule?

TRUTH AND DELUSIONS

If we take the Bible seriously, we can't ignore the fact that our holy God of truth, the God who condemns lying and liars, at times sent delusions to certain people. Without facing this paradox squarely, we end up with an incomplete view of God and an incomplete view of the truth.

This is what the halakic question looks like: God is a God of truth who cannot lie. God sends delusions so that people will believe lies. How can God be a God of truth if he deliberately sends lie-confirming delusions?

The God of Truth

This paradox takes us way outside our comfort zone to think that in some cases, God might intentionally mislead people. But if God always tells the truth, why does he bless certain people in the Bible who don't tell the truth?

If we grab onto the A side of this paradox and say that God always and only speaks the truth, we run into problems with certain passages of the Bible. We stumble over stories where God approves of people who deceive others. "I guess the outcome was good even though the person lied," we theorize, "but I'm sure the person sinned and needed God's forgiveness." But the Bible doesn't call these deceptions sin, and we don't see the deceivers asking for or receiving forgiveness. So were their lies actually sins in the eyes of God?

Furthermore, if God is only interested in a straightforward presentation of facts, why doesn't he line up his truthful revelation in an orderly fashion in the Bible? He buries some truth, putting it where it's hard to find, and he baffles us by setting the truth about his nature and his work in paradox. As we have seen, the teacher of Proverbs tells us, "It is the glory of God to conceal a matter."[1] Making everything crystal clear to us does not seem to be God's top priority. There is value in the struggle to discern what he's up to, but we can easily wonder why a God of Truth would make us go to so much effort to find the truth.

If we focus only on God's truthfulness, we are left with no wiggle room. Truth seems to have no gray areas or soft spots. The fact that God is Truth seems to rule out any form of deception for any reason.

We get much of our understanding of truth from the Bible, which is the written revelation of God. But that same Bible portrays a God who sends delusions. If we rule out one-half of this paradox, we do so at the expense of discounting this revealed truth.

Part of our uneasiness could arise from our definition of "truth." The human mind can tend to equate truth with accurately shared information—*facts*. If a flower is described accurately in a botany textbook, we view that as truth. After reading the description, we know more about the flower's color, growing season, size, and fragrance. But do we then know the truth about the flower? Do we know all there is to know and understand about that flower? Not at all, and a flower is an incredibly simple thing compared to God and the life he invites us to live.

The widespread assumption that truth is the accurate transmission of information also affects our dealings with other people. We measure a person's truthfulness not by a standard consistent with God's behavior but according to our own earthly definition. If a person refuses to provide all the details to someone who might use the information for evil ends, we might consider the person who holds back the information to be a liar. But is that God's standard?

This is not a theoretical situation. The ten Boom family of Amsterdam sheltered Jewish people in their home during the Nazi occupation of the Netherlands. The family saw it as their Christian responsibility to protect Jewish citizens by providing them sanctuary, which at the time was against the law. Further, whenever the Gestapo would come to the door and ask if they knew of any Jews in the area, the ten Booms knew that answering with all the facts would send innocent people to the gas chamber. When they evaded the questions or provided inaccurate responses, were they lying? According to the human definition of truth, they were liars; although to everyone who hears their story, they were God's heroes.[2]

When we bring this matter down to the level of everyday life, we see the tension between factual accuracy and truth in our own lives. If a friend comes up and asks how he looks, the standard of factual accuracy would require us to express in great detail exactly how he appears to us at that moment. His trousers are wrinkled or too tight or too short. His shirt clashes with his pants. The color of his clothing bleaches out his too-pale complexion. His glasses appear to date back to the 1980s. His hair needs a trim; the gray at his temples makes him look old; and why doesn't he do something about that mole? That's the complete story, and it's factually accurate based on our honest observations.

But that description, for all its detail, is superficial at best. It captures only our friend's outward appearance in one moment of one day. It doesn't go below the surface to capture his intelligence, his compassion, his sense of humor, or his patience with those who lack tact. Plus the "truthful" response cited above hurts his feelings. Does real truthfulness require us to batter him with every fact we observe about his appearance?

Are factual accuracy and the truth one and the same? If three witnesses to the same auto accident give three different accounts of the event, does that make at least two of them liars? The argument for truth can quickly get muddled by our adherence to the "fact-as-truth" standard.

The God of Delusions

Even if we draw some distinctions between bare facts and the truth, we are still not out of the woods. This paradox confronts us with a God who sends delusions. And if that is the case, how can we expect mere mortals to seek out the truth or to uphold it once they find it? Doesn't the idea of God-sent delusions call into question God's goodness, fairness, and decency? And if God does send delusions, how can we ever know what's real? If we can't trust God, whom *can* we trust? And how do we know that some parts of the Bible aren't actually delusions?

If we take the view that God on occasion deceives people and that factual truth is not really important, we end up with a reckless and inscrutable God. What tricks does he have up his sleeve? Why would a God who knows all truth not tell it? Why would a God who hates "lying lips" turn around and use delusion as a tool? What else is delusion? The Virgin Birth? The Resurrection? The historical Jesus?

We might indeed reach the conclusion that factual truth isn't that important, that it's enough if we have good intentions. As long as we don't hurt anyone, why shouldn't we stretch the truth? If embellishing our résumé will land a job we deserve to get anyway, what's the harm? If exaggerating our accomplishments helps impress a new friend, so what? If nobody asks about that leak in the basement when they're thinking of buying the house…well, let the buyer beware.

This confusion extends to how we should act with regard to others. Can we lie to avoid getting someone else in trouble or hurting someone's feelings or over-committing our schedules? As long as our intentions are good, does it really matter what we say to one another? If our boss asks whether we're checking out other job opportunities, and we know he has fired other employees who were looking around, can we say, "I wouldn't even consider another job if it were offered"?

While looking only at the B side of this paradox, we might give up on the idea of truth altogether. Many have, some of them professing Christians. In our era, it's common to hear people say: "There's your truth and my truth. They're both equally valid. It's all a matter of what works for a person." Even worse, there are many who believe there is no truth, no absolute reality. To them, everything on some level is an illusion. It's all a matter of how you perceive it or "construct" it with your words.

Our culture is so disillusioned with truth that every person is invited to invent a truth that best suits his or her preferences. Even factual accuracy is no longer held in high esteem. In a culture where marketing, political campaigns, and business deals rely on half-truths or outright lies, we've become cynical about "facts." It's as if we expect to be lied to, so we simply factor that into the daily transactions of life.

If we read in the Bible that God sends delusions, what does that do to our society's general disregard of truth? Maybe God was the first spinmeister. This idea is nothing if not troubling.

Surely there is more to this paradox than we see on the surface.

WHAT SCRIPTURE SAYS

Belief in a God who is truth alone leaves us vulnerable and obsessed with factual detail. We have to tell the "truth" even if it hurts people and destroys relationships. Meanwhile, grabbing on to the other strand of this paradox gives us a God of delusions who can't be trusted. We have to question truth, even when its relevance is obvious. Neither side of the paradox, by itself, satisfies our souls. Both strands are needed to build a whole life around a whole God.

Truth Alone with No Room for Lying

If we're going to know anything about God, we have to know that he is "God, who does not lie."[3] The writer of Hebrews takes this idea a step further when he declares outright that "it is *impossible* for God to lie."[4] Now, if God is all-powerful, why would it be impossible for him to lie? Because he is a holy, honest, truth-telling God. To lie would contradict his character.

When God says something—anything—we can believe it is true. "For the word of the LORD is right and true," declared the psalmist.[5] It's always exactly, perfectly right. When the Bible says that liars offend God and will be punished, we can count on it. "Your words are trustworthy," we are reminded.[6]

If we think God allows himself a little latitude with the truth, we are mistaken. "*All* your words are true," the psalmist said to God.[7] We don't have to worry about which words are true and which ones are delusions. They're *all* true. God doesn't lie.

His truth is the final word. When it's our word against his, we lose. "Though everyone else in the world is a liar, God is true. As the Scriptures say, 'He will be proved right in what he says, and he will win his case in court.'"[8] If God says we are to be holy as he is holy, and human experts tell us it's perfectly normal to think impure thoughts, someone is lying.[9] And it isn't God.

Not only is truth important to God, but he defines truth a little differently than we do. According to the Bible, the following things are the truth:

- *God's Word.* "Your word is truth."[10] In a world full of ideas and ideologies and philosophies, there is one set of teachings we can count on. The Bible sets the standard. We have to work to understand it, but everything it says is truth.

- *Jesus.* "Jesus answered, 'I am the way and the truth and the life.'"[11] The truth is more than the written word. It is Jesus, the Living Word. When we want to know what God has to say on a subject, we can look at Jesus. If he is doing something, we're safe in doing it. If he condemns something, we're safe in condemning it. To find Jesus is to find the truth. To follow him is to walk in truth.[12]

- *The Holy Spirit.* "The Spirit is the truth."[13] When the Holy Spirit speaks, people who want the straight story should listen. We're told that the Spirit was the One who inspired the writers of the Bible,[14] and the Spirit was with Jesus, guiding him and inspiring him.[15] We're told in this verse that the Spirit doesn't just speak the truth—he *is* the truth. We can count on him 100 percent of the time.

These three, according to John's writings, are the core definition of the truth. "There are three that testify," wrote John: "The Spirit, the water and the blood."[16] There are three that make up the truth—the Holy Spirit, the water of the word,[17] and the blood of Jesus.

We find that God opposes those who tell lies. "Lying lips are an abomination to the LORD, but those who are truthful are his delight."[18] There are no harmless "white lies." He hates lies and the lips that utter them. God's response to lies is chilling: "You destroy those who tell lies," the psalmist says of the Lord.[19]

God intends his people to be without illusion or confusion. "But when he, the Spirit of truth, comes, he will guide you into all truth."[20] We can't find the truth without the help of the Holy Spirit. But we have the incredible teaching that, with him, we can find *all* truth.

We see also that God expects his people to speak the truth and be hard on those who deal in lies and deception. "Speak the truth to each other," the prophet Zechariah commands.[21] God wants the community of faith to be a truth-telling community. If we can't expect to find the truth with fellow believers, where do we look?

The positive command is to speak the truth. The negative command is to avoid falsehood. "Therefore each of you must put off falsehood and speak truthfully to his neighbor."[22] We have to look honestly and clearly at what we are thinking and saying and take off the parts that are false, like a set of dirty clothes. "Surely you desire truth in the inner parts," prayed King David.[23] God wants us to be truthful, right to the core.

We are told that we shouldn't lie, and this includes not deceiving other people.[24] We have to give up game playing and saying what we don't mean, all hallmarks of a world that devalues the truth. We have to let liars know that we won't be associated with them. "No one who practices deceit will dwell in my house," the psalmist affirms.[25]

God's whole orientation, Jesus' whole orientation, is toward the truth. The apostle John reminded his readers, "We know also that the Son of God has come and has given us understanding, so that we may know him who is true. And we are in him who is true—even in his Son Jesus Christ. He is the true God and eternal life."[26] The Holy Spirit gives us understanding so that we can get our arms around the truth. And the way we do that is to embrace Jesus, "the true God."

There is no doubt that God speaks the truth, the whole truth, and nothing but the truth—and that he expects us to do the same.[27]

The God Who Sends Delusions

If we're serious about knowing the God of the Bible, we can't settle for a lopsided view. If we are to pursue God with our whole heart, we have to embrace all aspects of his character and his work as they are described in Scripture. In this case, it involves admitting that God at times deals in delusions. We see in the Bible that God launches delusions into a world that is begging for them.

The delusions sent by God are not minor affairs. "They refused to love the truth and so be saved. For this reason God sends them a *powerful* delusion so that they will believe the lie."[28] The reason he sends the delusion to those who refuse to love truth is chilling: *so that they will believe the lie.* He doesn't send delusions so we'll have an interesting topic for discussion around the dinner table or in a Bible study group. He sends them to convince people that lies are true—because they refuse to acknowledge that truth is true.

God has an array of delusions in his arsenal. "If you do not obey the LORD your God and do not carefully follow all his commands," the Bible warns, "the LORD will afflict you with madness, blindness and confusion of mind."[29]

- *Madness.* We will believe in things that don't exist, and we'll doubt the reality of things that do exist.
- *Blindness.* God will destroy our ability to see what's going on around us. The visual sense, which is critical for discerning the reality around us, will be gone.
- *Confusion of Mind.* God will cloud our thinking and leave us to wander in a maze of desperation. We won't know right from left or up from down.

Critic and essayist H. L. Mencken liked to remind people that democracy was based on the theory that the people deserved to get what they wanted—and that they deserved to get it good and hard.[30] If people press God far enough with their rejection of the truth, he'll let them go all the way into total delusion and depravity. "Furthermore, since they did not think it worthwhile to retain the knowledge of God, he gave them over to a depraved mind."[31] This is interesting, because it describes people choosing not to "retain" the knowledge of God. This tells us that he initially makes his truth available to all. They have it. But when they give up on the truth, they get depravity—one of the greatest delusions of all, the idea that a life of committed sin can satisfy, rather than lead to more sin, worse sin, slavery, and death.

In one of the most interesting (but little-discussed) stories in the Bible, rotten King Ahab was trying to get God-fearing King Jehoshaphat (each one ruling a segment of the Jewish people) to join him in a war. Jehoshaphat agreed with the basic concept but wanted to hear from a prophet before he fully committed to the plan. After listening to four hundred people saying, "Go," Jehoshaphat was still unconvinced and asked for a *real* prophet. Ahab reluctantly called in the prophet Micaiah, who told Ahab that he was in deep trouble. Micaiah described a most intriguing and disturbing conversation in heaven.

> Therefore hear the word of the LORD: I saw the LORD sitting on his throne with all the host of heaven standing around him on his right and on his left. And the LORD said, "Who will entice Ahab into attacking Ramoth Gilead and going to his death there?"
> One suggested this, and another that.[32]

Note that it was the Lord himself who asked the question that launched the thought process of the heavenly hosts. "Who will entice [him]?" is not a question we expect God to ask, but there it is. And it's not just enticement, but enticement to death. In this celestial brainstorming session, the spirits—presumably angels—put forth a number of ideas that might get God's approval.

And then "Finally, a spirit came forward, stood before the LORD and said, 'I will entice him.' 'By what means?' the LORD asked. 'I will go out and be a lying spirit in the mouths of all his prophets,' he said."[33] God wanted to know how the spirit intended to entice Ahab to his death. When God heard the plan, that this spirit would speak lies and delusions through Ahab's prophets, he approved it. " 'You will succeed in enticing him,' said the LORD. 'Go and do it.' "[34] Micaiah confirmed to Ahab that this is exactly what had happened. "So now the LORD has put a lying spirit in the mouths of all these prophets of yours,"[35] he announced. Ahab ignored Micaiah, followed the advice of the four hundred lying prophets, rode into battle, and was promptly killed—even though he was in disguise!

God approved a plan that involved a spirit filling Ahab's prophets with delusions and lies. The spirit apparently cannot do his deceptive work without God's prior approval. Micaiah summarized what happened by declaring unequivocally that it was God who put the lying spirit into Ahab's mouthpieces.

"Listen," God was saying, in essence, "if you don't want the truth, I've got a plan for you. You can believe lies that confirm your own illusions and delusions. And I'll help. I'll not only send a spirit who can persuade you, I'll make sure it's the spirit with the best and most effective plan."

Another example of God's using deception as a tool of truth is the story of the Hebrew midwives who were told to kill Jewish baby boys at birth. These women, because they "feared God," disobeyed the king of Egypt. But they not only disobeyed him, they told a whopper of a lie to his face. They said that Israelite women "are vigorous and give birth before the midwives arrive,"[36] which couldn't have been more factually *in*accurate.

At this point, we could expect God to say, "It's great that you're trying hard to save the babies. But listen, you've *got* to stop this lying!" We might expect God to demand their repentance, to admit they were wrong, to apologize to Pharaoh. But instead, we read that "God was kind to the midwives.... And because the midwives feared God, he gave them families of their own."[37]

Rahab, a prostitute from Jericho, saw that God was on the side of Israel and hid the Jewish spies in her home. When local authorities came to her door and asked if she knew where the spies were, she immediately handed the authorities a delusion: "They went that way." Again, there were no recriminations from God. On the contrary, she was saved from destruction, blessed, and ended up in the ancestral line of Jesus. And this was not in spite of her lie—it was *because* of her lie.[38] Her lie, which spared the lives of the Jewish spies, was the only reason that Rahab and her family lived.

David, future king of Israel, offered a delusion to protect his own life. When brought before a king he thought might kill him, David "pretended to be insane in their presence;…he acted like a madman, making marks on the doors of the gate and letting saliva run down his beard."[39] His deception was so successful that the enemy king said, "Look at the man! He is insane!… Am I so short of madmen that you have to bring this fellow here to carry on like this in front of me?"[40] David's explanation of this event and his deliverance are detailed in Psalm 34: "I sought the LORD, and he answered me.… He saved [this poor man] out of all his troubles."[41] In an interesting twist, he said the key to receiving blessings from God was to "keep your tongue from evil and your lips from speaking lies."[42]

When people want to believe in delusions, God will use their own deluded teachers to deliver the goods. "The LORD has brought over you a deep sleep: He has sealed your eyes (the prophets); he has covered your heads (the seers)."[43] God can put a people to sleep by simply deluding their leaders and letting delusion take its course. If the prophets and teachers and pastors can't see the truth, it's almost certain that they will lead the people further into the lie. "If a liar and deceiver comes and says, 'I will prophesy for you plenty of wine and beer,' he would be just the prophet for this people!" declared the prophet Micah.[44]

Amazingly, even God's basic message is masked to those who refuse to believe it. "For the message of the cross is foolishness to those who are perishing.… God chose the foolish things of the world to shame the wise."[45] The critically true message of heaven looks like nonsense to the resistant, to those who prefer lies over truth. It is part of God's design of life.

If we're going to know anything about God and truth, we have to see that he is the God who sends delusions.[46]

THE DEEPER MEANING OF BOTH/AND

What are the both/and truths that we find in this unsettling paradox? First, we are forced to admit that God is a God of unfailing truth who is also comfortable dealing in delusions. We see that God speaks truth, loves truth, and is truth. If we are liars or lying, we will find no solace in him. However, in Scripture we see that he sends powerful delusions that often confirm the lies we invent.

Truth Is More Than Factual Accuracy

This paradox forces us to think about our definition of truth. Is it the same as factual accuracy? Or is truth something more? Is a lie being factually inaccurate, or is a lie, too, something else—something more? A simple, cookbook definition of *truth* and *lie* is insufficient in the kingdom of God.

This paradox drives us to conclude that truth is a whole lot more than we have previously thought. Truth far surpasses factual accuracy; it is being aligned with the right—with what God is doing. Not only is "factual accuracy" too small a definition of truth—it isn't even an accurate definition! We can be factually accurate and still be quite wrong, quite outside the bounds of truth; for example, when we break a confidence with a friend or tell factually accurate stories to slander someone else.

At the same time, we are forced to conclude that a lie is something different, something a whole lot more, than we previously thought. A lie is not limited to being factually inaccurate. It is being aligned with the wrong—against what God is doing, functioning outside his will. The statements of the Hebrew midwives and Rahab were factually incorrect. In modern parlance, they all lied because their words were not literally "true." But their words and their intent were aligned with what God was doing—with ultimate Truth—and God blessed them for using the words they used.

Some have tried to argue that God blessed them in spite of their sinful lies, because their intentions were good. Those good intentions are thought to outweigh the wrongness of their lies. But the Bible doesn't even hint at this. God is comfortable with their approach, approves their actions, and blesses their work. God understands this: Just being careful to say words that are factually accurate does not make us people of truth. Likewise, depending on the circumstances and what God is doing in the moment, saying words that are factually inaccurate does not automatically make us liars.

Being aligned with what is right, being connected with God, and living in obedience to his will are the only antidotes to delusion.[47]

Those Who Hate Truth Are Given Delusions

Ironically, God can confirm his truth by sending delusions to his enemies. The enemies of God are the enemies of Truth. As such, they tell lies, and they believe lies.[48] The delusion takes people into the abyss, which can have a good outcome if they are finally willing to see God and his truth. How many people have said things like, "I finally saw that alcohol was killing me" or "I just never thought I'd get caught"? Or what about, "Drugs as an escape—what a joke" or "I didn't see the harm that raising my kids outside the church would do"?

We see God's willingness to delude the wicked in the story of Jehu and the prophets of Baal, a false god. Jehu pretended to be a Baal-worshiper: "Ahab served Baal a little; Jehu will serve him much," he said.[49] Under this banner, he invited the prophets of Baal for a great time of sacrifice to their god. When they arrived, they were greeted warmly. But we are told that "Jehu was acting deceptively in order to destroy the ministers of Baal."[50] Jehu took great pains to make sure that the temple of Baal had all the Baal-worshipers and no "servants of the LORD" inside.[51] Then he had his followers kill every false prophet and tear down the temple (and, we are told as an aside, "the people have used it for a latrine to this day"[52]). "So Jehu destroyed Baal worship in Israel."[53] And what did God think about this massive, bloody deception? "The LORD said to Jehu, 'Because you have done well…' "[54]

God only sends delusions to those who reject the truth, since these people already want to believe a lie. For those who are seeking God, this is a great comfort. We don't have to worry that God will send out random delusions that might catch us in a trap. We have to use discernment, to be sure, because there are many bogus teachers and teachings floating around out there. Plenty of delusions come from Satan. But if we're aligned with God, it simply isn't possible for us to be deluded. "For false Christs and false prophets will appear," warned Jesus, "and perform great signs and miracles to deceive even the elect—*if that were possible.*"[55]

We are protected when we are following God, but his enemies are vulnerable to every delusion. God won't let anyone who has a callous heart get in on his truth. This is what the Bible means when it describes God "hardening" someone's heart. God doesn't lock the gate to keep out someone who is seeking truth. But if the person is on a long journey of rejecting God and his truth, God will send delusions that confirm the lie that the person wants to believe.

God is willing to let us hear and believe all the absurd ideas that come along if we are looking for them and willing to believe them. Confusion for the willfully confused seems to be one of his operating principles. "He has made my paths crooked," these people might lament.[56] And once he sends a delusion, we will have a hard time finding our way back out of it. "Who can straighten what he has made crooked?" we read in the book of Ecclesiastes.[57] This is the most insidious danger of rejecting God—not that he will stop telling us the truth, but that he will start sending us delusions.

We Should Not Sell Out the Innocent

We are never required to cooperate with evil people by providing accurate information that they can use to destroy people. God does not expect us to side with evil under some false idea of what "truth" is. Rahab sent the spy hunters in a different (wrong) direction, and Christians often did the same thing in Nazi Germany. Rahab didn't ask God (or the people of Jericho) for forgiveness for her "lie," and no one who hid people from the Nazis needed to ask for forgiveness either.

We see that in God's universe, a lie is an attempt to cover up our own sin or another's, not an attempt to protect the innocent. For example, covering up our own mistake in the workplace by playing the game of CYA ("cover your assets"), when we know this is wrong and may hurt others, is a lie. But not telling an evil boss about a mistake that has no effect on others, or not giving him information that he could use to fire a coworker who made an honest mistake, might be something else entirely.

Truth Does Not Destroy People

We have seen that people have used words that are factually accurate with the intention of destroying others. If we tell someone the facts about another person,

God still might condemn us for breaking a confidence, for damaging a person's reputation, for delivering constructive criticism in an accurate but brutal way, or for sharing details of others' sin under the guise of "praying" for them.

Truth without justice is no truth at all. "Just *and* true are your ways...King of the ages."[58] Hard, cold facts without justice aren't truth; they are just hard, cold facts.

We sense this greater justice in Victor Hugo's great story *Les Misérables*. Embittered by being sent to prison for many years for stealing a loaf of bread to feed a starving relative, Jean Valjean is finally free. His life does not improve, however, and he ends up stealing the silverware of a kindly priest who has taken him in. When the police ask the priest to confirm the theft and press charges, the priest surprises Valjean. He says that the silverware is a gift and that, in fact, the culprit forgot to take some additional items that also were given to him. It is a moment of redemption for Jean Valjean, a light at the end of a long, dark tunnel, and it turns his life around. And it is all based on what many of us would call a lie.[59]

This priest is in some sense a picture of God, who can look at us and, even knowing we are full of sin, see something holy because of Christ. He is "the God who gives life to the dead and calls things that are not as though they were."[60] We look and see no life and no hope and no possibility. God looks and calls it life and hope and possibility, and his words make it so.

God is interested in our alignment with his will and his values, not about our self-righteous pronouncements. We proclaim something that is factually accurate, confident that we have spoken the truth. But God asks, "Is it just? Is it right? Will it advance my kingdom? Will it be 'helpful for building others up according to *their* needs, that it may *benefit* those who listen'?"[61] Truth is a textured web of interlocking principles, and telling the truth is a lot more difficult than taking care to maintain technical accuracy.

In the end, we see that God offers all people truth, but he sends delusions to those who want to believe a lie. God reveals all truth, so we have no reason to fall under any delusion. Jesus gives us his Spirit to guide us into *all* truth. "All that belongs to the Father is mine," Jesus taught his followers; "That is why I said the Spirit will take from what is mine and make it known to you."[62] If we want the truth, we can have it all. And if we prefer a lie, God will gladly send a delusion to our liking.

WHERE THIS LEAVES US

God offers truth to everyone, but we have to accept it in the form he offers it. We who know the truth are called to join the apostle Paul in preaching "Christ crucified: a stumbling block to Jews and foolishness to Gentiles, but to those whom God has called, both Jews and Greeks, Christ the power of God and the wisdom of God."[63] What often appears to unbelievers as truth is really a delusion, and what appears to them as delusion—a young, unschooled carpenter dying on a Roman cross to create a bloody path to heaven—is really the most important truth they could ever know and believe.

When our eyes are finally opened, we see that this Jesus, this "foolishness," is truly "the way and the truth and the life."[64] He doesn't just know truth and speak truth and defend truth—he *is* truth. Pilate had the wrong question when he asked Jesus, "What is truth?"[65]

The real question is, "*Who* is truth?"

And the only truthful answer is "Jesus."

FOR FURTHER THOUGHT AND DISCUSSION

1. How would you define truth? How has your definition changed from what it was before you explored this paradox?
2. How does God's truth differ from and exceed simple factual accuracy?
3. Why does God send delusions? How can people avoid being deluded?
4. How would you define lying? How has your definition changed from what it was before studying this paradox?

Nine

The Choice Is Ours, but the Choice Is God's

GOD'S CHOICES AFFECT OURS—AND VICE VERSA

This day I call heaven and earth as witnesses against you that I have set before you life and death, blessings and curses. Now choose life.

DEUTERONOMY 30:19

You did not choose me, but I chose you.

JOHN 15:16

Marcus is a new Christian who is looking for a church. At work last week, he had lunch with Raj, and they talked about differences among denominations.

"The church I visited last Sunday believes that God has already chosen who will believe in him and who won't," Marcus said. "The sermon was very convincing, but I couldn't help worrying if I had truly been chosen. What if I just *think* I'm a child of God, but maybe I'm not really?"

Raj explained that churches' teachings run the gamut from "God does everything" to "it's up to each person to decide."

"There are many passages in Scripture that support the teaching that every person has the opportunity to accept or reject God's salvation," Raj added. "Maybe you should visit my church."

"But how can you ignore all the verses about God choosing people?" Marcus asked. "There seems to be a major contradiction between God choosing who he wants in heaven on the one hand, and people having the freedom to choose God or to reject him. How can anyone know which view is right?"

"I guess I've never really given it that much thought," Raj admitted. He repeated his invitation for Marcus to visit his church, and then he headed back to his office feeling just as confused as his friend.

The paradox of who chooses whom provides a striking example of the problems that arise when we assume the answer is either A or B: Either God chooses us or we choose him. Christians have taken sides with one interpretation over the other, giving rise to one of the most hotly debated doctrinal differences between various Christian traditions.

Even a cursory reading of Scripture shows that there is a biblical basis for both sides of this paradox. Since playing one side against the other has not resulted in a doctrine that all Christians can agree on, let's see what comes to light as we apply halakic reasoning.

GOD CHOOSES AND WE CHOOSE

The seeming contradiction that Marcus pointed out is not a new one. Differing allegiances on the question have split the church for centuries, as Christians have sought the one, authoritative interpretation. God tells us that we have to choose him. God also tells us that he chooses us. How can God tell us that we have to choose him, when he also tells us that he chooses us?

Whose choice is it? And what does the answer mean for our lives on earth—and then after our earthly lives come to an end?

The Choice Is Ours

If the choice is really ours, why does God keep telling us that his choice overrides everything else? Isn't everything about us predetermined by God, or at least by his agents? Consider all the life-forming factors that we have no control over, from nature (including our DNA, our innate talents and aptitudes, and our personalities and temperaments) to nurture (our families, our communities, and our culture). None of us can choose where or when we are born, what family we grow up in, or what religion will influence us through our family and our culture.

But if we cling to side A of this paradox and say simply that God waits for us to choose, the results can be ugly. We might believe that we can reason our way to God, using logic and our intellect to plot a course to heaven.

Or we might decide that we don't really need God's involvement in our daily lives, since he has made us in his image and we have the ability to make right choices. We might conclude that we are what we choose to be, so if we don't like our circumstances, we simply make a change. If we're down, we pull ourselves up by our bootstraps. If we're up, we congratulate ourselves for our first-class thinking and carefully crafted self-image. God doesn't figure into our daily struggles and decisions. We generate our own help rather than rely on God's assistance. Good thinking yields good results.

This thinking can also affect our beliefs about the afterlife. Do we really need God's grace? We might believe we can reach God through our own efforts. Even though the Bible tells us that without God we can do nothing,[1] we still might think we can get to heaven through learning and by making careful, enlightened choices.

By this same line of thinking, we might conclude that we can also choose to reject our salvation, that we have the power to remove ourselves from God's family. No matter that Jesus said if we belong to him we have "eternal life and will not be condemned," because we have "crossed over from death to life."[2] No matter that he said, "*No one* can take [my sheep] out of my hand."[3] If we ignore Jesus' words and focus exclusively on the role of *our* choices, we can easily be consumed by the fear that our own decisions might take us from his hand.

The Choice Is God's

If the choice is God's, why does he keep telling us to make choices? Doesn't his great power make a joke of the idea of a human's free choice? Since we are flawed and finite beings whose wisest choices are still fraught with blind spots, doesn't God really have to intervene and dictate outcomes to make our lives follow the right course?

But if we cling to side B of this paradox and say that God chooses us, period, we can become lazy and detached. If it's all up to God, we don't have to do *anything*. He looked at the human race from the beginning of creation and chose who would be saved. Since it's already been determined who is in and who is out, why bother pursuing either God or a godly way of life?

We might go even further than mere apathy about moral living and end up believing that we are *powerless* to do anything right, even if we wanted to. Why oppose evil or resist temptation? God's in charge, and he'll deal with this ugliness eventually. If we're born with a rebellious nature, and it doesn't matter what we choose—since God's choice is the only one that matters—why try to fight our natural tendency to sin?

Then there is the inevitable question: What if God chooses someone for heaven who doesn't want to go? If God chooses people and that's that, then a person's desire or lack of desire for spending eternity with God is irrelevant. If God chooses someone, that person will go to heaven even if she denies the idea of God to begin with. Don't want to believe in God? Sorry, you have no choice!

Clinging to this side of the paradox can narrow our view of the miraculous, redemptive work of Jesus on the cross. Did he really die to offer forgiveness to everyone or only to the ones God had already chosen? If God had already decided who would get into heaven, why did he send his Son to die such an inhuman death? Why not just save the chosen ones and let the others spend eternity in hell? The sacrifice of God's Son, if we accept this view, seems unnecessary at best. The play was already over before Jesus came on stage.

We might not even see any reason to spread the word about Christ. What's the point of evangelism if God has chosen in advance which people he's going to save? After all, if God has already determined that you're not going to be saved, nothing we can do will change the ultimate outcome.

Well-intentioned Christians have held to some of these ideas, casualties of believing only half of the paradox.

What Scripture Says

As with every paradox that we find in Scripture, we can be confident that both sides of this seeming contradiction are true. God chooses, and so do we. We're free to make our own choices, but God also chooses us in advance.

We Are Free to Choose

It's clear in the Bible that we have some serious choosing to do, legitimate choices that are unencumbered by any limits on our freedom to decide for ourselves. And the choices that we make have huge consequences for our lives.

"This day I call heaven and earth as witnesses against you," God tells us in a courtroomlike fashion, "that I have set before you life and death, blessings and curses. *Now choose life.*"[4] God lays out dramatic alternatives in this statement. We can live or we can die. We can be blessed or we can be cursed. And the choice is up to us. Everything that exists is watching, waiting for us to choose.

God encourages us to choose life, of course, because he is a good and loving God. But he is clear in showing us that he will not make the choice for us, and he's equally clear that he won't let us avoid making the decision. "No decision" is a decision. If we don't choose life and blessings, we get death and curses.

Jesus makes this moment of decision clear to everyone who encounters him. "He who is not with me is against me."[5] Again, to avoid making a decision is to make a decision. There is no neutral territory. We can pick Jesus, or we can reject him. In the end, there is only that one eternally crucial decision: What will we do with Jesus?

If we choose to side with those who oppose God, we are also choosing to oppose God ourselves. "Anyone who chooses to be a friend of the world becomes an enemy of God,"[6] we're taught. We can choose to be "a friend of the world"—

not at all meaning a cosmopolitan, sociable person but rather someone who prefers the things that lead to curses and death.

Scripture that holds us accountable for making a choice—and guiding us to the right choice—makes no sense if we are not free to make choices. No good leader gives his followers orders that can't be obeyed, and God is the greatest leader of all. If he orders us to make a choice, he must also give us the freedom to choose. In fact, God makes it clear that his will for us is that we make good choices.[7]

We see in Scripture that people have the capacity to make good choices. "I have chosen your precepts," the psalmist says to God.[8] "I have chosen the way of truth," we're told in the same psalm.[9]

In looking forward to the coming of Jesus, our Savior and also our model, the prophet Isaiah spoke of the time "when he knows enough to reject the wrong and choose the right."[10] There comes a time when we know the difference between what's wrong and what's right. Little children don't yet have this capacity, but at some point everyone who is able to think and understand sees that there is a wrong and a right. We can reject the right and choose the wrong. Or we can be like Jesus, rejecting the wrong and choosing the right. Everyone can choose to be blotted out of the Book of Life, and everyone can choose to be written back in.[11]

We can make good decisions no matter what our circumstances are, like the "eunuchs who keep my Sabbaths, who choose what pleases me."[12] In human terms, eunuchs had very little power. They had many choices taken from them—their occupations, their daily routines, even their sexual lives. But they could still choose to please God or to displease him. What we choose to think about, how we choose to live our inner lives, is a choice that no one can take from us.

We find that we can also make bad choices. God says, again through the prophet Isaiah, "You did evil in my sight and chose what displeases me."[13] "You didn't stumble into this evil," he is saying. "You looked right at it and chose to make it your own." They have chosen "what pagans choose to do," said the apostle Peter.[14]

Our choices are so important that they set the stage for God's responses. In a stunning comment from the God who is love, we are told, "Then they will call to me *but I will not answer;* they will look for me *but will not find me.*" What could produce such a shocking response from our loving God? Because "they hated knowledge and did not *choose* to fear the LORD."[15] Fearing God is a good idea, but it is also a choice. If we choose not to fear him, he chooses not to be found.

If we choose to reject God and then call out to him when we are in trouble, we will get the terrifying answer, "Go and cry out to the gods you have chosen."[16] We can pick our gods, but we then have to live with our choice. If we pick false gods, we can't expect the one true God to come running as soon as we get into trouble.

We learn that we can't even *understand* God if we don't choose to do what he asks. "The fear of the LORD is the beginning of wisdom; all who follow his precepts have good understanding."[17] Many people say, "I'll choose God's way when I understand it." But God says, "You'll never fully understand it if you don't choose in advance to do it."[18] We can say to God, "I don't know what you want me to do, but whatever it is I'll do it." Making that choice opens the door to vast stores of wisdom. "I have more understanding than the elders," said the psalmist, "for I obey your precepts."[19]

God issues the invitation. He makes himself available to us. He calls us to draw near to him. But he doesn't force us to accept his offer. It's our decision.[20]

But what about those who live in a culture that worships other gods or prohibits all talk about the God of the Bible? Won't those who die in ignorance of God go to hell without having had a chance to choose him or reject him? As we read Scripture, we see that no one is beyond God's reach. Amazingly, we find that God puts people in their exact time and place because that is the perfect spot for them to find God. We're told that God "determined the times set for them and the exact places where they should live." But why did he do this? "God did this *so that* men would seek him and *perhaps* reach out for him and find him, *though he is not far from each one of us.*"[21]

There are no "God-forsaken" parts of the planet. His fingerprints are everywhere, in part because his nature is reflected in his creation. The apostle Paul points this out in the first chapter of Romans, where he teaches that no one can use the excuse that they haven't heard about God:

The wrath of God is indeed being revealed from heaven against
every impiety and wickedness of those who suppress the truth by
their wickedness. For what can be known about God is *evident* to
them, because God made it evident to them. Ever since the creation
of the world, his invisible attributes of eternal power and divinity
have been able to be understood and perceived in what he has made.
As a result, they have no excuse; for although they knew God they
did not accord him glory as God or give him thanks.[22]

In other words, even those who live in a pagan culture with no gospel witness
and no access to the Bible still can find God through his monumental declaration: the witness of his creation.

If anyone responds to God's work in creation and concludes that "there
must be a God," then God will give that person more spiritual insight and
knowledge of him.[23] And as long as a person sincerely pursues God and a relationship with him, God will respond with more and more knowledge of him.
"Whoever has will be given more," is Jesus' principle.[24] Jesus said those who
hunger and thirst after righteousness are blessed, because they will be satisfied.[25]
And the prophet Jeremiah said that those who seek God will find him as long as
they "seek me with all [their] heart."[26]

It's part of the mystery of God: He reveals himself to those who choose to seek
him, no matter what period of history they live in, and no matter what part of the
globe they occupy. The book of Job tells the story of a remarkable man of faith, a
man who clung to God despite the most vicious attacks of Satan. Although Job
probably lived before any Scripture had been written, among people with unclear
ideas about God, he remained obedient and faithful to God like no other human
had ever done. God had touched this man, and Job had responded to God with
his entire being. His faith was so complete that he was willing to lose everything
he had while remaining faithful to God. We don't know what God did to capture
Job's allegiance, but it's clear that God got through to this man.[27]

The prophet Samuel learned that people tend to judge situations based on
outward appearances and external evidence, while God looks on the heart.[28] It's

not a difficult task for God to look inside each one of us to see if our hearts are with him or against him—if we are choosing to live or die.

When it comes to the question of free will, we shouldn't pretend that we're helpless in the matter of accepting or rejecting God and his claim on our life. No matter what our circumstance, the choice is clearly ours.[29]

God Does the Choosing

The Bible is clear that the choice is God's, not ours. Jesus made that plain to his followers. "You did not choose me, but I chose you," he said, no doubt taking some of the wind out of their sails.[30] If they'd been thinking they were smart enough to spot the Messiah and join his inner circle, they were now disabused of that notion.

Peter says to us very directly, "But you are a chosen people."[31] That is really the identifying mark of the people of God, the fact that they are chosen and set apart by God. Moses added more detail to this idea when he encouraged the Israelites by saying, "The LORD your God has chosen you out of all the peoples on the face of the earth to be his people, his treasured possession."[32]

Over and over, God makes it plain that he has chosen certain individuals and groups of people. As we read the Bible, we find that he has chosen:

- *individuals.* "For I have chosen him,"[33] God said about Abraham, who is identified as "the father of us all."[34] God didn't set aside a people of his own possession by calling a multitude and forming a nation out of the crowd. Instead, he chose one man, Abraham, and formed a nation out of Abraham's descendents. Much later, God chose Moses to free his people, Abraham's offspring, from slavery.[35]
- *the twelve disciples.* Many people crowded around and followed Jesus. But he chose only twelve to join him in his ministry, and some of them hadn't been followers prior to being called.[36]
- *God's people as a whole.* Christians are "God's chosen people, holy and dearly loved."[37] "God the Father chose you long ago," in fact, so long ago that it was "from the beginning," "before the creation of the

world."[38] The fact that we felt the power of the gospel and were convicted of our sin and neediness by the Holy Spirit is evidence that God has chosen us.[39]

- *spiritual leaders.* God chooses the people who serve as spiritual leaders to his people. In Moses' day, it was the priests: "The LORD your God has chosen them to minister and to pronounce blessings in the name of the LORD."[40] In the early church, we see the examples of Matthias, who was "chosen to take over this apostolic ministry" as one of the Twelve, and Barnabas and Paul, who were "set apart...for the work to which I have called them."[41]

In a statement that is almost beyond fathoming, God the Father says about Jesus, "This is my Son, whom I have chosen."[42] Jesus had a unique, redemptive mission as God the Son.[43]

Jesus confirmed that he is part of the choosing process when he said, "No one knows the Father except the Son and those to whom the Son *chooses* to reveal him."[44] We can't choose to see God unless Jesus "chooses to reveal him" to us.

We often think that we call the shots in our lives, making decisions and choices that determine the course of our future. But Scripture shows us that God chooses very specific things for our lives. "How can we understand the road we travel? It is the LORD who directs our steps."[45] Why did we run across a statement that gave us just the spiritual insight we needed at a particular moment? How about that job offer that changed the course of our life, or the person who decided to mentor us—altering forever the person we would become? God may in fact be behind it all, choosing, directing, guiding our steps.

God has a specific plan for our lives, and he set this in motion long ago. "For those God foreknew he also predestined to be conformed to the likeness of his Son.... And those he predestined, he also called; those he called, he also justified; those he justified, he also glorified."[46] There is certainly calling, justifying, and glorifying, but it all begins with predestining.[47]

There is no question about it: The choice is clearly God's.[48]

THE DEEPER MEANING OF BOTH/AND

The choice is ours and the choice is God's. Both are taught in Scripture, so both must be true. But the tension between our free will and God's prerogative to choose (or not to choose) someone has caused more consternation among Christians than just about any other paradox in Scripture.

Gaining insight into the both/and truths will help clarify our thinking and prevent us from taking an extreme position by clinging to only one strand of the paradox. There is no "free will only" or "predestination only" on God's ship. There are two sets of choices described in Scripture, and halakic study can make clear how they work together.

Is it possible that we have a set of choices and that God has a set of choices? Perhaps he has given us things to decide that he leaves completely open, pending our decision. And perhaps he has reserved other decisions exclusively for his own domain. And it just might be that he has established these two sets of choices to play off one another. In other words, could his choices determine our available options, and our choices determine his responses? Let's consider some possibilities.

God Chooses to Give Us Life

We see that unborn and newborn babies and young children enjoy a place in God's grace, since they are not held accountable for their own choices until they can distinguish between wrong and right. There is an original sin nature in humans, which gives us a *penchant* toward sin.[49] But infants are not guilty of committing any sin, because sin is a *choice* to go against God's will for our lives. We have to be aware of the options and be able to make a choice before we can sin. A little one who dies early, before he or she has an awareness of obedience to God and rebellion against him, goes to live with God for eternity.[50]

It's similar to a professor who tells her class, "Everyone in this room starts out today with an A. It's yours to keep or lose." As infants we begin life with an A, a high grade with the God who made us in his image, who "made us only a little lower than God."[51]

People Choose Death over Life

If we begin life in God's grace, then it must be true that at some point we choose to be lost. God wants us to choose life, but instead we choose death. "The LORD replied to Moses, 'Whoever has sinned against me I will blot out of my book.'"[52] What book? The Book of Life.[53] All people who reach the point of making moral decisions choose to sin, to follow their sinful nature that predisposes them to disobey God. And with that initial choice, they get struck from the record of God's book.[54]

"May they be blotted out of the book of life and not be listed with the righteous," the psalmist fervently prayed about the wicked.[55] Somehow they had been in the book earlier. But when they reached the moment of choice, their decisions earned an F and they were kicked out of class.

We're told by the apostle Paul that some people "did not think it worthwhile to *retain* the knowledge of God."[56] We are all created in the image of God, and each of us has an inner sense of God's reality, but we can choose not to hold on to that knowledge. God provides plenty of reminders and corroboration of his existence, speaking to humanity through his creation, the Bible, the Holy Spirit, conscience, the church, other people, and Jesus, the living Word of God.[57] No one who lives to the age of moral accountability can honestly say, "But I didn't know."

God Chooses to Offer Us a New Life

God asks us to repent and confess our sins if we want to obtain eternal life. If we hear him speaking to us in any of the ways he reveals himself, we can choose life. Or we can choose to ignore him. If we choose to listen, we find that "whoever has will be given more, and he will have an abundance."[58] With each step we take, we are moving toward or away from God. If we seek him, no matter how feeble our attempts to discover him may be, he will show us more clearly the life he holds out to us, the abundant truth of who he is.[59]

We Can Choose to Be Reentered in the Book of Life

Although by sinning we choose to be blotted out of the Book of Life, God gives us a second chance in this life. After choosing rebellion against God, we can make another choice, a choice to be saved and written back into the Book of Life.[60] God will reenter our names, right over the area that has been blotted out.[61] Because he is a God of unfailing love, he is looking for an opportunity to rejoin us to his family and kingdom.

We can say to God, "According to your great compassion blot out my transgressions."[62] God hears our prayer and, based on our request, says, "I, even I, am he who blots out your transgressions."[63]

The apostle Peter boldly proclaimed, "There is no salvation through anyone else, nor is there any other name under heaven given to the human race by which we are to be saved."[64] Peter is telling us that the way to get written into the ultimate who's who is to choose to be saved by Jesus.

We Can Choose to Serve God

After the initial choice of life over death, we can choose whom we will serve. Every day, we can choose to be identified with Jesus, the living God. We still have a sinful nature, to which we can choose to listen. But now we have a spiritual nature, and we can choose God's way each moment of our lives.

"Man has free will," wrote Thomas Aquinas. "Otherwise counsels, exhortations, commands, prohibitions, rewards and punishment would be in vain."[65]

We learn from the Bible that no one can choose for us.[66] Choosing in the kingdom of God is a very personal matter.

But God Lays Out the Options

Although God invites every person to choose, we find that it is God's choice to send out the invitation. He chooses the options and then chooses to lay them out for us. We can't choose anything that he has not presented as a possible choice. And it is God who has chosen to give us the ability, the wisdom, and the power to make a good choice among the available options.

We see that "God so loved the world that he gave his one and only Son, that whoever believes in him shall not perish but have eternal life."[67] God started the process by choosing to love the world when it was lost in sin. He chose to send

Jesus to earth to open a way for us to return to God. And he chose to allow everyone an opportunity to choose him and believe in him.

With God having laid out the options, it is our choice whether we live or die. He makes it clear that "what may be known about God is plain to [humanity]."[68] Life or death, blessing or cursing—it's our choice.

God's Way of Salvation Requires a Choice

In addition, we see that God chooses the means of salvation. "He chose to give us birth through the word of truth," James tells us.[69]

We discover that God's salvation plan has two parts: "God chose you to be saved through the sanctifying work of the Spirit *and* through belief in the truth."[70] God's choice forces us to make a choice in response. It is his choice to send the Holy Spirit who can sanctify us, but it is also his choice that we have to *believe* the Holy Spirit if we want to be sanctified. A God who could have made us animals driven by instinct and without choice—a God who could have chosen not to make us at all—chose to make us noble beings with the ability to choose, to believe.

We see this interplay of choices again: "For it is by grace you have been saved, through faith."[71] God chooses to provide grace, and he expects *us* to respond with faith. Some have been confused by the second part of the verse, which says "and this not from yourselves, it is the gift of God."[72] The gift, God's starting choice, is *grace*—and we can't earn it by our efforts. To offer it is God's choice alone, and we can be very glad that he chose to offer it to us all.

But we can choose to believe. In fact, we're encouraged to believe, commanded to believe, commended for having great faith, and condemned if we have little or no faith.[73] None of that would make any sense if faith were forced on us. "He who created us without our help will not save us without our consent," wrote Augustine.[74]

God chooses to respond to us and give to us based on our choices. Jesus explained: "Ask and it will be given to you; seek and you will find; knock and the door will be opened to you."[75] If we don't choose to ask, seek, or knock, we won't receive, find, or enjoy a life of open doors. God leaves room for our choices, but he has chosen how he will respond to our choices.

We can choose a flight destined for Los Angeles or a flight destined for Paris, but once we board the jet we shouldn't be surprised when it lands at its announced destination. God offers us routes, and we can choose which to take—the one that puts us in his kingdom or the one that promises eternal separation from him. We cannot, however, choose to change the way God responds to our decision for life or a curse.

"They have chosen their own ways,...so I also will choose harsh treatment for them," the prophet Isaiah quoted God as saying.[76] God responds to us depending on whether we choose for or against him. We can't choose hell and end up with heaven.

Our Choices Predestine Us to Receive Certain Results

So what do we do with the scriptures that talk about predestination? Predestination is taught in the Bible, but we need to ask: "What is it that we are predestined *for?*" We found that the salvation choice—life or death, blessings or curses—is ours to make, so that choice can't be predestined. We also discovered that our choices lead to predestined responses from God. What do we get if we put these truths together?

We see that we are free to choose our basic course, and based on our choice God has predestined a number of things for us to be and do. It's as if we are standing in front of a closed door that has a sign that says, "Whoever wants to come through this door—Jesus—can come right in." If we choose to go through the door, we find another sign that says, "I knew you were coming, so look at what I have prepared in advance for you!"

Does our choice to enter destine us to certain consequences? This halakic study pushes us in that direction. When we look closely at scriptures that talk about predestination, they seem to say that a person who believes the gospel is predestined to *blessings.* God honors our choice by choosing some amazing gifts for us. "He chose our inheritance for us," the psalmist teaches.[77] What is this predestined inheritance?

- God plans for us to be holy and blameless.[78] We are not told that he chose whether we would be saved. Instead, those who are saved have been predestined by God to be holy.
- He predestines us to be conformed to the likeness of his Son.[79] God sees that some of us will choose him, and he predestines us to end up looking like Jesus, as surely as children end up bearing the family likeness.
- He predestines us to be *adopted* as his daughters and sons.[80] God didn't have to make those who believe a part of his family. But we can be *very* thankful that he made this choice a part of our destiny.
- He chooses us out of the world.[81] God does not say that he chose us to be saved or damned, but rather that he chose to free us from the death grip of a corrupt world, to live in his presence. "Blessed are those you choose and bring near to live in your courts!" the psalmist shouted.[82]
- God gives us the ability to obey him. "To God's elect…who have been chosen according to the foreknowledge of God the Father…*for obedience* to Jesus Christ."[83] For all who choose him, he predestines a willingness and ability to do whatever Jesus asks them to do.
- God chooses us to go and bear fruit. "You did not choose me, but I chose you," was a verse we looked at earlier. Here's the remainder of that verse: "and appointed you *to go and bear fruit*."[84] We are not chosen to be saved but to live a life that makes a difference. "For we are God's workmanship," wrote Paul, "created in Christ Jesus to do good works, which God prepared in advance for us to do."[85]
- He predestines us to be people who live to praise his glory by our lives. "In him we were also chosen, having been predestined…in order that we, who were the first to hope in Christ, *might be for the praise of his glory.*"[86] We are predestined to live as shining lights that bring praise to God's glory.

The Holy Spirit is God's ever-with-us guarantee that he has given us a breathtaking inheritance as adopted members of his family.[87]

Jesus said, "For many are invited, but few are chosen."[88] We, the many, are invited to come to God's dinner party, but few accept. And God only chooses those who accept his invitation to receive the gifts he has decided in advance to give anyone who attends the feast.

We also see in the Bible that once we choose God, we can't unchoose him. "I give them eternal life, and they shall never perish; *no one* can snatch them out of my hand," Jesus said.[89] We freely place ourselves in the grasp of One so powerful in his love that *nobody*—not even we ourselves—can tear us away. "And God *raised*"—past tense—"us up with Christ…in order that in the coming ages he might show the incomparable riches of his grace."[90]

WHERE THIS LEAVES US

God chooses to give us the power and freedom to make choices and then holds us accountable for the choices we make. He does everything to help us make the best choice, but he leaves the decision in our hands. If he didn't do this, it would be unreasonable for him to condemn us for making wrong or bad choices. And if we don't have the freedom to decide, it doesn't make sense for him to tell us to choose.

Some have struggled with God's foreknowledge versus our free will. We can "find it difficult to conceive of [God's] previous knowledge of actions which man freely originates. The difficulty…led some to deny the foreknowledge of free actions, and others to deny human freedom."[91] But with this halakic, we don't have to deny either. God can know what we will do (or not), but we are still completely free to do it (or not).

Our choice is not everything, since it is empty and impossible without God's grace; and yet our choice is not nothing, since we can indeed accept or reject that grace.

And our choices have consequences. Perhaps the biggest is how these choices affect God's choices about us. He includes all people in his invitation, and he excludes all who will not accept the invitation. If we don't choose him, he will at some point stop listening to us and will leave us to our own self-centered and self-destructive will. If we choose him, however, there is no end to the life and blessings.

As we have seen, our choices and God's choices, in the end, intertwine. "From the beginning God chose you to be saved *through the sanctifying work of the Spirit and through belief in the truth.*"[92] And what is the result of these blended choices, of his choice to sanctify us and our choice to believe he'll do it?

Nothing less than heaven on earth, and eternal life with God in the ages to come.

FOR FURTHER THOUGHT AND DISCUSSION

1. How would you define *free will* after studying this paradox? What is the most important choice that God gives us?

2. How would you define *predestination* after studying this paradox? Among the things that God has predestined for his children, which are you most thankful for?

3. Describe in your own words how our choices and God's choices blend, how they work together, how they feed off one another.

4. Which ideas in this chapter conflict most with your earlier understanding of free will in light of God's sovereignty? How does studying this paradox alter your understanding?

5. Of the seven predestined inheritances discussed in the latter part of this chapter, which one surprised you the most? What made it so surprising?

Ten

It's Faith Alone, but We Must Have Good Works

What Does God Really Require of Us?

Workers earn what they receive. But people are declared righteous because of their faith, not because of their work.

Romans 4:4-5, NLT

So you see, we are made right with God by what we do, not by faith alone.

James 2:24, NLT

As Stephen listened to the teacher of an adult Bible class discuss the eleventh chapter of Hebrews, the "faith chapter," several questions came to mind. He raised his hand to catch the teacher's attention.

"I agree that a person must have faith to accept Christ," Stephen began. "But don't you think good works are necessary to be a Christian? I mean, how do you explain all the things the people in this chapter *did* for God?"

"Good works are done because we love God, but they are not required to be a Christian," the class leader explained with confidence. "Faith alone in Jesus as God's Son—and in his saving work on the cross—is all we need. Good works will not get you to heaven."

No one else joined the discussion, so Stephen left it alone. But he went home with the same questions and doubts. If God isn't interested in our carrying out good deeds, then why is the Bible full of stories about God's people performing acts of goodness, often at great personal cost? Why are we commanded to do good works and to earn rewards? *There must be more to it than faith alone,* Stephen thought as he pulled into his driveway.

Can a person who professes faith in Christ lead a life that is seemingly devoid of good works? If a person's life lacks outward evidence of consistent obedience to God, are we right in doubting the authenticity of that person's faith?

Likewise, what are we to think about people who devote their lives to acts of service to others but claim no special relationship with God? Are they saved but don't know it, or are they simply generous, good-hearted people who need to be introduced to Christ?

Faith and works often are mentioned in the same breath, but how they fit together has given rise to ongoing debate among Christians. Can you have one without the other? That's what this paradox is all about.

FAITH AND WORKS TOGETHER

If you're looking for a challenging theological debate, you don't need to look further than the question of faith and works. The Protestant Reformation, the sixteenth-century Council of Trent, and much of church history since then have all revolved around this one issue. This is much more than an academic discussion. The answer to this paradox has a direct bearing on how we live the Christian life.

We are told that we're saved by faith and not by works. We are told that we're saved by works and not by faith. How can we be saved by faith and not by works when we're told that we are saved by works and not by faith?

Salvation by Faith Alone

If we are saved by faith alone, what prevents someone from asserting his or her belief in God's saving grace and then living like someone who has no concept of God? Couldn't we "believe" on some intellectual level but not at a level that affects our daily life? Doesn't true faith require more than mere intellectual assent?

Jesus told would-be followers to consider the cost of following him,[1] which many Christians would understand to be a base-level commitment that changes our worldview, our attitudes, our words, and our actions. How does a faith that requires nothing more than belief leave us with anything but a selfish life that is only *called* Christian?

If we choose side A of this paradox and say that people are saved by faith plus nothing, we can end up with a "head" faith that relies on mental assent to the message of the gospel, but with no "heart" component that governs how we live our daily lives. We can easily reduce faith to nothing more than agreeing with a proposition, creed, or statement of faith.

Why should we bother to serve others, to put the needs of others ahead of our own, to sacrifice for the good of others, if our simple profession of allegiance to the death and resurrection of Christ has guaranteed us a place in heaven? The low percentage of giving—of both money and time—in many churches may answer this question in part. If we focus on side A of the paradox, we might ignore the biblical exhortations about running the race to win rewards.[2]

What effect might a faith-only Christianity have on relationships among Christians? Seeking and granting forgiveness could easily get shoved aside. Why should we go through the difficulty of confession, repentance, and forgiveness to restore broken relationships? After all, we're already forgiven by God, and those actions gain us nothing.

And why worry about sin? Good works, bad works—what difference do they make if our place in eternity is already determined by our act of faith? We can end up with a flawless statement of faith and a badly flawed life. We can put our confidence in agreeing to a confession of faith while living like those who make absolutely no claim to religious faith.

This can take us, in the end, to what Dietrich Bonhoeffer called "cheap grace."[3] Believe now, change later. This is head faith without heart change, verbal assent without a life commitment. There's no reason to count the cost of discipleship when there *is* no cost, when nothing is required except a simple declaration: "I believe."

Churches can find themselves railing against unbelief and unbelievers even as their own members live shoddy and disgraceful lives. These churches can take great pride in their doctrinal purity. "If you don't agree with everything on our doctrinal statement, your faith is lacking. In fact, we're not even sure you're really a Christian if you question any of our beliefs." Since good works are deemphasized—they're nice things to do, but not critical for a Christian—people can say they believe while living for themselves rather than for God. This is what comes of overemphasizing the first half of the paradox, that what people do isn't critical to their salvation.

Salvation That Requires Good Deeds

If we choose side B of this paradox and say that people are saved by works rather than by faith, we still have problems. We can easily end up with a performance-based religion that measures our inner life by our outward results. This can lead to a rules-based system that gauges the validity of a person's faith by how much good they appear to do.

If we are saved by works, how can we have confidence in our salvation? How many good deeds are enough to get a person into heaven? How will we know if we've built up enough credit before we die? What if we arrive at heaven's front gate only to find that we're two good deeds shy of enjoying eternity with God? And what if bad actions cancel out good works? How can we ever keep the ledger straight? Can enough bad actions cancel out heaven?

Basing the Christian life on works leads to "running a tab" for ourselves and for others. We might think we're doing pretty well—volunteering for committees, writing out a big check to the church once in a while, visiting the sick.

Surely those will override that little gossip session we were part of last week. And things look even better when we consider what others are doing, or not doing, to build up their spiritual bank account. If that other guy's going to heaven, then we've got it made!

Works-based religion leads to rules-based religion. We calibrate our progress toward heaven with a manifesto of higher standards and line-item listings of all the things that good Christians do. We can use the manifesto to discern whether we're doing "enough," then turn and use it to assess those around us. Since we can't measure their inner lives, we focus on outward behavior. If they look pretty good, we get worried about our own performance. But we forget how easy it is for any one of us to fake it, that the person who looks the best on the outside might have the darkest heart of all.

We might conclude that if good works get a person to heaven, *more* good works will assure a better seat in heaven. We can end up with a competitive version of Christianity, where my good works not only look better on earth, but promise a bigger ultimate payoff than yours. In a religion based on good deeds, piety can come to mean "I'm doing my best to look holier than other people," instead of "I'm doing my best to align my life with God."

An allegiance to doing good things can produce churches that are focused on activities and programs at the expense of deepening the faith of those who worship there. Leaders can easily find themselves measuring Christian commitment based on church attendance, hours of service, and participation in church activities rather than by whether a person strives to follow Jesus in all her words, actions, and allegiances.

Such churches can make people feel spiritually secure on the basis of being a member of a congregation when they might have a complete absence of authentic faith in Christ. These churches can produce a wide breadth of membership that has little or no depth. A congregation can be populated with people who act like Christians but have no relationship with God.

Clinging to one side of this paradox, no matter which side it is, leaves a person with only half the picture. We sense that we've missed something very large. And we're right.

WHAT SCRIPTURE SAYS

When we study the Bible with a fixed interpretation in place, it's easy to downplay or completely disregard passages that challenge our assumptions. But taking this approach can blind us to the full truth that God wants us to grasp. Paradoxes have a way of opening our eyes to the deeper meaning of God's message. This is certainly the case when we are weighing the value of faith against works and vice versa. The Bible is strongly focused—on both sides of this paradox.

We Live by Faith Alone

If there is one clear theme in all of Scripture, it is that we are saved by God's grace through faith. Period. Nothing else can be added.

"When people work, their wages are not a gift," the apostle Paul wrote to the Roman Christians. "Workers earn what they receive. But people are declared righteous because of their faith, *not* because of their work."[4] The message couldn't be clearer. We are "declared righteous"—made ready for heaven—by our faith. Salvation is a gift from God, not a salary paid for work we have done.

The way to life is hearing God's words and believing them. "I tell you the truth," declared Jesus, "whoever *hears* my word and *believes* him who sent me has eternal life and will not be condemned."[5]

It's clear that receiving Christ is a matter of believing that he is who he says he is and then welcoming him. "Yet to all who received him, *to those who believed in his name,* he gave the right to become children of God."[6] The path to eternal life, the way to become a part of God's family, is faith.

Faith is what gives us life. In fact, it's how we live if we are truly God's children. "The righteous will *live* by his faith," declared the prophet Habakkuk.[7] Our faith isn't just a ticket to heaven; it's the rule of life on earth.

"For in the gospel a righteousness from God is revealed, a righteousness that is *by faith from first to last.*"[8] Our life with God doesn't start by faith and finish by works. And it isn't a combination of faith plus doing good things. Another translation of the same verse says, "This Good News tells us how God makes us right in his sight. This is accomplished from *start* to *finish* by faith."[9]

These verses make it clear that faith is the key, but they also raise a question: What is faith? We discover that it is much more than simply hearing God's Word: "The message they heard was of no value to them, because those who heard did not combine it with faith."[10] We can learn everything there is to know about God's plan for salvation and still not receive the gift of eternal life. Hearing the gospel transforms our lives only if we *believe* it. And notice that this verse makes no mention of performing good works. The message isn't made valuable to us because we suddenly start doing good things. It's made valuable to us because we "combine it with faith."

Since faith is the key, it's essential to grasp the Bible's definition of faith. We are taught that "faith is being sure of what we hope for and certain of what we do not see."[11] Faith is a decision to believe, a commitment to a life that we want but cannot now see. And this has always been the only way to God. The next verse adds the comment that "this is what the ancients were commended for."[12] There aren't different ways to God depending on what era of history you live in—faith now versus works in ancient times. There is no new covenant replacing the old covenant. There is just faith—always and for all time.

"God saved you by his special favor *when you believed*," Paul wrote to the Ephesians. "And you can't take credit for this; it is a gift from God. Salvation is not a reward for the good things we have done, so none of us can boast about it."[13] God's special favor (his grace) is a free gift that is activated by our faith. But we can take no credit for this grace. He offers us a simple agreement, stripped of all human effort or contribution. Our role is simply to accept the gift in faith.

But what about good works? The Bible commends acts of righteousness, so we can't very well toss good works onto the trash heap. God's law for righteousness, laid out in the Scriptures, is the authoritative picture of what a good life looks like. And just because faith is the rule for salvation, it doesn't mean we can downplay the law of righteousness. We're told that "the law is holy, and the commandment is holy, righteous and good.... We know that the law is spiritual...that the law is good."[14] God gives us no easy way to dismiss the rightness and power and beauty of the law.

But he does make it clear that the law won't get the job done. "So we are made right with God through faith and *not* by obeying the law," Paul told the Roman Christians.[15] Faith is the vehicle that makes us "right with God." "Don't think the law has anything to do with salvation," Paul seems to be saying.

We can be sure that "a person is not justified by works of the law but through faith in Jesus Christ."[16] Obedience to God does not "justify" us. It does not clear away the mounds and mounds of sin. The Scripture goes on: "So we, too, have put our faith in Christ Jesus that we may be justified by faith in Christ and not by observing the law, because by observing the law *no one will be justified*."[17] No one.

Paul taught that "the Gentiles, who did not pursue righteousness, have obtained it, a righteousness that is by faith; but Israel, who pursued a law of righteousness, has not attained it. Why not? Because they pursued it not by faith but *as if it were by works*."[18] One group didn't even try to obey the law, and they were declared righteous by faith. The other group tried hard to obey the law, and they were declared unrighteous because they missed the way to connect with God—by faith.

Performing good works that far surpass the ordinary is no substitute for faith. "Many will say to [Jesus] on that day, 'Lord, Lord, did we not prophesy in your name, and in your name drive out demons and perform many miracles?' Then I will tell them plainly, 'I never *knew* you. Away from me, you evil-doers!'"[19] Jesus doesn't deny that these people performed great works, which include speaking up for God, driving out evil, and performing miracles. Instead, he brings it all back to the fact that he doesn't "know" these people. There is no relationship between him and them. Their work, as great as it was, could not substitute for faith, and his response to their claims is far from friendly.

The choice is between the "righteousness" of our works and God's righteousness, between a cheap imitation and the real deal. The Bible encourages us to "be found in him, not having a righteousness of my own that comes from the law, but that which is through faith in Christ—the righteousness that comes from God and is by faith."[20] If we want phony righteousness, we can work for it. If we want real righteousness, we have to believe.

"Did you receive the Spirit by observing the law, or by believing what you heard?" Paul asked the Galatian Christians.[21] He expected only one answer, "by believing." The Spirit *never* comes to us because we are doing good things. He *only* comes because we have believed what we have heard, the message of God's grace in Christ.

The Bible tells us that Christ came to erase the idea that we can work our way to heaven. "Christ is the *end of the law* so that there may be righteousness for everyone who believes."[22] The law is a dead end if we are trying to find our way to heaven. In answer to the biggest question of a broken man's life, "What must I do to be saved?" the apostle Paul said to this jailer—and to those in the prison who had not moved, even though their chains had come loose and the prison doors had come open—"Believe in the Lord Jesus, and you will be saved."[23]

How could it be any clearer? We are saved by faith—period.[24]

We Must Have Good Works

If you are part of the Protestant tradition, the doctrine of salvation by faith alone is as familiar to you as your address or phone number. So the preceding discussion of the role of faith in salvation makes perfect sense. It's a comfortable fit.

But as we read Scripture, we notice a startling paradox. It is clear in the Bible that faith without works is dead. Not anemic, not incomplete, not limping along. But lifeless, an empty shell—dead. In fact, without works there is *no* faith. "So you see," wrote James, "we are made right with God by what we do, *not by faith alone.*"[25] He not only says that works are the way to be made right with God, but specifically denies the singular role of faith. One word-for-word translation says, "You see that a man is justified by works and not by faith alone."[26]

The Bible goes on to tell us that the kind of "believing" that doesn't involve good works is absolutely dead. "In the same way, faith by itself, if it is not accompanied by action, is dead."[27] To make sure we understand, James gives us a startling analogy: "As the body without the spirit is dead, so faith without deeds is dead."[28] When a body is without the spirit, we put it in the ground and cover it with dirt. So we see that faith without works belongs six feet under.

How do we know if people are saved? By their profession of faith? No. Jesus told us that we can identify people who are right with God by the fruit they produce, not by what they claim to believe. "By their fruit you will recognize them," he explained.[29] It's not enough to claim to be a grapevine or a fruit tree. There must be good fruit on the branches, or your profession is at best suspect.

"Not everyone who says to me, 'Lord, Lord,' will enter the kingdom of heaven," warned Jesus, "but only he who does the will of my Father who is in heaven."[30] There are many people who pray and go to church and worship but who don't do the will of God in their daily lives. Jesus' judgment is clear: These people, regardless of their humble-sounding profession, are not on their way to heaven.

Jesus drills this point into our souls with detailed examples:

- In the parable of the wise and foolish builders, Jesus shows that the difference between those whose lives are broken by the storms of life and those whose lives stand firm is in what they *do.*[31]
- In the parable of the sower, Jesus shows that it's not enough to receive the Word and sprout a little shoot; we have to *produce a crop.*[32]
- In the parable of the sheep and the goats, Jesus shows that the difference between the sheep, who receive eternal life, and the goats, who go to eternal punishment, is once again what they *did.*[33]

The absence of good works doesn't indicate that we're sloppy Christians— it indicates that we *aren't* Christians. "Anyone who does what is good is from God. Anyone who does what is evil has not seen God."[34]

Jesus said that the only way people would know that we're his followers is by watching what we do. "This is to my Father's glory, that you bear much fruit, showing yourselves to be my disciples."[35] We don't present ourselves as his disciples by claiming to be his disciples or by insisting that we believe the right things. We present ourselves as his disciples by what we are, by what we do.

Actions are the great measuring stick of authentic spiritual life. "He who does what is right is righteous, just as [Jesus] is righteous. He who does what is sinful is of the devil."[36] Look at what people do, and you'll know what they are. "Anyone who does not do what is right is not a child of God," taught the apostle John, "nor is anyone who does not love his brother."[37] The failure here is one of deeds, not belief.

And talk is cheap. "They claim to know God," the apostle Paul wrote to his young friend Titus, "but by their actions they deny him."[38] In the kingdom of God, actions don't just speak louder than words—actions speak while the words don't even whisper.

The apostle Paul addresses the great work of the Christian life, which is love. "If I speak in the tongues of men and angels, but have not love, I am only a resounding gong or a clanging cymbal.... If I have a faith that can move mountains, but have not love, I am *nothing.*"[39] Most people are happy if they maintain just a little faith, but Paul tells us that even a mountain-moving faith without love, and all that love does, produces *nothing.* He goes further, saying that even if he has the greatest faith imaginable but is missing love, he *is* nothing.

The final condemnation that those who reject God will hear is this: "Depart from me, you who are cursed, into the eternal fire prepared for the devil and his angels. For I was hungry and you gave me nothing to eat."[40] These people will answer with words that sound reverential and humble: "Lord, when did we see you hungry?" Jesus' answer? "I tell you the truth, whatever you did not *do* for one of the least of these, you did not do for me."[41] If we don't see Christ in the needy people around us and do something about their needs, we have failed the entrance test to the kingdom of heaven.

We're supposed to "consider how we may spur one another on toward love and good deeds."[42] Why bother? Because good deeds are the stuff of the Christian life. They are what distinguishes Christians from everyone else. A world full of Christians focused on doing good deeds, and spurring others to do the same, is a world that would look much different from the one that surrounds us. We live in a world that is full of church programs and church members—but too few good works.

James, someone who keeps pounding away at the importance of good works, tells us that "faith without deeds is useless."[43] *Useless.* It simply can't help us at all. "What's the use of saying you have faith if you don't prove it by your actions?" he asks. *"That kind of faith can't save anyone."*[44]

In answer to the biggest question of their lives, "Brothers what must we do [about Jesus]?" the apostle Peter told a large crowd, "Repent...and be baptized....

Be saved from this corrupt generation!"[45] We have to do something; we have to be different. There's no doubt. Faith is powerless to save us unless it is demonstrated in good works.[46]

The Deeper Meaning of Both/And

What are the both/and truths that become clear as we dig deeper into this paradox? Are we saved by faith or works? The biblical answer, from what we have seen so far, seems to be yes.

There is no question that we have to have faith. Something has to change deep inside us, deep inside our souls, where convictions are formed and allegiances are solidified. We must adhere to the truth that "without faith it is impossible to please God, because anyone who comes to him *must believe* that he exists and that he rewards those who earnestly seek him."[47] Faith is absolutely essential.

There is also no question that we have to *act* on our faith. Something has to change on the outside, where others will see it, out where relationships are built and lives are changed and things are done to advance the kingdom of God. There is no escaping the need to "produce fruit in keeping with repentance."[48] Works are absolutely essential.

So how do we put those two ideas together to find the both/and truth?

There Is a Sequence

Halakic reasoning suggests that there is a necessary sequence in the manifestation of faith and works. If so, what are the possibilities?

- *Works Before Faith.* From what we saw earlier, this can't be it. "God saved you by his special favor *when you believed,*" we learned. "And you can't take credit for this; it is a gift from God. Salvation is not a reward for the good things we have done, so none of us can boast about it."[49]
- *Works at the Same Time as Faith.* This too seems to miss the mark. "Did you receive the Spirit by observing the law, or by believing what you heard?" we are asked.[50] The receiving, the starting point, is believing rather than doing.

- *Faith Before Works.* Could it be faith before works, then good works flowing from faith? "So you see," we are taught by James, "we are made right with God by what we do, not by faith *alone.*"[51] Faith has its role; it is the crucial starting point, but works are part of the equation. And it shouldn't take long before the works kick in. "In the same way faith, if it doesn't have works, is dead by itself."[52]

If we carry this thought a bit further, we begin to see that it isn't faith *alone,* but rather faith *first.* And then the works must come—immediately—or the "faith" is not real.

We saw that works do not save us. They *can't* save us. They are not the vehicle of salvation that God has provided. Works are not even enough to earn us a ride in the baggage car. "All our righteous acts are like filthy rags," moaned Isaiah.[53] "They cannot redeem themselves from death by paying a ransom to God," the psalmist said. "Redemption does not come so easily, for no one can ever pay enough to live forever and never see the grave."[54]

But if we are truly saved by faith, the works will flow. Genuine, saving faith can't help but produce good works. Works show that we're truly part of God's kingdom. "Therefore...be all the more eager to make your calling and election sure," urged the apostle Peter.[55] Prove it, he's telling us. Make it real. *Show* it's real. Works are an important way, he is telling us, to be "sure of what we hope for and certain of what we do not see."[56]

Paul did set up a contrast between grace and works. "And if by grace, then it is no longer by works; if it were, grace would no longer be grace."[57] But he was not saying that works have little to do with the Christian life. He was not even saying that they have no part in distinguishing whether someone is a real Christian. He was merely saying that we've got to get the starting point right. If we start with works, we cancel out our faith in God's grace. If we start with faith in God's grace, the works indeed should and *will* flow.

This order—faith followed by works—doesn't mean there is a gap between them, that we believe to obtain salvation and then work hard in our own strength for the rest of our lives. "After beginning with the Spirit, are you now trying to attain your goal by human effort?" Paul challenged the Galatians.[58] He is telling us that we have to begin with the Spirit and end with the Spirit, with spiritual works flowing from a spiritual connection.

Real Faith Inevitably Produces Action

We find that there are not two ways of getting to heaven, faith and good works. There may be a sequence of faith producing good works, but there is no exclusivity, no one or the other. "Now someone may argue, 'Some people have faith; others have good deeds.' I say, 'I can't see your faith if you don't have good deeds, but *I will show you my faith through my good deeds,*'" wrote James.[59] There is only one way of getting to heaven, and it involves faith that is authentic enough to produce good works.

Paul told the Galatian church, "The only thing that counts is faith expressing itself through love."[60] It is the two working together that make up the whole package of the Christian life—faith working and expressing itself through love. Love, according to the apostle John, is all about works: "Little children, we must not love in word or speech, but in deed and truth."[61]

We find that genuine faith *always* leads to action. Paul talks about the "service coming from your faith,"[62] about "your work produced by faith."[63] Genuine good deeds derive from real faith. He told Timothy about "God's work—which is by faith."[64] We can't do God's work unless we believe, but if we really believe, we *will* do God's work.

The major point of Hebrews 11 is not to show us that faith is a good thing (which it is), but that faith leads to good *actions.* "By faith Abel *offered* God a better sacrifice than Cain did."[65] "By faith Noah…*built* an ark to save his family."[66] "By faith Abraham, when called to go to a place he would later receive as his inheritance, obeyed and *went,*" and "by faith Abraham…*offered* Isaac as a sacrifice."[67]

In this action of offering Isaac as a sacrifice, James picks up the theme. "Don't you remember that our ancestor Abraham was declared right with God *because of what he did* when he offered his son Isaac on the altar? You see, he was trusting God so much that he was willing to do whatever God told him to do."[68] That's the deep connection, a trust in God so real that we're willing to do whatever he tells us to do. James went on: "His faith was made complete by what he *did*—by his actions. And so it happened just as the Scriptures say: 'Abraham *believed* God, so God declared him to be righteous.'"[69]

Good works finish what faith begins. "Prove by the way you live that you have really turned from your sins and turned to God," said John the Baptist.[70]

And we see that there is no contradiction and no competition between faith and works. Abraham was declared right with God "because of what he did." Good enough. And he was declared right with God because he "believed God." Also good enough. But how can it be both? How can he be declared right with God for two different reasons? Because in God's mathematics, believing and doing count the same—believing and doing are not separated from one another. Believing produces right action. Right action can only be sustained by real belief.

Rahab believed God was on the move against her city of Jericho, and she believed what the Israelite spies told her. Was her faith alone enough? Not according to James, who asks, "Was not even Rahab the prostitute considered righteous for what she *did?*"[71] She acted on her faith by helping the spies escape and by joining Israel. To say she believed God was bringing his people to Jericho and then to do nothing would have proved nothing—except that she had no faith.

The book of Hebrews shows clearly that the life of Moses is a study in faith that leads to action. "By faith Moses' parents *hid* him for three months after he was born."[72] "By faith Moses...*chose to be mistreated* along with the people of God rather than to enjoy the pleasures of sin for a short time."[73] In one of the biggest steps of faith of all time, "By faith the people *passed through the Red Sea as on dry land.*"[74] To say that we believe God is leading us to the Promised Land but then to stay put on Pharaoh's side of the sea is a profession of faithlessness—a slap in the face of a God who expects us to start walking.

Often when people have professed faith, done nothing, and then dropped out of the Christian life, Christians have said, "They've lost their faith." The problem with this assumption is that Christ says no one can snatch his sheep from his hand.[75] People who "drop out" are like fig trees that produce no fruit and are cursed,[76] like land that produces nothing good. "Land that drinks in the rain often falling on it…[and] produces thorns and thistles is worthless and in danger of being cursed."[77] They aren't former Christians. They are *non*-Christians, just as lost as before they professed a deedless, lifeless faith.

We see that works follow a living faith like fruit follows a living tree. There might be a lag before the fruit becomes visible, so we should give people the benefit of the doubt for a time, like the gardener who said to the man who wanted to destroy a barren tree, "Let's give it another year. I'll dig around it and fertilize." The gardener will invest more time, hoping for growth. But eventually, if no fruit appears, the jig is up, and the gardener will "chop it down."[78]

Works Are Good Only When They Are Built on Faith

We find that real works, works that are good and really count, have to come from God, and that our connection to him is our faith. "All that we have accomplished you have done for us," said the prophet Isaiah.[79] It is illusion to think we can do good works that count for eternity if we conjure them up out of our own resources. God says simply, "Your fruitfulness comes from me."[80]

We learn from this paradox that works without faith will fail us. "All who rely on observing the law are under a curse," Paul taught the Galatians. "Clearly, no one is justified before God by the law."[81]

In reality, our salvation, our relationship with God, is a matter of grace *and* law. "Do not merely listen to the word, and so deceive yourselves," wrote James. *"Do what it says."*[82] The result of doing? "If you keep looking steadily into God's perfect law—the law that sets you free—and if you do what it says and don't forget what you heard, then God will bless you for doing it."[83]

We see in the great teaching about the kinds of fruits we should expect to see in a Christian that these are fruits of the Spirit, not the fruits of human effort. They start with faith, with letting God's Spirit lead us. But when we look at this fruit—"love, joy, peace, patience, kindness, goodness, faithfulness, gentleness and self-control"[84]—we see clearly that all of these things involve action. You can't demonstrate the Spirit's kindness, for instance, by doing nothing kind.

In the end, we see that the Protestant Reformers brought a needed corrective to a trend that was placing too much emphasis on doing good deeds. But like so many correctives, perhaps this revolution went too far the other way, skipping past "faith first" and jumping to "faith alone." The necessary component of good works somehow may have gotten lost in the reemphasis on saving faith. The counterreformation may have started by saying that faith isn't saving faith unless it produces fruit in good works. This also may have gone too far the other way, saying that good works are necessary to be saved, rather than that they are the necessary *proof* of salvation.

God expects us to believe with our whole hearts. And then, if that faith is real, to act on it—unsparingly, unstoppably. Real faith demands real fruit and, at the same time, provides the only ground in which that fruit can grow.

Where This Leaves Us

I grew up in a church that emphasized good works,[85] and in college I found myself in a church that emphasized the role of faith alone. Perhaps I was drawn to that second church as a reaction to the focus of the first. Such a reaction can easily occur when we are trying to solve a both/and paradox with an either/or response. But it's not faith or works, it's faith *and* works. Only halakic reasoning can help us merge these two great truths into one greater truth.

We learn from the Bible that the entire Christian life is lived by faith—from "first to last," from the moment of salvation until the end when we finally see Jesus. But if we think that faith and works stand in contrast to each other, we can be confused on several points:

- We might think that there can be spiritual birth (the moment of salvation) that doesn't necessarily lead to the good works of a changed life.
- We might think that the burden is really on our shoulders to get good "grades" on earth so we'll earn a scholarship to heaven.
- We might, like the Galatians, think that we came to Christ by faith but that from here on we have to depend on our own efforts. In essence, we trade the free gift of God, which is activated by faith, for a life of bondage to the law.

- We may miss the full meaning of eternal life. Dallas Willard writes that many have "left unexplained how it is possible that one can rely on Christ for the next life without doing so for this one."[86]

Jesus gives us the final summary on this great paradox by showing that these two great principles, faith and works, are intricately and intimately woven together. In answer to the question, "What must we do to do the works God requires?" he answered, "The *work* of God is this: to *believe* in the one he has sent."[87] Faith ends up not just spurring good work—faith *is* good work in the kingdom of God.

And then comes the payoff. "Those who remain in me," he said, "and I in them, will produce much fruit.… My true disciples produce much fruit."[88] How much good fruit? More than we can even imagine. "I tell you the truth," he emphasized, "anyone who has faith in me will do what I have been doing. He will do even greater things than these."[89]

Good works don't produce faith. But true faith is made visible by the work that it does.

FOR FURTHER THOUGHT AND DISCUSSION

1. In looking at the subject of faith and works, how would you summarize the halakic conclusions raised in this chapter?
2. How would you answer the question, "Are we saved by faith, or are we saved by works?" Why?
3. What is the difference between professed faith and genuine faith?
4. When are works "good," and when are they not?
5. Have you ever found yourself swinging from one side of this paradox to the other? If so, what has this study taught you about your relationship with Christ? about various denominations and strands of Christianity?

Eleven

We Must Flee Evil, and We Must Fight It

In Spiritual Warfare, Timing Is Everything

～～～

I would flee far away and stay in the desert; I would hurry to my place of shelter, far from the tempest and storm.

PSALM 55:7-8

The wise conquer the city of the strong and level the fortress in which they trust.

PROVERBS 21:22, NLT

The ringing telephone startled Ed out of a sound sleep. His brother Phil was calling from another state. He was troubled about a situation at work and needed some advice.

"I don't think I can take it anymore," Phil confided. "My boss is making my life miserable. Should I stand up to him and risk getting fired, or just try to get a transfer to another department?"

Ed wondered if it was just a personality conflict or whether his brother might be caught up in an ethical issue. As Phil told more of the story, it became clear that his boss was singling him out for mistreatment because of his Christian faith.

"The situation is clearly unfair," Ed told his brother. "But I'd hate for you to lose your job just for calling him on his religious bigotry."

"So you think I should try for the transfer?" Phil asked.

"I don't know. The Bible does say we're supposed to take a strong stand against our enemies. So you have biblical grounds for challenging the way he's treating you. But the Bible also talks about fleeing from evil men, which would indicate that transferring to another department would be the best option. This is a tough call."

"Well, you're a lot of help," Phil said. "I still have no idea what to do."

Ed stifled a yawn. "Maybe you should pray about it."

"Believe me, I have. I just wish the Bible were a little clearer on what to do."

"Yeah, me too," Ed said. "Then maybe I could get back to sleep."

The existence of evil is a constant challenge for Christians. The dark forces claim victims with alarming regularity—and many would say the problem is growing in intensity. But what are we to do about it? Should we keep a safe distance to avoid being caught up in the sin? Or should we do battle against the forces that are destroying lives, including the lives of many people we love?

Actively fight evil or carefully protect ourselves from being drawn into evil? Which is the biblically mandated course of action?

RESISTING AND FLEEING EVIL

True to the activist nature of the Christian faith, many of us have been encouraged to take a firm stand by aggressively fighting evil. At the same time, we often are advised to run from evil to avoid the taint of sin. During the Revolutionary War, George Washington defeated a far superior enemy by knowing when to fight and when to run away, by knowing that both tactics were essential to a warrior's arsenal. Those who win in the end seem to know when to attack and when to retreat.

Here is our halakic question: We are told to flee from evil. We are told to fight evil. But how can we run away from evil and still fight it?

We Must Flee Evil

Fleeing evil makes sense, because a Christian is to have nothing to do with the deeds of darkness.[1] But if we flee from evil, won't evil win? Who will fight it if Christians won't? How can we hope to fight it when we have so often been a *part* of it? "Sin in a Christian's life makes a coward of him!" said Henrietta Mears.[2]

If we pick side A of the paradox and say simply that we should flee from evil, we might believe that Christians are commanded to be spiritual cowards. We don't have a responsibility to be a positive influence in the world. After all, we're too tiny and too weak to really make a difference.

With the view that Christians are to flee from evil, we might even begin to think that God's power is insufficient to defeat his enemies. We can fall into *Star Wars* thinking, where the forces of good and evil are paired off in a battle of equals, where God is doing his best just to hold his own against a "dark side" that is roughly his match. "When the elephants fight, the people hide," says an old African proverb. Wouldn't we be wise just to avoid this wrestling match between God and the Evil One?

We might find ourselves believing that the corrupt world system and the devil are winning the battle. We can conclude that the enemies of the good and godly life are not only fierce (which they are), but that they can't be defeated (which is patently untrue). But when we look around at our world they certainly *seem* to be winning.

Withdrawing from the fight can lead us to allow our enemies to box us in as we flee evil. We can even box ourselves in by creating a safe, insulated realm, shut off from the world and its evil. Or we can react in just the opposite way, concluding that if we're not to oppose evil, then what's the harm in blending into the corrupt part of the culture? Too many Christians have pursued this course to such a degree that they are now indistinguishable from the larger society.

Clinging to the "fleeing evil" side of this paradox can prompt us to create a long list of rules designed to protect us against our relentless foes. We can tell ourselves that by constructing a strict system of what to do and what to avoid we are insulating ourselves from the effects and power of evil. But in doing so, we could miss the great truth that Christianity is much more about possibilities than limitations, much more about freedom than controls.[3]

There are many ways to make hiding from evil a lifestyle, and many excel at it.

We Must Fight Evil

If we pick side B and say simply that we should fight evil, we might think it is our job to defeat the devil. We're the ones God expects to bring down the foes of righteousness. We can forget that "the battle is the LORD's"[4] and come to think that the safety of the kingdom of heaven is our responsibility. If we don't stand guard, who will? A best-selling novel suggested that angels themselves increased or decreased in power based on the prayers of human beings. But when angels appear in the Scriptures, they are so awesome that they are constantly saying to humans, "Don't be afraid."[5]

We might assume that victory is a matter of human will power. We'll just say no to temptation and sin. We can resist it; in fact, we are commanded to do just that. We begin to rely on unrealistic and ineffective tools to combat our own addictions and rotten desires. Overcoming the evil within is up to us.

The "resist evil" side of the paradox might even lead some Christians to deliberately expose themselves to wickedness so they'll have extra opportunities to fight it. Believers often subject themselves to the one temptation to which they are most vulnerable, leading to disastrous results. "Do not think of yourself more highly than you ought," warned the apostle Paul, "but rather think of yourself with sober judgment."[6] How often do we make bold statements about "never doing that again," and then find ourselves doing that very thing again in spite of our forceful declaration?

We could go so far as to believe that we have the power to stomp on the devil. At a men's conference years ago, I heard a dynamic speaker exhort us to "grab the devil by the neck, throw him down on the ground, and put our foot on his throat." He shouted, "I'm going to stomp on you, devil!" There is a scripture that says, "Bold and arrogant, these men are not afraid to slander celestial beings; yet even angels, although they are stronger and more powerful, do not bring slanderous accusations against such beings in the presence of the Lord. But these men blaspheme in matters they do not understand."[7] This bravado is foolish because it minimizes the ferociousness of our enemy. We see that even angels refuse to engage in such boasting.

As we pursue the path of resisting evil, we again might place our confidence in adhering to "higher" standards, such as a sexual purity program that includes symbols of a commitment we make to avoid certain sins. Purity is essential, but there is a temptation to rely on the power of our will rather than God's power to overcome the temptations we face. We can delude ourselves into thinking that the act of making a pledge will guarantee our safety. But our enemy is incredibly crafty, and he wants nothing more than to devour us.

We might even believe that pledging to adhere to a higher standard is the way for everyone else to resist evil, so we tell others: "You have to do this if you want to be holy!" Our original effort to fight evil can quickly become a fight against other Christians who see things differently from us. We see too many periods in Christian history when the enemy advanced up the hill against God's people only to find the Christians pointing their guns at each other.

Fighting evil. We can overestimate our ability to do it. We can go out to fight with inadequate weapons and not even see that we're about to be captured—or killed.

WHAT SCRIPTURE SAYS

When we search for a biblical basis for the best way to respond to evil, we see that both sides of this paradox are well represented in Scripture. But as we read passages that warn us to flee as well as passages ordering us to the front lines of battle, it's easy to become confused. Run to safety? Run to the battle? Yes. The Bible is very clear on what we are to do.

Be Careful to Flee Evil

There can be little doubt about this straightforward biblical teaching: When in doubt, run away. Because we're so weak in our human limitations, we're told to run to a place that is really strong. "The name of the LORD is a strong tower; the righteous run to it and are safe."[8]

We read that the early church fled in the face of persecution. "On that day a great persecution broke out against the church at Jerusalem, and all except the apostles were scattered throughout Judea and Samaria."[9] We don't see the apostles telling the people to make their stand, to hold their ground, to resist until every last believer is slaughtered. The people just go. As a result, the message about Christ was carried to faraway places.

Jesus himself escaped from danger. "All the people in the synagogue were furious.... They got up, drove him out of the town, and took him to the brow of the hill on which the town was built, in order to throw him down the cliff."[10] What was Jesus' response? Did he brace himself for a fight? No. He "slipped away through the crowd and left them."[11] The stories of Christian martyrs inspire us with the example of their courage and faith. But as we study martyrs, we see that they were willing to suffer pain or death when bearing witness to Christ called for such a sacrifice, when there was no other way. Short of that, however, they, too, slip through the crowd and escape.

What if the crowd pursues the escaping believer? We're supposed to run again. "When you are persecuted in one place, flee to another," Jesus encouraged.[12] Christianity offers no general call to martyrdom. Instead, it offers an escape plan. Jesus is assuming persecution will come if our belief in him becomes known. But he is also assuming that we will wisely move away from that persecution. If a college class or workplace or neighborhood has become intolerable, it's all right to drop the class, change jobs, or move to another area.

There are some temptations that are so fierce that when they come after us we are given one biblical directive—run away. "*Flee* from sexual immorality,"

Paul encouraged.[13] This is not a fight that a mere mortal can hope to win. There's another: "Flee from idolatry."[14] There is no reason for a Christian to remain in a place with false gods. Idolatry is not just the worship of hand-crafted idols or of natural phenomena such as trees, the sun, or the stars. Paul warned the Colossians to avoid "greed, which is idolatry."[15] Idolatry is putting something—anything—ahead of God. We are supposed to flee any influence or pressure to give allegiance to anything that could or would replace God.

Paul warned Timothy to "flee the evil desires of youth."[16] We are supposed to run from whatever took us down the road to sin when we were young, probably in part because those temptations will be likely to get us again.

Paul singled out a particular sinkhole of youth that often stretches into adulthood, a penchant to start, join, or prolong arguments: "Don't have anything to do with foolish and stupid arguments," he warned, "because you know they produce quarrels."[17] God wants us to learn to run from these when we're young and to keep running for the rest of our lives. Foolish and stupid arguments are always just a step behind us and gaining ground. We should run away so we won't be drawn into them.

There's more. Paul was concerned that his young friend Timothy might feel the need to fight for God by arguing with false teachers and lying prophets and heretics. Much of what passes for religion is simply an "unhealthy interest in controversies and quarrels about words," Paul pointed out.[18] So he warned Timothy to avoid this: "But you, man of God, flee from all this."[19] Likewise, he told Titus to "avoid foolish controversies and genealogies and arguments and quarrels about the law, because these are unprofitable and useless."[20] John carries this to the point of banning such people from a believer's home. "If anyone comes to you and does not bring this teaching, do not take him into your house or welcome him. Anyone who welcomes him shares in his wicked work."[21] Giving these people a forum encourages them—and corrupts us.

When we're attacked by temptation, we have the good news that God always provides an escape route.[22] We see a wise decision to run when Joseph made a quick exit from the room, leaving his coat behind him, when Potiphar's wife tried to seduce him.[23]

We shouldn't just run away from evil; we should *hide* from it. "I would flee far away and stay in the desert," wrote the psalmist; "I would hurry to my place of shelter, far from the tempest and storm."[24] We often don't want to take the time or make the effort to get that far from the tempests of life. We want to say a quick prayer and get on with our lives, perhaps moving just inches away from evil. That's not far enough, God is telling us.

Often the danger of evil comes not in a physical threat but in the form of a verbal attack. The psalmist says of God's protection: "You hide them in the shelter of your presence, safe from those who conspire against them. You shelter them in your presence, far from accusing tongues."[25] As we flee evil, we need to join the psalmist in praying, "Hide me from the conspiracy of the wicked, from that noisy crowd of evildoers. They sharpen their tongues like swords."[26]

Fleeing could involve physically moving to another place as well as running to God in prayer. There may come a time when we need to leave a place because the downward pull—the memories, the acquaintances, the vivid reminders of offenses—is simply too great to endure.[27]

We see in the Bible that we are to avoid putting ourselves into temptation's way. The recovering alcoholic shouldn't stand and fight evil by hanging out in bars to witness to his friends. The person who frequently becomes angry shouldn't settle for just trying to resist her outbursts of temper. Rather, she should figure out what situations are likely to set her off and try to avoid them. Instead of trying to control her temper when heavy traffic slows her down, she should leave home earlier in the morning. There is great encouragement in the Bible for those who take pains to avoid evil.[28]

In the end, if we don't run, hide, or avoid evil, we can't expect to be protected. But if we do these things, we can ask for complete deliverance. "O LORD my God, I take refuge in you; save and deliver me from all who pursue me."[29] There is just no substitute for fleeing and for finding a good place to hide.[30]

Make Sure You Fight Evil

There can be little doubt about this straightforward biblical teaching: When in doubt, fight.

Spiritual life is, at its core, a battle. "Fight the good fight of the faith," Paul encouraged Timothy.[31] We are designed to take down evil.

The fight against evil goes beyond developing a heart of wisdom. What do wise people do? "The wise conquer the city of the strong and level the fortress in which they trust."[32] Wise people fight a two-stage war. First, they "conquer the city of the strong" by leaving their own little world to go where the evil people live. We can't remain isolated from evil, pretending that it doesn't exist. We find the strong and then we defeat them. We stop their plans and end their evil deeds. Christians shouldn't be content to live in silence near pornography shops or abortion clinics or neighborhoods where any group of people is oppressed and discriminated against. There is a time to stand up and overcome such evils.

And second, the wise will "level the fortress in which they trust." We don't leave any remnants of the evil behind. This may be why we're given the example of the Hebrews entering the land of Canaan, who were advised "to wipe out all its inhabitants from before you."[33] We don't take a swing at evil and then leave it alone so it can nibble away at us. We don't pervert the noble principle of tolerance by saving a place at the table for evil. When a public official stands for something evil, we vote the rascal out of office. When a business supports a rotten cause, we write them letters or boycott them or organize a protest. Abolitionist Sojourner Truth urged people to speak truth to power. So we speak. And we don't quit until the evil is "leveled."

The great Old Testament warrior Nehemiah was encouraged by a concerned party to run away from evil. He was told, " 'By night they are coming to kill you.' But [Nehemiah] said, 'Should a man like me run away?... I will not go!' "[34] Anyone who has ever taken a stand to challenge injustice has probably been warned to leave the field of battle. Nehemiah had real enemies who opposed his rebuilding of the wall around Jerusalem. When he was warned that his enemies were "coming to kill you," he could easily have retreated in order to protect himself. In our culture, God's enemies threaten to criticize us, ostracize us, slander us, gossip about us, or try to hurt us in various ways. But we should say strongly, "I will not stop!"

We don't just hold our ground against evil. We are taught a model of opposition, one that takes the initiative to move the fight forward. "As the Philistine moved closer to attack him, David ran quickly *toward* the battle line to meet him."[35] We don't wait for God's enemies, no matter how large, to make a move. We run forward. We have the power to do it. "I have given you authority to trample on snakes and scorpions and to overcome *all* the power of the enemy," Jesus advises us.[36] And we don't just have the power to take out snakes and scorpions. "Through you we push back our enemies; through your name we trample our foes," the psalmist declared.[37] We keep going until evil either falls or runs, and until it is gone.

Amazingly, not even the devil can budge us. Paul used battle language in his advice to the Ephesians:

> God is strong, and he wants you strong. So take everything the Master has set out for you, well-made weapons of the best materials. And put them to use so you will be able to stand up to everything the Devil throws your way. This is no afternoon athletic contest that we'll walk away from and forget about in a couple of hours. This is for keeps, a life-or-death fight to the finish against the Devil and all his angels.
>
> Be prepared. You're up against far more than you can handle on your own. Take all the help you can get, every weapon God has issued, so that when it's all over but the shouting you'll still be on your feet.[38]

The apostle Paul warns us to "be self-controlled and alert. Your enemy the devil prowls around like a roaring lion looking for someone to devour. *Resist him,* standing firm in the faith."[39] The Evil One "prowls around." The very name *devil* means "deceiver." But when he gets near, he roars in an attempt to paralyze us and make us easy prey. If we're "self-controlled and alert," if we're "standing firm in the faith," we have nothing to fear. In fact, good news: We're going to make *him* run away. "Resist the devil, and he will flee from you."[40] When we resist, he runs away from us—just as he did when Jesus stood against him in the desert.[41]

The reason we can do this is that we have better weapons than the wicked have. We win because "the weapons we fight with are not the weapons of the world. On the contrary, [the weapons of the righteous] have *divine power to demolish strongholds.* We demolish arguments and every pretension that sets itself up against the knowledge of God."[42] Christians annihilate evil.

As we prepare for battle, we need to make sure we are fighting against true evil and not just human incompetence, ignorance, or pettiness. Too much of what Christians have called fighting evil is really a battle over personal preference (for example, trying to get a city council to open each meeting with a prayer) than it is with a biblical imperative. And even when a clear biblical absolute is being violated, we have to make sure we're fighting the battle God's way. We're told, "The weapons we fight with are *not* the weapons of the world."[43] This means that we avoid bludgeoning people into righteousness and that we renounce the slander and character smearing of which many have been so fond. To guard against that error, we learn about God's state-of-the-art military technology, superpower weapons like "the sword of the Spirit, *which is the word of God.*"[44]

We know that if we don't give up, we will overcome evil. And if we have wisdom, when evil people and temptation and persecution come against us, we know we'd better fight.[45]

The Deeper Meaning of Both/And

What are the both/and truths that we find in this puzzling paradox? First, it's clear that we are to both flee evil and fight it. The key is to know when each strategy is called for. The prophet Elijah illustrates the importance of correctly reading each situation. He showed great wisdom when he hid from an evil king, Ahab.[46] He showed great cowardice, however, when he ran away and hid from Ahab's evil queen, Jezebel, when God wanted Elijah to resist.[47] We have to study any situation closely and trust the leading of the Holy Spirit to know if fight or flight is the best option.

We Should Flee from Temptation

Some enemies leave us with only one legitimate option, and that is to run. Our will power and other personal resources will not be sturdy enough to hold off the assaults of these temptations. We saw earlier that sexual immorality, idolatry, greed, false doctrines, the evil desires of youth, and foolish and stupid arguments are things from which we should *always* flee. These temptations appeal to our sinful nature[48] and work to destroy us from within. Our sinful nature is like a terrorist, looking for the opportunity to use our bodies against us as "instruments of wickedness."[49] These things violate "the perfect law that gives freedom."[50]

We should flee to God, hide in him, and ask him to deliver us from the:

- *penalty of sin.* If we don't flee to God from the enemies bent on destroying us, we face constant penalties in this life and—if we never choose to know God—when this life is over and we stand before the Judge.
- *pain of sin.* The memory of sin and the guilt it brings are too much for us to bear. We have to run to God and ask him to heal the pain.
- *power of sin.* The power of sin is still effective against us even after we entrust our lives to Christ. While our spirits are transformed, the Evil One, the corrupt world system, and our own sinful nature are still there to bring us down if we do not constantly avail ourselves of God's power.
- *plague of sin.* Sin brings destruction and disaster upon the person who habitually gives in to it. Consider the physical consequences of alcoholism, drug addiction, sexual promiscuity, and chronic anger.
- *persistence of sin.* Since Satan never gives up, at least in this life, the hard-won lessons we learned earlier in our lives, the protective walls we built, the self-control we fought to achieve, can all evaporate if we aren't constantly vigilant.
- *pervasiveness of sin.* Temptation can come at any time and in any place. We can be reading the Bible or kneeling in prayer and be tempted by a terrible thought.
- *presence of sin.* By committing our souls to Christ, we find that our lives are "hidden with Christ in God" so that "when Christ your life appears, then you too will appear with him in glory."[51]

We Flee from the Attacks of Our Enemies

Our security comes from running to God, not from engaging our enemies in a battle that isn't worth fighting and that we can't win. So it's clear in Scripture that we are to run away from—and hide from—the intrigues, conspiracies, attacks, and persecutions of our enemies.

We should flee toward the Lord so that *he* can deal with our enemies—possibly by using others. "When the men come out against us, as they did before, we will flee from them," Joshua told the Israelite army. "When we flee from them, you are to rise up from ambush and take the city. The LORD your God will give it into your hand."[52] They think they've got us, but God's got them. Paul advised us to "leave room for God's wrath."[53] We hide behind God and let him hand out the punishment.

Fleeing to God Is the First Step in Fighting Evil

We also see in this paradox that there is a sequence: First comes the flight, then comes the fight. We flee from evil and then run to God where we can stand firm, and the devil who has been chasing us is forced to flee. We have to flee to the Rock—God—the only place where we *can* stand firm. In military terms, this means we fall back to a defensible position. The order is always: Run to God, *then* stand firm.

If we run to God—if we let him be what he wants to be, the ultimate Bodyguard—he will make our enemies afraid of us. They know where we're hiding, and they won't try to come in after us.

As we flee to God, we will find ourselves in the company of other believers. We find real strength to fight life's battles when we assemble with others who find their refuge in the Almighty. We are told: "Let us not give up meeting together…but let us encourage one another."[54] There is power in numbers, for the simple reason that Jesus promised to be in the midst of the smallest of groups—even two or three of us gathered together.[55]

But we flee evil to find hope, not to escape from the world. "My prayer is not that you take them out of the world [a hope of far too many Christians today] but that you protect them from the evil one," Jesus prayed.[56] There is no biblical warrant for cowering inside the church's walls. The writer of Hebrews reminds us that "we who have *fled to take hold of the hope* offered to us may be greatly encouraged."[57] We run *to* hope, not just *away* from hopelessness.

The Turn from Fleeing to Fighting

There is at times a turning point from fleeing to fighting, as we see in a battle between the Israelites and the Gentiles who were occupying Canaan. "They *turned around* and *attacked* the men of Ai."[58] God's people ran until the enemy exposed itself to destruction, and then they turned on that enemy and destroyed it.

To fight God's battles in God's way, we first flee to God in prayer,[59] then we listen and do exactly (and only) what he tells us to do. If we find ourselves in a situation where we are being drawn into the wrong, we leave, even abruptly if necessary.

We can see the turning point from fleeing to fighting in an interesting command of Paul's. "Have nothing to do with the fruitless deeds of darkness, but rather expose them," he says.[60] How can we have nothing to do with them, and yet expose them? It's a paradox within a paradox. We personally have nothing to do with these deeds—we flee from their corrupting influence. But when we're far enough away, hidden and personally disentangled from the evil, we shift to fighting—to pointing out the evil, to warning others about it, and to taking steps to end its influence.

We are to recognize and resist the tempter's schemes, and then "stand firm." For example, we may be driving home at the end of a tough day, feeling frustration as we leave work and head toward our families. We can pull the car off the road and sit there until the frustration and anger are gone. Or we can take a detour on our way home to stop at the health club and run on the treadmill until the tension of the day has lost its hold on us. Whatever steps we take, we need to resist the temptation to take our frustrations out on others.

There Is a Time to Battle God's Enemies

Deceptions, seductions, and temptations are designed to destroy us, and we should not fight when we feel even a shred of attraction to them. But when our souls are safe and we are facing enemies that would destroy the helpless, the poor, the abused, orphans, widows, or children, it's time to run *at* them. It's time to take the offensive, as David did against Goliath, no matter how big or scary the opposition appears to be.

We see, in fact, that we should *never* run away from God's work because of threats or fears. "We did not give in to them for a moment," Paul boasted.[61]

God is so much in favor of us not fleeing in the face of *his* enemies that he encourages us, in effect, to do things that could cause others to persecute us. "Everyone who wants to live a godly life in Christ Jesus *will* be persecuted," we're told.[62] If we're *not* persecuted, this might be a clue that we're not really all that serious about living a godly life.

We are not required or expected to sit idly by and let evil people destroy us or our civilization. There comes a time when we can and should defend ourselves. "The Jews assembled in their cities…to attack those seeking their destruction. No one could stand against them, because the people of all the other nationalities were afraid of them."[63] Some will ask us to be tolerant and to respect their freedom to victimize others. But in their insane world, tolerance means "accepting evil." We cannot stand aside, aloof, and allow that to continue.

We Never Use the Weapons of the Violent World

God has given us weapons, but we have to know how to use them. For example, we are supposed to "pray continually,"[64] but "when you pray, do not keep on babbling like pagans, for they think they will be heard because of their many words"[65]—another paradox within a paradox. Our prayer should be an ongoing conversation with the living God, not a ritual that we suspect might bring magic results. And we don't use prayer to put off running to God when he expects us to run. We don't fight temptation by praying a lot while we're engaged in sin. Instead, we stop sinning and run from the temptation that seduced us. Prayer is *never* a substitute for fleeing.

If we wisely use the weapons God has given us, instead of using human weapons such as anger, judgment, and criticism, we'll find that we can pull down strongholds. The spiritual strongholds in our world include a whole range of bad ideas, such as false peace, anti-God arguments, pretensions to self-righteousness, and addictions. We have to use new and different weapons in new and different ways if we want to defeat these foes. And we have to face the fact that some of the weapons God gives us are unusual and counterintuitive: "If someone strikes you on one cheek, turn to him the other also," Jesus teaches.[66] This nonviolent action is a weapon, but it doesn't look like one to the untransformed mind.

We Need to Attack the Right Enemies

We must remember to fight the right enemies. With so much real evil in the world, we shouldn't waste our ammunition on the quirky ideas of our fellow Christians in various churches and denominations (and they all have a few eccentricities). We shouldn't be fighting weak or ignorant Christians. We shouldn't be fighting side issues that have no importance to the kingdom, like trying to rigidly define rules about worship music or which Bible translation to use.

The Bible authorizes us to establish guidelines at some reasonable level for our personal behavior, but it warns us that it is not all right to project our own guidelines or preferences onto others: "Whatever you believe about these things keep between yourself and God," we're commanded.[67]

If we violate our own personal boundaries, we sin, since "if people have doubts about whether they should eat something, they shouldn't eat it. They would be condemned for not acting in faith before God. If you do anything you believe is not right, you are sinning."[68] We may need personal boundaries to help us develop self-control. If we grow more mature in Christ and don't need these boundaries any longer, we can dispense with them and know that we are not sinning as a result.

This fleeing and fighting business takes effort to understand and apply. But understanding and applying this paradox is central to the well-lived Christian life.

WHERE THIS LEAVES US

We learn from this halakic study that a bad fight is the one we fight in our own strength, while a good fight is a fight of faith. God's name is a strong tower; we run to it in faith and we are delivered from the enemy. We fight by letting God fight for us—"The battle is the Lord's."[69]

This paradox tells us there is "a time for war and a time for peace,"[70] a time to fight and a time to run away. But it also tells us that we must have different responses to different attacks. We respond differently when we are facing:

- *temptation.* The one clear option is to run and hide. Trying to fight it will leave us exposed and destined to lose.
- *the Evil One.* When demonic power comes against us, we need to run to God, our strong Tower, hide in him, and thus resist the devil.
- *our own enemies.* When people who hate us assault us—spiritually, emotionally, verbally, even physically—we run to God and hide in him. His defense will be stronger and his wrath much more effective than ours could ever be.
- *God's enemies.* When people who hate God and goodness assault the kingdom of God, we need to run toward them and let God's power work through us to bring evil down.

There is another paradox at work here: We are weak and we are strong. We have to know when and how we're weak, and what to do about it (flee). And we have to know when and how we're strong, and what to do about it (fight). We'll run and hide when we're weak, in part so we'll be able to attack and fight God's enemies when we're strong. If we fight at the wrong time or in the wrong way, we won't be able to make a difference when we're called upon to be warriors for God.

When God tells us to run, we'd better flee and not fight. And when he tells us to fight, we'd better fight and not run. The good news is that as we act in obedience to God, whether fleeing or fighting, *we will always win.*

FOR FURTHER THOUGHT AND DISCUSSION

1. In your own life, can you think of areas in which you should be fleeing? How will you do it? Have you tried to fight in these areas in the past? If so, what was the result?
2. Can you identify acts of evil and injustice that you feel called to fight? What are they? How will you go about fighting them?
3. If you were mentoring a new believer in Christ, how would you summarize this important paradox for him or her?

Twelve

Innocent As Children but Knowing the Score

The Right Time and Place for Openness or Guardedness

I tell you the truth, unless you change and become like little children, you will never enter the kingdom of heaven.

Matthew 18:2-3

Stop thinking like children.... In your thinking be adults.

1 Corinthians 14:20

LaSandra's friend was worried about her teenage son's plan to do a report on the occult for English class.

"He says he wants to learn more about the subject in order to talk with other teenagers who are interested in it," the concerned mom explained. "But I don't know if it's a good idea."

"Are you afraid he might be influenced by learning about occult practices?" LaSandra asked.

"Not really. He's grounded in what he believes. It's just that I'm not sure I want my kid learning about some of the terrible things that go on in the world."

"I see what you mean," LaSandra replied. "But the Bible tells us to be shrewd as snakes in order to face our enemies. That might mean that we should be knowledgeable about the different ways Satan snares people, so we'll know how to approach different people as we share our faith."

"But the Bible also says we need to be innocent and unsoiled by the world and to flee from evil," the friend added.

LaSandra wanted to respond, but she realized that she didn't know what to tell her friend. Should a Christian teenager study the occult for a school paper, or should he choose a different subject?

It's hard to think that being innocent could be harmful to a Christian or to the kingdom of God. Isn't too much knowledge of the world problematic, since it can lure believers away from God and into destructive beliefs and habits?

As we read Scripture, we see that it commends shrewdness as well as innocence. But it does not always seem clear which circumstances call for which response. Childlikeness or shrewdness? How can we know when each one is appropriate?

INNOCENT AND SHREWD

This is one of the most challenging paradoxes we confront as we try to be faithful followers of Jesus. On the one hand, we're told to avoid bad stuff and not even think about it. Yet we are to be street-smart, familiar with the schemes of those who do evil. So what on earth should we do?

We are told in Scripture to be innocent as doves, as innocent and straightforward as children. We are told to be as shrewd as snakes, as clever and nuanced as adults. How can we be as innocent as doves if we are to be as shrewd as snakes?[1]

Get this one right and you can lead a pure life while influencing an impure world. Get it wrong and you can be so heavenly minded that you're no earthly good—or so earthly minded that you're no heavenly good.

We Must Be Innocent

We live in a broken and corrupt world. Isn't "be innocent" just another way of saying, "Be gullible and naive so others can take advantage of you?"

If we pick side A of this paradox and say simply that we should be innocent, we might trust anyone who claims to be looking out for our best interest. We could take at face value people who have ulterior, self-serving motives. "Ephraim is like a dove, easily deceived and senseless," the prophet Hosea declared.[2] With the deceptions and complexities of our world, we can easily become just like Ephraim—gullible and senseless, the type of people who are easily deceived.

Clinging exclusively to innocence, we also could remove ourselves from any effort to right the wrongs that are all around us. We might simply refuse to help relieve poverty, stand against greed, or speak up for those who can't speak for themselves.[3] We might go even further and choose not to even *know* what is going on around us. Ethnic cleansing? Horrible thing. Please don't tell me about it. Bigotry? Nasty people. Please don't share the gory details. Murder, rape, drunk driving, drug dealing, and destruction of the environment? I know those things are out there, but knowing more about them won't make things any better.

We can take this another step by forgetting that we don't have to go out into the world to find corruption. It's right here, inside each one of us. But we might use innocence as an excuse not to confront our own wrong attitudes.

At another level, we can become judgmental toward those who try to engage with the world. We might categorize these believers as worldly or unholy or even backsliders. We might assume they care more about righting societal wrongs than they do about spreading the gospel (as though those are two different things). In our retreat from a world that really is full of corruption, we can create our own worlds that are long on standards, self-righteousness, and criticism of others, and short on involvement, understanding, and positive influence in a needy world.

Such an isolationist policy—clinging to innocence and rejecting shrewdness—carries with it significant danger. We read in one biblical story that a people called the Danites conquered the "peaceful and unsuspecting people" of Laish and burned their city.[4] The people of Laish seemed decent enough, a peaceful people. Who wouldn't like folks such as that? But they were "unsus-pecting," and as a result they were conquered by outsiders.

We Must Be Shrewd

If we study the ways and wiles of the world, how will we keep ourselves from becoming cynical or being defiled by the things we are studying? Won't greater familiarity with worldly schemes make us cautious around others, causing us to avoid opportunities to make new friends and share our faith? Won't we become guarded and suspicious around any new acquaintance, trying to figure out his or her motives and possibly underhanded strategies? Won't we imagine enemies lurking around every corner?

If we pick side B of this paradox and focus on becoming shrewd, we can also become wise in our own eyes.[5] Being constantly on the lookout for the ulterior motives of others might keep us free of harm, but it will *certainly* also keep us free of relationship. We might grow cynical, believing that relationships are a matter of people's using each other for personal gain or advancement. We'll keep others at arm's length, possibly even concluding that people are so conniving that it's useless to try to reach them.

We can also become hardened, more attuned to life's school of hard knocks than we are to God's lessons of grace and mercy. God says, "Go," but our experiences say, "No." We've had our fill of people taking advantage of us!

We might put confidence in our shrewdness rather than in God's wisdom. We can overlook God's warning: " 'Because you think you are wise, as wise as a god, I am going to bring foreigners against you, the most ruthless of nations.' "[6] While we concentrate on the destructive path of evildoers, we can be blind to the destruction about to rain down on us by relying on our own "wisdom."

Perhaps worst of all, we can become the very thing that we say we hate. We claim we loathe people who wound and take advantage of others, but our own distrustful attitude takes the preemptive course of gaining the upper hand. We make sure that things always work out in our favor. Our cheap cunning can turn us into people who are rightfully loathed by others.

WHAT SCRIPTURE SAYS

On the face of it, this paradox presents us with an unappealing choice. We can be innocent doormats, allowing God's enemies to walk all over us while we're oblivious to their schemes. Or we can wise up to the ways of the world and grow cynical and hard, assuming the worst of others and keeping people at arm's length. Neither option appeals to a Christian who desires genuine relationships and who wants to open avenues for the message of God's kingdom.

Living As Innocent Children

There is no question about it: God expects us to be *very* out of touch with evil and corruption. He is blunt in telling us that there is no entrance into his kingdom without first becoming like a child. "[Jesus] called a little child and had him stand among them. And he said: 'I tell you the truth, unless you change and become like little children, you will *never* enter the kingdom of heaven.'"[7] And Jesus doesn't just want us to become like children—he wants us to become like *little* children.

The apostle Paul takes this requirement even further, making it clear how little we should be: "In regard to evil be *infants*,"[8] he commanded. An infant is as innocent as you can get. An infant doesn't watch the news or read the papers or think about all that is wrong in the world. A crime can take place in the same room where an infant is lying, and unless things get extremely noisy, the infant won't realize that anything is amiss. The world of evil simply doesn't exist for her.

That's how innocent *we're* supposed to become. "But I have stilled and quieted my soul; like a weaned child with its mother, like a weaned child is my soul within me."[9] If we don't grow to be as innocent as little children, Jesus stuns us by saying that we will "never enter the kingdom of heaven."[10]

Jesus confirmed this notion a second time:

> People were bringing little children to Jesus to have him touch them, but the disciples rebuked them. When Jesus saw this, he was indignant. He said to them, "Let the little children come to me...*for the*

kingdom of God belongs to such as these. I tell you the truth, anyone who will not receive the kingdom of God like a little child will never enter it."[11]

God's deal is fairly simple and straightforward: We receive the kingdom of God like a little child, or we don't receive it at all.

God actively hides things from the sophisticated but makes a special point of showing them to the young. "At that time Jesus said, 'I praise you, Father, Lord of heaven and earth, because you have hidden these things from the wise and learned, and revealed them to little children.'"[12] It appears that all our street-smart awareness doesn't make us any wiser, because wisdom comes to "little children."

He won't even let us into his presence to commune with him or worship him unless we've severed our ties to sin. "Who may ascend the hill of the LORD? Who may stand in his holy place? He who has clean hands and a pure heart."[13] The apostle Peter warns us to "make every effort to be found spotless, blameless and at peace with him."[14]

God makes it plain that innocence involves much more than simply not participating in evil. It extends to avoiding knowledge about the inner workings of evil. God commended one group of believers by telling them, "You…have not learned Satan's so-called deep secrets."[15] Part of innocence is choosing to be deliberately unaware of the subtleties of evil.

We who love to learn and think are faced with the troubling notion that we might have to lay aside some things we have learned and thought. "Trust in the LORD with all your heart," said the Teacher, "and lean not on your own understanding."[16] Innocence involves trusting God, even when our own understanding tells us to do things differently. At least at times, God expects us to be instrument-rated pilots, who do what we are told from the control panel and the control tower rather than from what our eyes tell us to do.

When Jesus gave a physical example of what he meant by innocence, he picked one of the most unsuspecting and vulnerable of birds. "Therefore be…as innocent as doves," he said.[17] Paul said, simply, "Avoid every kind of evil."[18] *Every* kind. That's innocence. Avoiding lying while welcoming lust, avoiding gluttony while welcoming gossip, and avoiding greed while welcoming laziness are not ways that will align us with God.

We have to face it. God expects us to be completely innocent. Period.[19]

Living As Street-Smart Adults

It's obvious from reading Scripture that God expects his people to be as savvy as anyone, including the shrewdest unbelievers. He positively hates the idea of our acting in an immature way. "Brothers, *stop thinking like children,*" the apostle Paul commanded, "[and] in your thinking be adults."[20] In other words, act your age!

"When I was a child, I talked like a child, I thought like a child, I reasoned like a child," Paul stated matter-of-factly. But growing up means losing these ways of thinking and talking. "When I became a man, I put childish ways behind me."[21] It's all right to act like a child when you are one. But if you're an adult, you'd better grow up.

God wants to teach us a lot, but our stubborn clinging to spiritual infancy can anger him. "We have much to say about this," the Hebrew Christians were told, "but it is hard to explain because you are slow to learn.… You need milk, not solid food! Anyone who lives on milk, being still an infant, is not acquainted with the teaching about righteousness."[22] Remaining a spiritual infant means that we'll never have even a passing acquaintance with God's teachings on righteousness.

The writer went on. "But solid food is for the mature, who by *constant* use have trained themselves to distinguish good from evil."[23] Only young children think that life is clear-cut, black or white. Growing up spiritually means that we wrestle with the complexities of life and powerful ideas like paradoxes, and train ourselves by constantly asking what they mean and how we can apply them.

God wants us to grow up, and soon. Solomon, as a boy-king, prayed, "So give your servant a discerning heart to govern your people and to distinguish between right and wrong."[24] This was the great prayer of Solomon that pleased the Lord.

It's a *very* tough world out there, and Jesus warns us to get ourselves in the proper mind-set to deal with it. "I am sending you out like sheep among wolves.

Therefore be as shrewd as snakes."[25] Those guys in the world are *tough*, he is saying, and you're as defenseless as sheep. A sheep will never defeat a wolf in hoof-to-fang combat. So Jesus suggests that we find another way to survive, and his recommendation is shrewdness. Specifically, he calls to mind the shrewdness of a snake, which is able to slip away from harm unseen, defend itself with surprising suddenness, or strike a foe from out of nowhere.

We should be sharp about how the world really works, and clearheaded and clever in how we respond to it. If we can't beat the wolves with our strength—and we can't—then we'd better do it with our shrewdness.

Being shrewd, we'll be discerning enough to recognize that wolves usually dress up to look like sheep. "Beware of false prophets who come disguised as harmless sheep," Jesus warned, "but are really wolves that will tear you apart."[26] We can't go by appearances. "Not all people who sound religious are really godly," Jesus pointed out.[27] The most effective wolf is the one who can look and sound the most like a sheep.

Jesus loved people, but he didn't trust all of them. "He knew what people were really like. No one needed to tell him about human nature."[28] We should approach life in the same way. "They have betrayed you; they have raised a loud cry against you," said the prophet Jeremiah. "Do not trust them, *though they speak well of you*."[29]

God makes a special point to be shrewd with people who clearly depart from the straight path. Speaking to God, King David observed that "to the crooked you show yourself shrewd."[30] And God expects the same astuteness from us. We should be able to identify crooked people and be on our guard around them. Most Christians, unfortunately, don't seem to understand this. "For the people of this world are more shrewd in dealing with their own kind than are the people of the light," Jesus taught.[31] Being willfully ignorant in the face of crookedness is no Christian virtue.

And don't think you're safe at church. Even there you can't let down your guard. "From your own number men will arise and distort the truth," Paul told the elders of the church at Ephesus. "Remember that for three years I never stopped warning each of you night and day with tears."[32] People with whom we've shared worship, Bible studies, and ministry projects can shock us with their gossip, slander, and maliciousness.

Some people will distort the truth in an effort to destroy churches. "I urge you, brothers," Paul wrote to the Roman Christians, "to watch out for those who cause divisions and put obstacles in your way that are contrary to the teaching you have learned. Keep away from them."[33] Jesus echoed a similar warning: "Beware of people, for they will hand you over to courts and scourge you *in their synagogues.*"[34] Where else would wolves go but to sheep pens? Where else would destructive people go but to the meetings of God's people?

Even church leaders can turn out to be wolves in sheep's clothing. "Be on your guard against the yeast of the Pharisees and Sadducees," Jesus warned.[35] The "yeast," he taught them, was the Pharisees' and Sadducees' teaching. In the first century, these people were the most learned of the religious teachers. *Don't be gullible,* Jesus was saying. *Take things you hear with a grain of salt, even if the person has a reputation as an expert in the Scriptures.* This was not just a problem within the Jewish community. The apostle John warned: "Do not believe every spirit, but test the spirits to see whether they are from God, because *many* false prophets have gone out into the world."[36] This makes it all the more crucial for us to be as shrewd as snakes, considering how many actual snakes are out there.

We are relentlessly encouraged to be street-smart. "A prudent person sees trouble coming and ducks; a simpleton walks in blindly and is clobbered."[37] Shrewd people pay attention and know that one protection from foolish suffering is to be savvy. "Discretion will protect you, and understanding will guard you,"[38] they know. Much of the difference between wise people and fools comes down to whether they can see what's going on around them.[39]

And we're supposed to stay shrewd at all times. "Test *everything,*" we're told, and "hold on to the good."[40] There's an undeniable insistence in the Bible that we know the score, in every situation, at all times. We're to be like the "men of Issachar, who understood the times and knew what Israel should do."[41]

We have to face it. God expects us to be very, *very* shrewd.[42] Period.

THE DEEPER MEANING OF BOTH/AND

We're to be as innocent as young children and as shrewd as people of the world. What a jarring combination! With two direct, paradoxical commands such as these, we need the deeper understanding that comes through halakic reasoning. What are the both/and truths that we find deep within this paradox?

We Respond Appropriately to People

God expects us to be both innocent *and* shrewd. If we are innocent without being shrewd, we will deal with others from a place of ignorance, not wisdom. If we are shrewd without being innocent, our cynicism will keep others at a distance.

If we are both, we will be cautiously but genuinely open to new people we meet. At first, we will offer our hands but not our hearts. We won't be easily open to others, and we won't be easily closed to others. We won't assume the worst, but we won't assume the best until experience warrants it.

If we follow God's requirements, we will choose an appropriate approach—innocence or shrewdness—based on the people with whom we are dealing. "To the pure you show yourself pure, but to the crooked you show yourself shrewd," the psalmist told God.[43] If we have someone dealing with us in a straight-up, genuine way, then we should respond in the same way. But if someone is dealing with us in a questionable way, then we should respond with shrewdness.

Like Little Children, We Are Uninterested in Evil

We are to be like little children. "How can an old man go back into his mother's womb and be born again?" Nicodemus asked Jesus. Jesus answered that "no one can enter the Kingdom of God without being born of water and the Spirit."[44] Innocence comes from being washed with the water of the Word of God and allowing the Holy Spirit to lead us into all truth.[45]

Little children are people of faith. They believe that mountains can be moved, and they don't spend their days thinking about evil. They are open to God, his love, and his miraculous power. As Jesus said, "Everything is possible for him who believes."[46] We can always be protected from evil in all its forms by focusing on our holy God and his power, and by never focusing on evil.

When it comes to the details of evil, we should be like infants. Instead of taking a baby outside and rolling her in the dirt, parents usually adopt the opposite extreme: They can be nearly neurotic about keeping the baby germ-free. Likewise, as we have the faith of a child, we need to keep ourselves from being polluted by the world. Wallowing in the details of evil (as Christians sometimes do under the guise of "knowing how to reach them") is never helpful to our souls. We are to be wise, but only "wise about what is good."[47]

And more than avoiding detailed knowledge of evil, we have to get away from evil. Doves, which are vulnerable to attack, know their only hope is to flee. "Oh, that I had the wings of a dove! I would fly away and be at rest," said the psalmist.[48] People who are innocent doves rely on God for protection: "Do not hand over the life of your dove to wild beasts," they pray.[49]

Consider also the possibility that innocence can be a form of shrewdness, because it keeps us from thinking about and participating in things that can destroy us. "Live such good lives among the pagans," wrote the apostle Peter, "that, though they accuse you of doing wrong, they may see your good deeds and glorify God on the day he visits us."[50] In God's upside-down kingdom, we don't defend ourselves or win people over by arguing about the evil that surrounds us, but rather by our good-natured, productive innocence.

We Adopt the Best of Childlikeness and Maturity

We see that we are not to let childlike innocence become an excuse to avoid growing up spiritually. But how can we be little children and mature adults at the same time? Biblical teaching seems to lead us to be paradoxical enough that we will adopt and combine the best of being a little child *and* a mature adult. What might this look like?

- *Little Child.* We remain blissfully unaware of the *details* of evil. When the nitty-gritty of sin flows from our televisions, radios, newspapers, and magazines, we respond with the disinterest of a *tiny* child. Instead, like a child, we trust God and believe what he says. We don't allow ourselves to become bored with the world or with the God who created it "good." We join little children in faith and love and wonder, and we give others the benefit of the doubt.

- *Mature Adult.* We stay relentlessly aware of the *presence* of evil. We wrestle with God's truth until we understand it. As we go deeper into God's truth, our ability to discern holiness and evil is sharpened. While we meet every person with initial openness, we keep our skepticism and street savvy close at hand. We understand that life demands constant use of God's principles, and training in how to use them.

We Distinguish Truth from Deception

Truth can show up in the unlikeliest of places, and we don't want to miss it. "Even among fools [wisdom] lets herself be known," we are taught.[51] We are warned to avoid the deception of hypocritical liars, even as we take seriously any truth they might happen to utter.

A snake is not always bad. The devil came disguised as a snake in the Bible, but Jesus used a snake as a picture of himself. "Just as Moses lifted up the snake in the desert, so the Son of Man must be lifted up, that everyone who believes in him may have eternal life."[52] Jesus is reminding his listeners of the sculpture of a bronze snake that Moses put on top of a pole during an infestation of snakes in the Israelite camp.[53] If people were bitten but then looked at the bronze snake, they lived; but they had to look, just as we have to look to Jesus for spiritual revival and survival.

We see that we shouldn't protect children and new Christians from *truth*. We should protect them from harm by *exposing* them to the truth. Exposing them to unpleasant truth can protect them from even less pleasant harm.

Like Snakes, We Are Aware and Astute

How, exactly, are we to be like snakes? We are not to emulate snakes in the sense of being treacherous or poisonous. But we are to be as shrewd as snakes in being "astute or sharp in practical matters...keen; piercing...artful."[54] Snakes are alert to their environment and aware of predators, and they know how to respond to dangerous circumstances. They are shrewd because they don't give away their movements or their intentions. "There are three things that are too amazing for me, four I do not understand," said the Teacher. One of them was "the way of a snake on a rock."[55]

Snakes know what to do. They know when they are overmatched, and when that's the case, they move quickly and secretively to escape. And they know when they have the advantage. When this is the case they strike, keenly and piercingly. Their shrewdness gives them the advantage in both situations.

If we're not careful, we can erroneously perceive the Christian life as a conflict between innocence and knowledge. We can think we will remain innocent by remaining ignorant. But God himself knows about evil. Of course, he doesn't "know" evil in the sense of being complicit in it. But he is not ignorant. In fact, innocence is the opposite of guilt, not the opposite of knowledge.

It is possible to remain oblivious to the evil going on around us and still be deeply involved in hardheartedness and personal rebellion. In a final, terrible irony, obliviousness to evil can sometimes make us accomplices of evil, like the people who lived in the shadow of the Nazi death camps and chose not to "ask too many questions." Conversely, it is completely possible, by God's grace, to live in a world that throws sin in our faces every day while we remain innocent, clean, without guilt.

Shrewd parents keep their children from knowing about certain things, but these are things that are inappropriate for children at a certain age. It takes wisdom to know when a child is mature enough to be given knowledge, strong enough that he or she will not be harmed or tripped into sin.[56] And not every child at the same age will be ready for the same knowledge. There might be different starting points on the road to shrewdness, different levels of knowledge about how the world works. Paul addressed this issue as one of being "stronger" or "weaker"[57]—some people can handle things that others can't. (Of course, *no one,* adult or child, is old enough to be inquisitively immersed in the details of sin or intentionally exposed to vile material.)

We Are Savvy Enough to Avoid Danger

We're given so many reminders to be shrewd that we see the need to distinguish between biblical innocence and dangerous naiveté. Too many well-meaning adults try to shield children and even themselves from reality, and in the process they open the way for reality to devour those who haven't developed discernment. "The gullible believe anything they're told," we're taught.[58] If we foolishly cling to naiveté, we will be susceptible to things like flattery that cover up the evil intentions of others.

This paradox suggests that we shouldn't define "trusting" as "sharing everything about ourselves with others." For example, we shouldn't share things about ourselves that can be turned against us. We should instead be like Queen Esther, who "had kept secret her family background."[59] How many have harmed their reputations by unwisely sharing their sins with a large group as they give their "testimony"? How often have people put their fragile souls into the hands of those who selfishly abused them? People who know the score define "trusting" very differently; they trust only the trustworthy.

The devil will send his troops in disguise, and we need to be savvy to figure this out. "Warfare is the Way of deception," taught Sun-Tzu, the ancient expert on warfare.[60] The world has always had quantities of people who are "false apostles, deceitful workmen, masquerading as apostles of Christ."[61] If we are shrewd, we will work hard to understand not the details of evil, but rather how evil operates and masquerades as light.

We learn the life-saving truth that false teachers will introduce their ideas *secretly*. They seldom announce their twisted take on the truth, and no age is immune from false prophets and teachers. Peter tells us: "They will secretly introduce destructive heresies."[62] We never know when or how they will arrive. "For certain men…have secretly slipped in among you," wrote Jude.[63] They hope to find listeners who are either gullible or cynical—missing either shrewdness or innocence. Ironically, either extreme makes us susceptible to harm.

Those who are untrustworthy ask for our confidence when they don't deserve it, and at times when they intend to abuse it. They ask for our sympathy when they have brought destruction on their own heads. When I was writing an earlier book on illusions,[64] I made the astonishing discovery that the word *disillusioned* is in the dictionary but not the word *illusioned*. And yet, how can we ever be disillusioned unless we were first illusioned?

If we are shrewd we will be concerned with pleasing God first, rather than the people around us. If we count on the praise and encouragement and help of everyone who comes along, we are destined to be disillusioned. If we count on the praise and encouragement and help of God, we are destined to remain illusion-free. We have a safe haven of shrewdness, within which our rock-solid innocence can grow. Shrewdness becomes a powerful way to protect our innocence.

We find that we become shrewd in great part by listening to God's Word, the Bible. This is how we "test the spirits" and make sure we're hearing the truth.[65] "So be on your guard," Jesus warned. "I have told you everything ahead of time."[66] Shrewd people know they've been told everything ahead of time, including how to be fiercely innocent.

"So don't be too good or too wise!" said the Teacher. "Why destroy yourself?"[67] Don't swing to an extreme: Don't be too "good" (innocent) or too "wise" (shrewd). Either path alone will fail. "So try to walk a middle course," the Teacher advised.[68]

The middle course is to be shrewdly innocent doves, who know what can defeat them, and to be innocently shrewd snakes, who haven't become evil in the process of really knowing the score.

WHERE THIS LEAVES US

We can delude ourselves by thinking we are innocent when in reality we're either naive or ignorant. We can hide out from the world, have no impact, and be destroyed when the evil that people do catches us unprepared. It's not that ignorance is no excuse. The truth is, ignorance is a deadly excuse.

Or we can think we're being shrewd when in reality we're being manipulative or arrogant. We can employ the world's ways and then be shocked when people learn about our manipulation and ostracize us for our exploitative approach. We can be cocky and overconfident, only to be beaten down in the school of hard knocks.

Are we to be innocent? Yes. Are we to know the score? Most definitely. Our course is clear: We are to love, trust, and be vulnerable with people, even as we are skeptical and cautious and on our guard. We're to be shrewdly innocent in all our relationships and efforts. Just like a mature adult.

And just like a little child.

FOR FURTHER THOUGHT AND DISCUSSION

1. How would you define biblical innocence? What about shrewdness?

2. As you think about your everyday life, where do you think you might be missing innocence? Have you been believing everything you hear, trusting the untrustworthy, or being naive about the way some people operate?

3. How can the idea of innocence be misunderstood in the Christian life? How can this idea be taken too far?

4. As you think about your life, where do you think you might be missing shrewdness? Have you been watching out for number one, doing it to the other guy before he does it to you, or getting what you want by any available means?

5. How can the idea of shrewdness be misunderstood in the Christian life? How can this idea be taken too far?

6. How would you finish the sentence: "A shrewdly innocent person is someone who…"?

PART III

Our Knowable, Unknowable
GOD

Thirteen

The Center
of God's Character

How We Get from Here to There

A primary characteristic of orthodoxy is a capacity for paradox.
Kenneth Arnold

Only the paradox comes anywhere near to comprehending the fullness of life.
Carl Jung

As we have plunged into ten paradoxes dealing with God's nature and character, his dealings with us, and our own responsibilities as people of faith, I hope you have caught a glimpse of how big God is compared to the way we typically picture him. When we begin to touch God's mystery, we see our sense of awe and reverence deepen.

It's impossible to explore paradoxes while avoiding questions and surprises. As we examined the ten paradoxes in this book, it's very possible that you reached conclusions that differed from what I suggested. That's to be expected, since halakic reasoning can lead to a wide array of conclusions. And all of our conclusions added together still might only begin to scratch the surface, since

God's character itself is a paradox. If you disagreed with any of my conclusions, "I heartily beg that what I have done here may be read with forbearance; and that my labors in a subject so difficult may be examined, not so much with a view to censure, as to remedy their defects."[1]

The paradoxes in this book serve as a starting point from which you can begin a lifelong journey. You can pursue the character of God in the myriad of biblical paradoxes that you see as you read Scripture. You no longer have to fear that the Bible is inconsistent or contradictory. You never again have to dread questions that occur to you as you read the Bible. With halakic reasoning, you can embrace those questions and use them as a path that goes deeper into God's nature—a nature that loves paradox, lives paradox, *is* paradox.

The Beauty of Both/And Thinking

As the world limped into the 1980s after years of business decline, outrageous inflation and interest rates, oil cartels, and government-created monopolies, there were a few "truisms" that were still widely believed.

"You get what you pay for." "You can have it cheap or you can have it good." "You can get it fast or you can get it right." No one preached this more than U.S. companies, which, though bruised, were still powerful.

Then an amazing thing happened. A number of companies, primarily in Asia, decided to change the rules. Taught by American quality experts such as W. Edwards Deming and William Juran, these companies embraced paradoxes that flew in the face of "true" capitalism: "You can get more for what you pay." "You can have it cheap *and* you can have it good." "You can get it fast *and* you can get it right."

These companies delivered on such unorthodox ideas. As they streamlined processes and systems and removed steps that added little or no value, they did the "impossible." They reduced costs and improved quality at the same time. There was less waste and bureaucracy, fewer layers of management, and smaller numbers of people involved. Quality shot up while price sank like a stone.

These companies saw that the two sides of the both/and proposition were very closely connected and that they reinforced each other. They were able to say: "If you make it cheaper, you will make it better" and "If you get it fast, you will get it right."

So what do these axioms of business have to do with God and his Word? Many of us have felt that the Bible is *way* too confusing. Many of us have understood the apparent contradictions that we studied in this book to be *real* contradictions. We have tended to avoid the hard questions, preferring instead to accept an easy answer such as, "We're too finite to understand the infinite" or "We'll have to wait for heaven to get the story on that."

Why We Struggle with Paradox

To get the most from your own study of biblical paradoxes, you need first to recognize the problems that can prevent you from fully grasping and applying the power of paradox. Some of the following may affect you strongly, and others may not affect you much at all. Here are a few of the problems that might deter you from fully embracing paradox.

The Problem of Faith and Reason

For years we've assumed there are things we can understand and there are other things we just have to accept on faith. But that assumption sets things in opposition that very much belong together. God doesn't ask us to believe *or* think, but to believe *and* think. He wants each of us to have a reasonable faith and a faith-full mind. He doesn't ask us to believe nonsense, and he doesn't ask us to avoid wrestling intellectually with our faith. "The confusion begins when…people are asked to sacrifice reason in order to accept senseless combinations of words as divine wisdom," wrote Paul Tillich.[2]

Throughout this book we have tried to use both our faith and our reason. Throughout any successful walk with God, we do the same. Paradox, because it is persistent and impossible to completely ignore, forces us to *think clearly* and *believe well.*

The Problem of Mystery

As physical beings living in a physical world, we tend to shy away from mystery. We don't want to deal with anything that is "out there" beyond our understanding. There is something inside that rebels when a person trots out something confusing or contradictory and tries to justify it with "Just trust me—it's a mystery." Our reason demands more.

On the other hand, we love mystery. We are drawn to things that are beyond our reach, outside our easy grasp. Life without mystery and wonder is a pretty dull existence. But we will never lack for mystery, because we belong to a God who offers us plenty of it. "Human salvation demands the divine disclosure of truths surpassing reason," wrote medieval philosopher and theologian Thomas Aquinas.[3]

We need to ban the casual, ambiguous way people use (and abuse) the word *mystery.* As we learn to differentiate paradoxes from contradictions (real or contrived), we should be able to see more clearly what remains. What remains is the Truth, breathtaking and mind-bending, wilder and more powerful than we ever imagined. Such a Truth, which expands understanding into awe, transcends simplistic, formulaic answers. As such, this Truth can touch the deep doubts, the big questions, and the paralyzing confusion that life presents.

The Problem of Credibility

We'd like to be able to believe in something and someone, and as Christians that "something" is the Bible and that "Someone" is God.

Many things can attack our ability to believe that the Bible is the inspired and infallible Word of the living God. There are teachers, some claiming to be Christian, who expend great amounts of energy showing people how faulty the Bible is, how a story in one gospel account differs from the same story in another gospel. Others, with better intentions but inferior theology, try to teach us their own confused, clashing ideas. And there are teachers and pastors whose theology might be solid, but whose personal lives contradict the message they are teaching. We were let down, so how can we trust any teachers and the principles they try to teach us?

But nothing eats away at credibility more than unresolved contradictions. To entertain the possibility that God just can't get it right, so he keeps changing things, strikes fear in the hearts of those who want a God who is, above all, consistent. We dread the possibility that some of the apparent contradictions in Scripture are real contradictions. How can the Bible be inspired and infallible if it is full of uninspired fallibilities?

If biblical paradoxes are not real contradictions, and we see this clearly, how much stronger will our thinking, believing, and living be?

The Problem of Feeling Unqualified

Many have been led to believe they lack the intelligence, experience, and specialized education required to do original thinking. People can end up wondering, *How can we possibly know even a fraction of what a Ph.D. knows?* Isn't this sort of work better delegated to the theologians and philosophers and pastors? Shouldn't these things be debated in universities and seminaries rather than in Bible study groups and Christian homes? Who are *we* to presume that we're qualified to explore paradox?

Many teachers and writers nurture this weakness with their rote sermons and simplistic writings. They don't respect people's ability to think and wrestle and wonder. "We have to spoon-feed them," they think, "or they just won't get it." One best-selling author said proudly, "I write books for people who don't read." In other words, keep it simple because people are stupid.

Forget all of this. As we have seen, biblical paradoxes are surprisingly accessible to any honest seeker who wants to think and know and believe. Remember the words of one of Jesus' prayers: "I praise you, Father, Lord of heaven and earth, because you have hidden these things from the wise and learned, and revealed them to little children."[4]

The Problem of Arrogance

American humorist Kin Hubbard used to say that it wasn't what we don't know that ends up hurting us, but what we "know" that just isn't so.

And so it is with the life of faith and thought. One of the hardest decisions for any human being is to look at a long-held belief or conviction and say, "It's not true, so *off with its head.*" Arrogance can keep us from sending falsehood to the executioner's block.

But in another paradox, the root of arrogance turns out, surprisingly, to be ignorance. Some of the most ignorant people on the planet are some of the most arrogant. When we don't know very much and don't know how much we don't know, it's easier to convince ourselves that we know it all.

On the other hand, a person can know a vast amount about a subject and still be arrogant. The vastness of their knowledge can puff them up[5] until they can't learn anything new. It's why great discoveries in a field are often made by people outside the center of the field, and why the best questions in a meeting are often asked by the person who knows the least about the details of the issue at hand.

Arrogance works hard to keep us ignorant. It provides a shield against learning anything that is new, different, or—heaven forbid—challenging to the accepted dogma or body of knowledge. We can't learn anything more because we believe we already *know.*

Arrogance often leads to dogmatism. If I've got the truth and other people don't, why shouldn't I insist that they agree with me? Dogmatism can become a defense against learning as well.

"Only the arrogant and the dogmatic find paradox hard to accept," wrote Richard Foster.[6] If we really want to understand paradox, we have to root out arrogance and dogmatism from our souls. The potential reward in knowledge is great.

Are you willing to go back and revisit any of the halakic conclusions in this book that you've kept at arm's length?

The Problem of Insecurity

If our security rests in our religious heritage or our traditions, we might view paradox as a threat to what our lives stand for. If our security resides in the tightness of our personally designed and controlled world, there will be no room for the rowdiness of paradox.

Insecurity can be housed in a facade of strength. One of the ironies of life is that often the most ruthless people are the most insecure. Their insecurity drives the ruthlessness, which can be directed at anyone who has the audacity to suggest there might be more to know and believe.

If we have grounded our security in incomplete beliefs—for example, in only one side of a biblical paradox—we need to be bold, to reach out for the possibility of a new way of thinking.

The Problem of Complacency

If we're satisfied with the current state of our Christian spirituality, then we'll see paradox as unnecessarily upsetting the equilibrium. Paradox tells us something about God or ourselves that we'd perhaps prefer not to face, so it's easier not to face it. The problem is not that there are problems. The problem is expecting otherwise and thinking that having problems is a problem.[7] Mark Twain liked to remind people that every difficult problem had a simple and easy solution—that happened to be wrong.

It makes us feel good to think that problems and their solutions are simple. Easy answers and formulas are inspiring, at least up to the moment when we realize they do absolutely nothing to address the real issues of our lives. In Western culture, especially, we rely on rational processes to reduce an incredibly complex world to a list, and to develop solutions to millenniums-old problems *that we don't even understand.*

"How many there are," wrote François Fénelon, "who, in consequence of too soft an upbringing in Jesus Christ, and too great a fondness for the milk of his word, go back and abandon their interior life as soon as God undertakes to wean them!"[8] Don't let complacency cause you to abandon your interior life. It's good to be content—but only with the *whole* truth.

The Problem of Illegitimate Desires

If we really want something—a car or house or piece of furniture or the newest technological wonder—we can start to work out all the reasons that we should have it, and we can ignore or develop defenses against all the reasons that we shouldn't have it. And we can do the same thing with the spiritual life. At times there are things we really want. If we want them badly enough, we can begin to color our theology to support and justify our desires.

There is a huge difference between wishful thinking and biblical hope. If we think things are better than they really are, we will "hope for the best" even as we're choosing for the worst. We might want a God who is merciful whether or not we have met his conditions for mercy, and in spite of the fact that we have made a long run of decisions deserving judgment.

As we consider our desires, we need to ask: "Is the thing we want something that God is offering?" Wanting the right things, wanting the whole paradox, wanting to live life God's way—all are crucial if we are to have a rich and authentic spiritual life.

If we want what God wants us to have, we can have it. And if we want what God doesn't want us to have, we can have it—but when we get it, we won't want it.

The Problem of Substituting Examples for Thought

Examples, even biblical examples, are a meager substitute for thought. For instance, we can look at the story of Jesus forgiving the woman accused of adultery[9] and use it to "prove" that God doesn't judge sin or sinners. We can look at the story of the young men carrying out the dropped-dead corpses of Ananias and Sapphira[10] and use it to "prove" that God doesn't give sin the slightest break. And we would be wrong on both counts. People often use examples to support their claims that God never changes or that he always changes, that he always heals or never heals anymore, that he saves everyone or saves only a few fortunate people.

Here's the truth about examples: They can *illustrate,* but they can never *prove.* We need to consider the full teaching of the Bible, in all its paradoxical richness, if we want to know the truth.

The Problem of Discounting Parts of the Bible

Some Bible teachers tell us that the Bible is all the Word of God, but that some parts of it are more applicable than others (or that some parts of it are no longer applicable). This teaching comes in many forms: "That was a different age, so this passage of Scripture is no longer binding on us" or "That was the *Old* Testament." This approach sets one part of the Bible against another, canceling out text that is "older" in favor of sections that are "newer."

These teachers might hold that "the Old Testament was about law and works and judgment, and the New Testament is about faith and grace and love," when in fact *both* testaments are about *all* of these things. What should we make of a book titled *The New Testament, with Psalms and Proverbs?* Are *only* Psalms and Proverbs—of all the books in the "Old Testament"—still relevant? Wouldn't it make just as much sense to have *The Old Testament, with John and Jude?* God has a better way of dealing with paradoxes and discomforting ideas than to drop half of the paradox off the radar screen.

The Bible might contradict these teachers, and the Bible might contradict you, and the Bible might contradict me, but the Bible will not contradict itself. We don't have to dismiss sections of the Bible that seem to run counter to other sections. God's Word is whole and applicable and authoritative. Any teaching to the contrary has fallen for an artificial contradiction.

ADDITIONAL PARADOXES FOR PERSONAL STUDY

This book serves in part as an introduction to biblical paradoxes, with examples of halakic reasoning applied to ten of the most troubling paradoxes we encounter. But the Bible is full of paradoxes, and you will find your faith enriched as you study these on your own or in a group.

Taking all of Scripture as the whole counsel of God, giving every section equal standing, you can pursue truth through biblical paradox. Here are additional halakic questions. Start with one that piques your interest or challenges your assumptions.

- *Judging.* God tells us not to judge. God tells us to judge. How can God tell us not to judge when at the same time he tells us to judge?[11]
- *Praying.* We're told to "pray continually." Jesus condemned those who thought they would be heard because of their many prayers. How can

we pray continually, if people are condemned for praying many
prayers?[12]

- *Signs.* Jesus condemned people who asked for signs. Over and over
  God gives people signs and honors their requests for signs. How can
  God condemn people who ask for signs when he gives signs to guide
  people and in answer to their requests?[13]

- *Freedom.* God sent Christ to set us free. God expects us to be his slaves.
  How can we be free if God expects us to be his slaves?[14]

- *Good Works.* We are told to let our good deeds shine before everyone.
  We are told to do our good works in secret. How can we let our good
  deeds shine before everyone if we are supposed to do our good deeds
  in secret?[15]

- *Distance.* We're told that God is a holy God from whom we are to keep
  our distance. We're told that we should boldly approach his throne.
  How can we keep our distance from God when he tells us to boldly
  approach his throne?[16]

- *Understanding.* We're told we can't understand God or his ways. We're
  told that we have "the mind of Christ." How can we not understand
  God or his ways if we have the mind of Christ?[17]

- *Evil.* We are told to "expose" the deeds of darkness. We are told that it is
  "shameful even to mention what the disobedient do in secret." How can
  we expose evil if we're not even supposed to talk about it?[18]

- *Death.* We are told that we will return to dust and be no more. We are
  told that we will stand in our own flesh on this earth after we're dead.
  How can we be alive and here after we're dead and gone?[19]

- *Length of Life.* We are told, "All the days ordained for me were written
  in your book before one of them came to be." We are told that if we
  keep God's commands in our hearts "they will prolong your life many
  years." How can we extend a life that has a predetermined end?[20]

- *Money.* We are told that "the love of money is a root of all kinds of evil."
  We are told that "money is the answer for everything." How can we

appreciate money as the answer for everything when loving it is the root of all kinds of evil?[21]

- *Jealousy.* We are told that jealousy is a sin. We are told that God is a jealous God. How can jealousy be a sin if God himself is jealous?[22]
- *Strength.* We are told to "be strong in the Lord and in his mighty power." The apostle Paul wrote, "I delight in weaknesses." How can we be strong if we are to delight in weakness?[23]

Where This Leaves Us

As you can see, there are plenty of additional biblical paradoxes that will give you an opportunity to test your halakic reasoning skills. As King David wrote, "They enter the mystery, abandoning themselves to God.... The world's a huge stockpile of God-wonders and God-thoughts."[24] So press on. Enter the mystery and explore the stockpile.[25]

Bible translator Eugene Nida said, "An awful lot of Christians don't think. Preachers just want them to say Amen." Nida, who has worked on translations in more than two hundred languages, drew this enchanting conclusion: "It's terribly important to have different translations to get a good argument started."[26]

Just as democracy requires people who are willing to serve as the "loyal opposition" to the party in power, the church needs believers who are willing to speak up for forgotten truths and against false orthodoxies, to risk disharmony for the sake of greater unity and truth. So here's hoping your exploration of paradox will lead to many spirited discussions, to "good" arguments, and to daring forays into the mystery and deeper truths of Scripture. May your conversations be seasoned and kept fresh with the salt of paradox.

For Further Thought and Discussion

Developing a halakic study with a friend or small group can be exciting. You can start with the paradoxes that are explored in chapters 3 through 12 to become familiar with the approach and to begin making your own discoveries in the mystery of God. Then launch your own study of additional biblical paradoxes, using a few that are suggested earlier in this chapter. You might also want to ask your pastor or priest to delve into paradoxes and halakic studies in sermons or in a special study group at church.

1. Looking back over this chapter, what would you say is the main reason you have struggled with paradox? What are some practical things you can do to overcome this struggle?

2. Which was your favorite of the ten paradoxes that we studied in this book? What made that your favorite? Who will you share it with— and how?

3. Which new paradoxes from the list in this chapter are your top choices for personal study? What additional paradoxes in the Bible have come to your mind?

Fourteen

Celebrating Our Mysterious Companion

AN INTIMATE RELATIONSHIP WITH THE LORD OF PARADOX

The most beautiful thing we can experience is the mysterious.
ALBERT EINSTEIN

God being All-mystery and All-encompassing, His will and the searchings of humankind into His cosmos cannot be in conflict—any more than the geometrical and the intuitive minds are in conflict when rightly understood.

JACQUES BARZUN

I f you were given an opportunity to erase any ten verses in the Bible, which would they be?

The fact that many Christians can answer this question, perhaps even easily, says many things. It says that the Bible is an unsettling book, and that God uses it to teach us unsettling things. It points out that each of us has particular points of discomfort and, as a result, that there are biblical truths we would prefer to dodge or ignore. And perhaps it says we have not fully absorbed the idea that discomfort can be a good thing.

Perhaps instead of erasing these verses, we should *underline* them. And perhaps, instead of avoiding the paradoxes in God's nature, we should celebrate our paradoxical, mysterious Companion.

We can try to recreate this remarkable God in our own unremarkable image. We can try to erase parts of paradoxes we don't like, parts that make God seem alien and incomprehensible. "When we are faced with the mystery of God, our minds ascribe to God attributes and characteristics that are more familiar," wrote pastor N. Graham Standish. "This acts to take away some of God's mystery."[1]

But God is still God, and we are not. He thinks and acts like God; in our very best moments, we can only remotely approximate this. He is God, full of mystery, who in answering one of our questions can drive us to ask a dozen more.

Still, he wants to be our Friend, Brother, and Father. He wants no distance between us, nothing to hinder a festive communion.

Is God complex, or is God simple? Of course he is. He is full of mystery, an enigmatic Being—astoundingly complex. And he is full of companionship, an affectionate Being—simple and approachable. We have to do a lot to know him, and we have to do almost nothing for him to love us.

"In him we live and move and have our being," we read in Scripture.[2] Our lives are "now hidden with Christ in God."[3] We are always drawn to him, to his life, to his mystery. "I am *always* with you," wrote the psalmist of his relationship with a loving, ever-present Lord.[4] We must always seek to understand him more deeply and to love him more splendidly.

"We will come to him and make our home with him," Jesus said.[5] He comes to board with us, to take meals together, to tell us what he is thinking, to warm himself in the deep red fire of friendship. While sitting together before the glowing blaze, he will take the time to unwrap the mystery, to show us the way. "Whether you turn to the right or to the left, your ears will hear a voice behind you, saying, 'This is the way; walk in it.'"[6] There will be no boredom and no coldness when he lives with us. "Here I am!" he tells us. "I stand at the door and knock."[7]

No one could be smart enough to think up a God who is at the same time so unfathomable and so intimate.

We can be like him. "The wind blows wherever it pleases," Jesus said. "You hear its sound, but you cannot tell where it comes from or where it is going. So it is with everyone born of the Spirit."[8] Jesus expects that people who don't know God won't understand us either. Because we follow God, we'll be unfathomable to them. And yet God asks us to throw ourselves into the work of loving these people until the glad day when they wake up.

Philosopher and critic Jacques Barzun summed up this dual expectation of God in a paradox: "Christ came to forgive sins as a spur to living the right life; this is a moral and social concern. He also preached giving up the world, a prerequisite to the soul's salvation. Can one follow both commands?"[9] Yes, we can. And we must. Because we are intimately involved with the Lord of Paradox.

At this moment, there are billions of us on this planet. And yet we can all say with the psalmist, "The Lord is thinking about *me* right now."[10]

And what is he thinking? That he loves us, that he wants to share his secrets with us. When the prophet Daniel was called upon to interpret a dream of King Nebuchadnezzar, Daniel proclaimed, "There are no wise men, enchanters, magicians, or fortune-tellers who can tell the king such things. But there is a God in heaven who reveals secrets.... The revealer of mysteries has shown you what is going to happen."[11] *Nobody can do for you what God is able and willing to do,* Daniel is saying. The king's response? "Truly, your God is the God of gods, the Lord over kings, *a revealer of mysteries.*"[12] God is full of mystery, overflowing with mysteries. And yet he is also the Revealer of Mysteries, the "God in heaven who reveals secrets."

God bundled his paradoxical nature into Jesus the Christ and sent him to walk among us, a mysterious Teacher and openhearted Companion. "Without question, this is the *great* mystery of our faith," the apostle Paul wrote to Timothy: "Christ appeared in the flesh."[13]

Broadcaster Paul Harvey reported seeing two bumper stickers on the same car. One, no doubt intending to warn potential tailgaters, said, "Keep your distance." The other stated an invitation, "Come to Jesus."[14] This is God's honest truth. He is lofty, so we should keep our distance. And he is among us, so we should come to Jesus.

As we walk with our mysterious Companion—thanking him for our greater understanding, bowing down before all we see that we don't understand—we can fall more deeply in love with the One who is loving enough to enthrall his uninformed children with his dazzling mysteries.[15]

So this is my closing invitation to you. Together, let's celebrate our mysterious Companion. Let's welcome a God so wise and brilliant, so intimate and loving, that he wants to walk with us and talk with us the whole way—as Jesus did with two of his followers after his resurrection, quoting "passages from the writings of Moses and all the prophets, explaining what all the Scriptures said about himself."[16]

Should we understand him or simply trust him, know him or stand in awe of him? You know the answer. *Yes. Absolutely.* He is the Lord of Paradox, and he wouldn't have it any other way.

Notes

Preface: The Shocking Truth
1. See Mark 10:15.
2. See Matthew 17:20; Mark 10:27; and Luke 1:37.
3. Proverbs 25:2.
4. As one example, see Matthew 22:41-46.
5. John 8:32.

One: Contradiction or Paradox?
1. Proverbs 26:4-5, NLT.
2. Philip Yancy, "Unwrapping Jesus," *Christianity Today,* 17 June 1996, 32.
3. *The American Heritage Dictionary of the English Language,* s.v. "paradox."
4. See Genesis 37:23-36.
5. For a wonderful treatment of this, see David McCullough, *The Path Between the Seas: The Creation of the Panama Canal, 1870–1914* (New York: Simon & Schuster, 1978).
6. *American Heritage Dictionary,* s.v. "paradox."
7. See Jonah 1:1–3:2; Luke 19:40; and Acts 9:1-6; 10:1-8.
8. For an in-depth exploration of this idea, read chapter 7. You'll love the awesome truth of Acts 17.
9. 1 Corinthians 2:16.
10. J. I. Packer, *God Has Spoken,* rev. ed. (1965; repr., Grand Rapids: Baker, 1993), 99.
11. Elton Trueblood, as quoted in Philip Yancy, "Living with Furious Opposites," *Christianity Today,* September 2000, 78.
12. Hebrews 11:1.
13. Proverbs 25:2.
14. See, for example, Romans 1:19-20, where we are told that "what may be known about God is plain to them, because God has made it plain to them...so that men are without excuse."

15. Matthew 13:10-11,13-15.

16. See Howard Gardner, with Emma Laskin, *Leading Minds: An Anatomy of Leadership* (New York: Basic, 1996).

17. Augustine, *On Christian Doctrine,* trans. D. W. Robertson Jr. (Upper Saddle River, N.J.: Prentice-Hall, 1958), 37.

18. For verses on the law, see Deuteronomy 32:46-47; Joshua 1:8; Psalm 1:2-3; Matthew 5:17-19; and Romans 8:4. For verses on salvation by faith, see Genesis 15:6; Habakkuk 2:4; Romans 5:1; and Ephesians 2:8-9.

19. Sören Kierkegaard, as quoted in Glenn Tinder, *Political Thinking: The Perennial Questions* (New York: HarperCollins, 1991), iii. Tinder adds, "The value of a paradox lies in the very fact that it is unacceptable. It compels us to keep thinking, to remain open to the mystery of being.... Again and again it forces us to think.... Rather than being discouraged, one should look about and see whether the truth is not near at hand" (20-1).

Two: The Spiritual Pursuit of the Both/And

1. Alan Lightman, "A Cataclysm of Thought," *Atlantic Monthly,* January 1999, 92.

2. Matthew 6:24.

3. D. A. Carson, "Matthew" in *The Expositor's Bible Commentary,* ed. Frank E. Gaebelein, 12 vols. (Grand Rapids, Mich.: Zondervan, 1976–92), 8:280.

4. Richard Rhodes, *The Making of the Atomic Bomb* (New York: Simon & Shuster, 1986), 131.

5. Martin Gilbert, *Churchill* (New York: Henry Holt & Company, 1991), 923.

6. *The Most Brilliant Thoughts of All Time,* ed. John M. Shanahan (New York: HarperCollins, 1999), 144.

7. Proverbs 26:4-5, NLT.

8. See Proverbs 26:4.

9. See Proverbs 26:5.

10. See footnote for Proverbs 26:4, *Catholic Answer Bible,* 658.

11. Matthew 22:41-46.
12. Mark 12:37.
13. Matthew 12:1-8.
14. Luke 22:19.
15. Matthew 26:26.
16. See Luke 22:25-26.
17. Mark 2:27.
18. Hosea 6:6.
19. Mark 2:27.
20. Quoted in *Fast Take* newsletter, 11 July 2000, found at www. fastcompany.com/fast.take/online/36/mongrel.html.
21. Kathleen Norris, "Why the Psalms Still Scare Us," *Christianity Today,* 15 July 1996, 21.
22. Ecclesiastes 3:1.
23. James Gleick, *Isaac Newton* (New York: Pantheon, 2003), 97.
24. Quoted in David McCullough, *Brave Companions* (New York: Touchstone, 1992), 26.
25. Psalm 119:18.

Three: The All-Knowing God Who Forgets
1. See Ephesians 3:12.
2. This term, by the way, never appears in the Bible "in either its nominal or its adjectival form." *The Wycliffe Bible Encyclopedia,* s.v. "omniscience."
3. "Unconditional love," even applied to God, is a term that is nowhere found in Scripture. He has *unfailing* love, but the benefits of that love are quite conditional, and we can choose to remain in it or exit its bounds (see John 15:9-10).
4. See Luke 17:3. In common practice, it's as though many people have forgotten the words "*rebuke* him, and *if* he repents"
5. See Galatians 6:7.
6. 1 Samuel 2:3.
7. Acts 15:17-18.
8. Psalm 147:5.
9. Colossians 2:3.

10. Isaiah 40:13-14.
11. Psalm 44:21.
12. 1 Chronicles 28:9.
13. Jeremiah 23:24.
14. Psalm 139:1-4.
15. Proverbs 5:21.
16. Isaiah 40:28.
17. Daniel 2:22.
18. Matthew 11:27.
19. John 16:30. See also John 21:17. What Peter does with all of this knowledge is truly amazing. We'll talk about that in a later chapter.
20. Psalm 90:8.
21. Psalm 19:12. For more on confession of sins committed unintentionally or unknowingly, see Leviticus 4.
22. Isaiah 29:15. See also Hosea 7:2.
23. Amos 5:12.
24. Hebrews 4:13. See also Jeremiah 16:17.
25. Amos 8:7.
26. Matthew 12:36, NAB.
27. 1 John 3:20.
28. Hosea 9:9.
29. For more on this side of the paradox, see Hosea 5:3; Amos 9:3; Matthew 6:8; 10:29-30; 12:25; Luke 12:6; 16:15; Acts 1:24; Romans 11:33; and 2 Corinthians 5:10.
30. Job 11:6.
31. Isaiah 43:25.
32. 1 John 1:9.
33. This is the author's translation/paraphrase for *purify*.
34. Jeremiah 31:34; see also Hebrews 8:12 and 10:17.
35. Ezekiel 18:22, NLT.
36. 2 Corinthians 5:17.
37. Ezekiel 33:16.
38. Psalm 103:12.
39. Habakkuk 1:13.

40. Genesis 18:20-21.

41. Genesis 22:12.

42. Deuteronomy 8:2.

43. Deuteronomy 13:3.

44. Matthew 24:36.

45. For more on this side of the paradox, see Genesis 3:9,11; 11:5,7; 2 Chronicles 16:9; Isaiah 1:28; and Jeremiah 23:39.

46. 2 Chronicles 32:31.

47. See Isaiah 1:18.

48. Jeremiah 2:22.

49. Psalm 103:8.

50. Revelation 20:12.

51. Isaiah 64:9.

52. See Leviticus 16:20-22.

53. Isaiah 1:18.

54. Philippians 3:13.

55. Habakkuk 1:13.

56. Genesis 18:21.

57. 1 Corinthians 14:20.

58. Revelation 2:24.

59. Ephesians 4:24.

60. 1 John 4:16.

61. Psalm 25:7.

Four: The God of Judgment Who Gives Us a Break

1. See 1 John 4:8.

2. See Isaiah 64:6.

3. See Romans 6:13. See also Romans 7:14-25.

4. See Paul's response to this sort of judgment in 1 Corinthians 4:3-4.

5. Romans 6:15.

6. See 1 Timothy 1:15-16, where Paul could be interpreted as saying that he was shown mercy *because* he was the worst sinner ever.

7. Numbers 32:23.

8. See Jude 14-15.

9. 2 Corinthians 5:10. See also Romans 14:10.

10. See Ecclesiastes 3:17.

11. See Romans 2:5-6.

12. Hebrews 2:1-3.

13. Hebrews 10:26-27.

14. Ezekiel 11:10,12.

15. 1 Peter 4:17.

16. See 1 Peter 1:17.

17. Acts 17:30-31. See also Romans 2:18-20.

18. See Isaiah 28:16-17.

19. See Jeremiah 9:24.

20. Romans 3:10. See also Daniel 5.

21. See Acts 5:1-11. See also 1 Samuel 2:27-36.

22. Psalm 2:2,4-5. See also Exodus 5–11 and Psalm 10:16.

23. Jeremiah 7:2-3. See also Revelation 2:5.

24. 1 Corinthians 3:13,15.

25. Revelation 20:12-13,15.

26. See Ezekiel 39:21-22.

27. In Ezekiel 11:10; 25:11; and 39:21-22, God's judgment brings glory to him and forces people to acknowledge that he is the Lord. The same is true of King Nebuchadnezzar's response after his episode of insanity in Daniel 4. If God ignored sin, we wouldn't know he is God.

28. Ezekiel 25:11.

29. See, for example, Judges 2:11-16.

30. Daniel 4:34. Daniel 4 gives the whole interesting story. See also the short book of Jonah, in which God brings his prophet to a point of obedience.

31. See 2 Samuel 12. Verse 14 refers to God's honor.

32. 2 Peter 3:7,10, NLT.

33. For other biblical references on this side of the paradox, see Lamentations 3:34-36; Matthew 16:27; Romans 6:23; Acts 17:31; 2 Peter 3:7; and Revelation 19:11.

34. Psalm 103:10.

35. James 2:13.

36. Ephesians 2:4-5.
37. Titus 3:5.
38. See Hosea 6:6.
39. See Psalm 28:2.
40. Psalm 57:1.
41. See Psalm 86:3.
42. See Psalm 9:13 and 40:11-12.
43. Psalm 25:6.
44. See Psalm 28:6.
45. See Psalm 116:1.
46. For more on the idea of "crying out," see Psalm 86:6; 130:2; and 140:6.
47. Exodus 33:18-19.
48. Luke 1:50, NLT.
49. See Psalm 119:132, NLT.
50. Nehemiah 9:30-31.
51. Jeremiah 12:1.
52. Micah 7:18-20.
53. See Titus 3:4-5. Further, God's mercy has a direct bearing on our practice of mercy toward others. "Be merciful, just as your Father is merciful" (Luke 6:36). This is never easy, of course, but the reward is one we don't want to miss: "Blessed are the merciful, for they will be shown mercy" (Matthew 5:7). See also 1 John 4:20, NLT.
54. Matthew 23:23.
55. See Luke 1:50.
56. 2 Peter 3:9,15, NLT.
57. See Psalm 5:7.
58. For additional references on this side of the paradox, see Deuteronomy 4:30-31; Nehemiah 9:13; 13:22; Psalm 69:16; 123:2-3; and Luke 1:69,72.
59. Psalm 103:3,9,12.
60. Deuteronomy 13:17.
61. Psalm 50:22, NLT.
62. Psalm 119:132.
63. Psalm 86:16.

64. Joel 2:13.
65. Luke 17:3.
66. James 2:13.
67. See James 2:13, NLT.
68. This statement has been made in various sermons by Adam Hamilton, pastor of Church of the Resurrection in Leawood, Kansas.
69. 1 Chronicles 21:8, NLT.
70. 1 Chronicles 21:13, NLT. See also 2 Samuel 24.
71. 2 Samuel 24:14, NLT.
72. There is certainly a warning about following or supporting a leader who is wandering off the path. Saying about a bad idea, "But the pastor said so," could bring you under God's judgment.
73. Psalm 89:31-33. See also Jeremiah 30:11 and 46:28.
74. Luke 7:47, NLT.
75. 2 Peter 2:9, NAB.
76. Exodus 6:6.
77. Ezekiel 33:17-20.
78. Zechariah 7:9-10.
79. Isaiah 42:1-4. These words are quoted about Jesus in Matthew 12:18-20.
80. Romans 8:1.
81. Romans 3:25-26.
82. For more on this, see my book *Walking Through the Fire: Finding the Purpose of Pain in the Christian Life.*
83. See Genesis 15:16.
84. Isaiah 30:18.
85. To see how to apply this in families, see my book *The Paradox Principle of Parenting: How to Parent Your Child Like God Parents You.*

Five: The Changeless God Who Changes

1. Stephen Charnock, *Discourses Upon the Existence and Attributes of God* (1853; repr., Ann Arbor, Mich.: Baker, 1979), 330-1.
2. A. W. Tozer, *The Knowledge of the Holy* (San Francisco: Harper & Row, 1961), 54.

3. Isaak August Dorner, *Divine Immutability: A Critical Reconsideration* (1856; repr., Minneapolis: Fortress, 1994), 106.

4. See Abraham, Genesis 18:16-32; Moses, Exodus 32:9-14; Hezekiah, 2 Kings 20:1-11; and Mary, John 2:1-10.

5. Lewis Richard Farnell, *The Attributes of God: The Gifford Lectures* (Oxford: Clarendon, 1925), 262.

6. For a basic introduction to process theology and its conclusions about God, see John B. Cobb and David R. Griffin, *Process Theology: An Introductory Exposition* (Philadelphia: Westminster, 1976).

7. For a basic introduction to openness theology and its conclusions about God, see Clark Pinnock and others, *The Openness of God: A Biblical Challenge to the Traditional Understanding of God* (Downers Grove, Ill.: InterVarsity, 1994).

8. Malachi 3:6.

9. Psalm 102:25-27, quoted in Hebrews 1:10-12.

10. Isaiah 14:24.

11. Psalm 33:11.

12. Psalm 110:4, quoted in Hebrews 7:21.

13. Job 42:2.

14. Titus 1:2.

15. 1 Kings 8:56.

16. Isaiah 45:23.

17. Hebrews 6:17, NAB.

18. Isaiah 54:10.

19. See, for example, Numbers 14:10-23,39-45 and 2 Kings 23:25-27.

20. Jeremiah 4:28.

21. Hebrews 13:8.

22. For more on this side of the paradox, see Numbers 23:19; 1 Samuel 15:29; Ezekiel 24:14; and James 1:17.

23. Hosea 11:8-9.

24. Psalm 106:44-45.

25. 2 Kings 20:1-2.

26. 2 Kings 20:5. See also verses 3-4.

27. See Genesis 18:16-33.

28. Jeremiah 18:7-8.

29. Jeremiah 26:13.

30. Jonah 4:2.

31. Jeremiah 18:9-10.

32. Joel 2:13-14.

33. For more on this side of the paradox, see Exodus 32:10-14; 2 Chronicles 12:5-8; and Amos 7:1-6.

34. Hebrews 13:8.

35. *Shaft*, motion picture, directed by John Singleton (Paramount Pictures), 2000.

36. See Bruce B. Miller II, "Rethinking God's Immutability," Southwest Regional Meeting of the Evangelical Theological Society, March 1988, 18, 20.

37. For instance, see Exodus 32:14; Jonah 3:10; and Jeremiah 18:7-10; 26:3,13,19.

38. See Dallas Willard, *The Divine Conspiracy* (New York: HarperSan-Francisco, 1998).

39. Matthew 27:46.

40. Hebrews 2:18. See also verse 14.

41. Matthew 7:7.

42. See John 15:9-12.

43. See Psalm 18:27. For more on the truth that God's love is both unfailing and conditional, see my book *The Paradox Principle of Parenting*.

44. Alan G. Padgett, *God, Eternity, and the Nature of Time* (New York: St. Martin's, 1992), 132-3.

45. See Revelation 21:1-4.

46. 2 Timothy 2:12.

47. Reflecting on this, theologian Isaak Dorner wrote: "In truth God without the free beings would prove himself not more but less in creative power, as having a smaller rather than a larger sphere of power and government." See Dorner, *Divine Immutability*, 144.

48. Genesis 1:31.

49. William Hasker, *God, Time, and Knowledge* (Ithaca, N.Y.: Cornell University, 1989), 182-3.

50. See Genesis 1:1.

51. Isaiah 57:15.

52. Nicholas Wolterstorff, "God Everlasting," in *God and the Good: Essays in Honor of Henry Stob,* ed. C. Orlebeke and L. Smedes (Grand Rapids, Mich.: Eerdmans, 1975), reprinted in Steven Cahn and David Shatz, eds., *Contemporary Philosophy of Religion* (New York: Oxford University Press, 1982), 77-98. Page citations refer to the Oxford University Press edition.

53. For more on this, see Charles W. Lowry, *The Trinity and Christian Devotion* (New York: Harper and Brothers, 1946; repr., Vancouver: Regent College, 1995).

54. Dorner, *Divine Immutability,* 176.

55. Commenting on this idea, Gerald Bray wrote: "God has perfect freedom, but nothing he does should be interpreted as being inconsistent with his nature." See Bray, *The Doctrine of God* (Downers Grove, Ill.: InterVarsity, 1993), 101.

56. 1 John 4:8.

57. We end up with some touching illustrations of the mutuality of relationship that God has with us. God wants us to remember what he has done for us, and he wants us to know that he will remember what we have done for him (compare Deuteronomy 4:9; 7:18 with Hebrews 6:10). We want God to remember us, just as God wants us to remember him (compare Nehemiah 13:14; Psalm 74:2; 106:4; and Luke 23:42, for example, with Deuteronomy 8:11-18 and 1 Corinthians 11:24-25).

    On God's ability to change in a true relationship, Saint Anselm wrote: "But what is the inconsistency between susceptibility to certain facts, called *accidents,* if from the undergoing of these accidents the substance undergoes no change?" See Anselm, *Monologion,* chap. 25 in S. N. Deane, ed., *St. Anselm: Basic Writings,* 2nd ed. (La Salle, Ill.: Open Court, 1962), 84.

58. Willard, *The Divine Conspiracy,* 253.

Six: The God Who Loathes and Loves the Wicked

1. See Luke 6:27-28.
2. See 2 Chronicles 19:2 and 2 John 10-11.
3. See 1 John 4:8.
4. Edmund Burke, quoted in Laurence J. Peter, ed., *Peter's Quotations: Ideas for Our Time* (New York: Bantam, 1977), 22.
5. Psalm 5:5.
6. Psalm 5:6.
7. Proverbs 18:21.
8. See Proverbs 15:4.
9. Psalm 11:5.
10. Romans 3:23.
11. Proverbs 16:5.
12. Romans 6:23 makes this clear: "For the wages of sin is death." So does Romans 1:32 (NLT): "They are fully aware of God's death penalty for those who do these things, yet they go right ahead and do them anyway. And, worse yet, they encourage others to do them, too."
13. Psalm 139:21. See also Matthew 12:30 and Luke 11:23.
14. Revelation 2:2, NLT.
15. Proverbs 15:26.
16. Psalm 119:113.
17. See Proverbs 12:22.
18. Proverbs 6:16,19.
19. Deuteronomy 25:16.
20. Proverbs 11:20, NLT. See also Proverbs 3:32.
21. Deuteronomy 18:12. For the list of offenses, see verses 10-11.
22. Hosea 9:15.
23. See Jeremiah 12:8.
24. 1 Corinthians 16:22.
25. Galatians 1:8-9. We don't get points for effort. God doesn't cut us any slack just because we're out there trying. Quite the opposite. And for preachers and teachers, there is even less room for them to be wrong. James says, "Not many of you should presume to be teachers... because...we who teach will be judged *more* strictly" (James 3:1).

26. 2 Chronicles 19:2.
27. 2 John 10.
28. 2 John 11.
29. Psalm 119:158. See also Psalm 31:6; 101:3; and 119:113.
30. Psalm 26:5. See also Psalm 101:4-5.
31. Titus 3:10.
32. Psalm 58:10. See also Psalm 52:6-7.
33. For more on this side of the paradox, see Leviticus 20:22-23; 26:30; Deuteronomy 7:10; 22:5; 23:18; Psalm 73:20; 94:23; 119:53; Matthew 23:27; Mark 9:42; John 8:44; Acts 23:3; and Titus 1:16.
34. Ezekiel 18:23a.
35. Ezekiel 18:23b.
36. Matthew 5:45.
37. A best-selling book bears the title *When Bad Things Happen to Good People*. God has another idea: *When Good Things Happen to Bad People.*
38. Luke 15:2.
39. Matthew 11:19.
40. See Matthew 9:11.
41. Matthew 9:12.
42. Matthew 9:13.
43. See Luke 8:2.
44. See Luke 19:1-10.
45. See John 4.
46. Jonah 4:11.
47. Mark 15:32.
48. Luke 23:42. To think about this in the context of what else was happening, read Luke 23:39-43.
49. Luke 23:43.
50. John 3:16, HCSB.
51. See John 3:17. See also Romans 5:6,8.
52. Luke 23:34.
53. John 15:13.
54. Luke 6:27-28.
55. Proverbs 10:12.

56. 1 John 2:9.

57. 1 Peter 3:9.

58. Proverbs 25:21; see also Romans 12:20.

59. José Luis González-Balado, comp., *Mother Teresa, in My Own Words* (New York: Gramercy, 1997), 38.

60. Acts 7:60.

61. For more on this side of the paradox, see Ezekiel 33:10-11; Matthew 5:33-34; Luke 7:36-50; 19:41-44; and 1 Thessalonians 5:15.

62. See Genesis 1:26-28; 2:7,25; and Psalm 8:5, NLT.

63. Jeremiah 13:23.

64. Jeremiah 4:22.

65. Romans 1:30.

66. Romans 11:22.

67. Deuteronomy 28:63. See also Psalm 37:12-13.

68. Proverbs 29:6.

69. Peter Kreeft, ed., *A Shorter Summa: The Most Essential Philosophical Passages of St. Thomas Aquinas' Summa Theologica*, trans. the Fathers of the English Dominican Province (San Francisco: Ignatius, 1993), 86.

70. Isaiah 9:17.

71. Acts 3:26. See also Romans 4:5 and 1 Corinthians 6:11.

72. Romans 2:4.

73. Genesis 15:16.

74. Psalm 138:6.

75. Mark 3:28-29, NLT.

76. John 15:26.

77. 1 John 2:22. People have written about "the Antichrist" for centuries and continue to do so today. However, the fact is that *anyone* who denies Christ is the antichrist. The apostle John is the only writer to use the term in the Bible, and he further explains, "*This* is the last hour; and as you have heard that the antichrist is coming, even now *many antichrists* have come" (1 John 2:18). There isn't just one "Antichrist." There are as many antichrists as there are people who have rejected—who are *against*—the Christ, Jesus.

78. 2 Peter 3:9.

79. Luke 13:34.
80. 1 Timothy 1:13.
81. 1 Timothy 1:16.
82. George Eliot, as quoted in *Whatever It Takes,* ed. Bob Moawad (Seattle: Compendium, 1995), 111.
83. See 1 Corinthians 6:15-17.
84. Jude 23.
85. Romans 12:21.
86. Luke 6:35.
87. Ezekiel 3:18.
88. 1 John 5:16.
89. Psalm 139:21.
90. *Webster's New Universal Unabridged Dictionary,* s.v. "imprecatory."
91. Psalm 10:15.
92. Psalm 31:17.
93. Psalm 68:2. See also Psalm 55:15; 58:6-8; 69:22-28; 83:9-16; 109:6-15; and 139:19.
94. Psalm 83:13,15-17, MSG.
95. Romans 12:19.
96. Genesis 6:3.
97. Luke 13:25,27.
98. Ecclesiastes 3:8.

Seven: The Prince of Peace Who Bears a Sword

1. John 14:27.
2. Matthew 10:34.
3. See Isaiah 9:6.
4. Jesus insulted people, see Luke 11:39-40,44,47. Jesus criticized leaders in front of their followers, see Matthew 23:15,17,24,27,33. Jesus made a whip to clear the temple, see John 2:14-16.
5. See John 16:33; Acts 14:22; and 2 Timothy 3:12.
6. John 14:27.
7. See Philippians 4:7.
8. John 16:33.

9. Zechariah 9:9-10.

10. Isaiah 53:5.

11. Colossians 1:20.

12. Ezekiel 34:25.

13. Isaiah 66:12.

14. Isaiah 9:6.

15. See Judges 6:24.

16. Micah 5:5. See also Revelation 1:4.

17. 2 Thessalonians 3:16.

18. Ephesians 2:14. See also verse 17.

19. Mark 5:34. See also Luke 7:50.

20. Leviticus 26:6.

21. Psalm 91:5,7,9-10.

22. Psalm 147:14.

23. John 20:19.

24. Luke 2:14.

25. Isaiah 26:12.

26. For more on this side of the paradox, see Isaiah 54:10; 57:19; Haggai 2:9; Acts 10:36; Romans 14:17; 15:33; and Galatians 5:22 (where we see that peace is part of the fruit of the Spirit). See also the greetings in so many of Paul's letters: "Grace and peace to you from God our Father and from the Lord Jesus Christ" (Romans 1:7).

27. Matthew 10:34.

28. Matthew 10:35-36. Jesus is quoting Micah 7:6, a passage that implies how evil people might react to the righteous.

29. Luke 12:52-53.

30. Luke 12:49,51.

31. Hosea 5:14.

32. Revelation 5:5.

33. Matthew 23:15,17,24,27,33.

34. Luke 11:39-40,44-45,47.

35. John 2:14-16. He was so angry, "His disciples remembered that it is written, 'Zeal for Your house will consume Me,'" we are told in John 2:17, HCSB.

36. Isaiah 10:26.
37. Matthew 21:12-13.
38. Mark 11:16.
39. Jeremiah 14:13-16.
40. Ezekiel 13:10,15-16. See also Jeremiah 6:14, repeated in Jeremiah 8:11.
41. See 2 Timothy 3:12.
42. Luke 6:26.
43. 1 Thessalonians 5:2-3.
44. For more on this side of the paradox, see 1 Thessalonians 5:3 and Revelation 6:3-4.
45. Ecclesiastes 3:8.
46. See Ezekiel 13:10,15-16.
47. See Job 1:6-12 and 2:1-7 for an example of a heavenly war.
48. Romans 3:17.
49. Luke 19:42.
50. Zechariah 8:19.
51. Luke 10:5-6.
52. Matthew 10:13.
53. Isaiah 53:5.
54. Colossians 1:20.
55. Hebrews 12:11.
56. Romans 12:18.
57. 2 Kings 16:18.
58. Luke 14:26.
59. Psalm 29:11.
60. Romans 5:1, NAB.
61. Psalm 34:14, quoted in 1 Peter 3:11.
62. Numbers 25:12.
63. Isaiah 32:17.
64. Psalm 85:10.
65. Psalm 85:8.
66. Isaiah 57:2.
67. Proverbs 16:7.
68. Romans 2:10.

69. Psalm 37:11.
70. Romans 8:6.
71. Philippians 4:7.
72. Philippians 4:6.
73. Hebrews 11:1. See also Mark 11:23-24.
74. Isaiah 26:3. Another translation of the verse renders "steadfast" with the phrase "whose thoughts are fixed on you!" (NLT).
75. See Matthew 8:23-27. See also Psalm 91:3-7,9-11.
76. Psalm 119:165.
77. 1 John 5:3.
78. Isaiah 48:17-18.
79. Isaiah 48:22 and 57:21.
80. See Romans 3:23.
81. Matthew 5:9.
82. Hebrews 12:14, NLT.
83. 1 Thessalonians 5:13.
84. Deuteronomy 20:10.
85. 1 Corinthians 4:21.
86. 1 Corinthians 4:21.
87. 2 Peter 3:14.
88. Numbers 6:23-26.

Eight: The God of Truth Who Sends Delusions
1. Proverbs 25:2.
2. See Corrie ten Boom with John and Elizabeth Sherrill, *The Hiding Place* (Minneapolis: World Wide, 1971).
3. Titus 1:2.
4. Hebrews 6:18.
5. Psalm 33:4.
6. 2 Samuel 7:28.
7. Psalm 119:160.
8. Romans 3:4, NLT.
9. See Leviticus 11:45; quoted in 1 Peter 1:15-16.
10. John 17:17.

11. John 14:6.
12. See John 18:37.
13. 1 John 5:6.
14. See 2 Peter 1:20-21.
15. See Matthew 4:1 and Luke 4:14-21.
16. 1 John 5:7.
17. See Ephesians 5:26.
18. Proverbs 12:22, NAB.
19. Psalm 5:6.
20. John 16:13.
21. Zechariah 8:16.
22. Ephesians 4:25.
23. Psalm 51:6.
24. See Leviticus 19:11.
25. Psalm 101:7.
26. 1 John 5:20. See also John 3:33.
27. For more on this side of the paradox, see Psalm 31:5; Isaiah 45:19; John 1:14,17; Colossians 3:9; and Revelation 19:11.
28. 2 Thessalonians 2:10-11.
29. Deuteronomy 28:15,28.
30. I've paraphrased this idea, a favorite of H. L. Mencken's. He said it, I believe, in multiple ways and on multiple occasions.
31. Romans 1:28.
32. 1 Kings 22:19-20; see also 2 Chronicles 18:18-22.
33. 1 Kings 22:21-22.
34. 1 Kings 22:22.
35. 1 Kings 22:23.
36. Exodus 1:19.
37. Exodus 1:20-21.
38. See the whole amazing story in Joshua 2:1-21, with the happy ending in Joshua 6:22-23.
39. 1 Samuel 21:13.
40. 1 Samuel 21:14-15.
41. Psalm 34:4,6.

42. Psalm 34:13.
43. Isaiah 29:10, quoted in Romans 11:8.
44. Micah 2:11.
45. 1 Corinthians 1:18,27.
46. For more on this side of the paradox, see Joshua 10:10 and Jeremiah 20:7.
47. See Deuteronomy 29:4.
48. See 2 Timothy 3:13.
49. 2 Kings 10:18. See the whole story in 2 Kings 10:18-30.
50. 2 Kings 10:19.
51. 2 Kings 10:23.
52. 2 Kings 10:27.
53. 2 Kings 10:28.
54. 2 Kings 10:30.
55. Matthew 24:24.
56. Lamentations 3:9.
57. Ecclesiastes 7:13.
58. Revelation 15:3.
59. See Victor Hugo, *Les Misérables,* trans. Lee Fahnestock and Norman MacAfee (New York: Signet Classics, 1986).
60. Romans 4:17.
61. Ephesians 4:29.
62. John 16:15. See also John 15:15 and 16:13.
63. 1 Corinthians 1:23-24.
64. John 14:6.
65. John 18:38.

Nine: The Choice Is Ours, but the Choice Is God's
1. See John 15:5.
2. John 5:24.
3. John 10:28, NAB. It's worth reading the entire passage: John 10:24-30.
4. Deuteronomy 30:19.
5. Matthew 12:30.
6. James 4:4.

7. See 1 Thessalonians 4:3. Many Christians talk about "finding God's will," as though it were some magical, detailed formula for life. This verse says, "It is God's will that you should be sanctified." His will concerns character, not a daily to-do list.

8. Psalm 119:173.

9. Psalm 119:30.

10. Isaiah 7:15.

11. See Exodus 32:33; Psalm 87:6; and Revelation 3:5.

12. Isaiah 56:4.

13. Isaiah 65:12.

14. 1 Peter 4:3. See also Isaiah 66:3.

15. Proverbs 1:28-29.

16. Judges 10:14.

17. Psalm 111:10. See also John 7:17.

18. We do need understanding to fully obey. See Psalm 119:34.

19. Psalm 119:100.

20. "Here I am!" declares the Lord. "I stand at the door and knock. If anyone hears my voice and opens the door, I will come in and eat with him, and he with me" (Revelation 3:20). He comes, stands, knocks, and calls out to us. But we have to make the choice to open the door. He won't pick the lock or knock down the door. An old French proverb puts it well: "The door to change is opened from the inside."

21. Acts 17:26-27.

22. Romans 1:18-21, NAB.

23. See Romans 10:17-18, where we're told that we have to hear the message before we can believe it, but we hear the message from those whose "voice has gone out into all the earth." Paul was quoting Psalm 19:4. If you read the first four verses of that psalm, you'll see that it is talking about God's creation—the heavens, the stars. In Romans 1:18-21, Paul condemned people for not knowing or acknowledging God, even though they had ample opportunity to see God's "invisible qualities" from "what has been made."

24. Matthew 13:12; Mark 4:25; and Luke 8:18.

25. See Matthew 5:6.

26. Jeremiah 29:13.

27. See the book of Job, a remarkable story of God's allowing Satan to test one of his most devout followers.

28. See 1 Samuel 16:7. See also Micah 6:8.

29. For more on this side of the paradox, see Exodus 32:26; 2 Kings 5:11-17; Proverbs 8:10; 16:16; and John 5:24.

30. John 15:16.

31. 1 Peter 2:9.

32. Deuteronomy 7:6. See also Psalm 33:12.

33. Genesis 18:19, confirmed in the great regathering of God's people in Nehemiah 9:17.

34. Romans 4:16.

35. See Psalm 106:23. For background on God's choosing other individuals, see Genesis 24:14,44 (Rebecca); Exodus 31:2 and 35:30 (Bezalel, chosen to build the tabernacle); 1 Samuel 10:24 (Saul); 1 Samuel 16:1; 1 Kings 8:16; 11:34; 1 Chronicles 28:4; 2 Chronicles 6:6; and Psalm 78:70 (David); 1 Chronicles 28:5-6,10 and 29:1 (Solomon); Haggai 2:23 (Zerubbabel); Acts 1:26 (Matthias, chosen to replace Judas); Acts 9:15 and 22:14 (Paul).

36. On Jesus' calling the Twelve, see John 6:70; also Mark 3:14; Luke 6:13; John 13:18; and Acts 1:2; 10:41.

37. Colossians 3:12.

38. 1 Peter 1:2, NLT; 2 Thessalonians 2:13; and Ephesians 1:4.

39. See 1 Thessalonians 1:4-5. Also 1 Corinthians 1:26-31; Romans 8:33; and 1 Peter 2:9. For additional references to God's choosing a people to call his own, see Deuteronomy 4:37; 7:6; 10:15; 14:2; 1 Chronicles 16:13; Psalm 105:6; 135:4; Isaiah 14:1; 41:8-9; 44:1-2; 49:7; Ezekiel 20:5; Amos 3:2; Matthew 11:27; Mark 13:20; Luke 10:22; 18:7; Acts 13:17; Romans 11:5; Ephesians 1:11; James 1:18; 1 Peter 1:2; and Revelation 17:14.

40. Deuteronomy 21:5. See also 18:5.

41. Acts 1:24-26 and 13:2. For additional references to God's choosing spiritual leaders, see 1 Samuel 2:28; 1 Chronicles 16:41; and 2 Chronicles 29:11.

42. Luke 9:35. See also Isaiah 42:1; Matthew 12:18; and 1 Peter 1:20; 2:6.
43. See 1 Timothy 2:5.
44. Matthew 11:27. See also John 15:19.
45. Proverbs 20:24, NLT.
46. Romans 8:29-30.
47. See 1 Peter 1:2, which ties the idea of God's choosing to the idea of his foreknowledge.
48. For more on this side of the paradox, see Ephesians 1:4-5,11-14,18; and 2 Thessalonians 2:13.
49. See Psalm 51:5.
50. See 2 Samuel 12:23. In this passage, David affirmed that he would again see his son, who died in infancy.
51. Psalm 8:5, NLT.
52. Exodus 32:33. See also Psalm 9:5.
53. See Revelation 3:5; 20:15; and 21:27.
54. See Romans 3:9-19; Revelation 13:8; and 17:8.
55. Psalm 69:28. See also Psalm 109:13-14.
56. Romans 1:28.
57. See Psalm 19:1-4 and Romans 10:17-18.
58. Matthew 13:12.
59. See Hebrews 11:6 and John 17:3.
60. See Psalm 87:5-6.
61. See Luke 10:20 and Hebrews 12:23.
62. Psalm 51:1. See also verse 9.
63. Isaiah 43:25.
64. Acts 4:12, NAB.
65. Peter Kreeft, ed., *A Shorter Summa: The Most Essential Philosophical Passages of St. Thomas Aquinas'* Summa Theologica, trans. the Fathers of the English Dominican Province (San Francisco: Ignatius, 1993), 111.
66. See Ezekiel 18:4.
67. John 3:16.
68. Romans 1:19.
69. James 1:18.

70. 2 Thessalonians 2:13. See also Ephesians 1:13, where we read that our belief triggers the Holy Spirit's "sealing" us.
71. Ephesians 2:8a.
72. Ephesians 2:8b.
73. See Matthew 6:30; 8:10; 15:28; 17:20; Mark 4:40; 5:36; 11:22; 16:14; and Luke 7:9.
74. Quoted in *The Viking Book of Aphorisms,* selected by W. H. Auden and Louis Kronenberger (New York: Barnes & Noble, 1993), 82.
75. Matthew 7:7.
76. Isaiah 66:3-4.
77. Psalm 47:4.
78. See Ephesians 1:4. He can do this in part because he is a God who forgets (see chapter 3 of this book).
79. See Romans 8:29-30.
80. See Ephesians 1:4-5.
81. See John 15:19.
82. Psalm 65:4.
83. 1 Peter 1:1-2.
84. John 15:16.
85. Ephesians 2:10.
86. Ephesians 1:11-12.
87. See Ephesians 1:13-14,18.
88. Matthew 22:14. In Jesus' parable, the invitation goes out to *everyone:* "Go to the street corners and invite to the banquet anyone you find" (Matthew 22:9). See also Matthew 22:1-14 and Luke 14:15-24.
89. John 10:28.
90. Ephesians 2:6-7.
91. Louis Berkhof, "The Attributes of God," in *The Living God: Readings in Christian Theology* (Vancouver: Regent College, 1995), 349.
92. 2 Thessalonians 2:13.

Ten: It's Faith Alone, but We Must Have Good Works

1. See Luke 14:25-33.
2. See 1 Corinthians 9:24-27.

3. See Dietrich Bonhoeffer, *The Cost of Discipleship* (New York: Simon & Schuster, 1976).
4. Romans 4:4-5, NLT.
5. John 5:24.
6. John 1:12.
7. Habakkuk 2:4.
8. Romans 1:17.
9. Romans 1:17, NLT. See also 2 Timothy 3:15.
10. Hebrews 4:2.
11. Hebrews 11:1.
12. Hebrews 11:2.
13. Ephesians 2:8-9, NLT.
14. Romans 7:12,14,16.
15. Romans 3:28, NLT.
16. Galatians 2:16, NAB.
17. Galatians 2:16.
18. Romans 9:30-32.
19. Matthew 7:22-23.
20. Philippians 3:9.
21. Galatians 3:2.
22. Romans 10:4.
23. Acts 16:30-31.
24. For more on this side of the paradox, see John 3:16; 11:25; Romans 4:13; Galatians 2:20; and 1 John 5:1.
25. James 2:24, NLT.
26. James 2:24, HCSB.
27. James 2:17.
28. James 2:26.
29. Matthew 7:16.
30. Matthew 7:21.
31. See Matthew 7:24-27.
32. See Mark 4:1-20.
33. See Matthew 25:31-46.
34. 3 John 11.

35. John 15:8.
36. 1 John 3:7-8.
37. 1 John 3:10. See also Revelation 3:1-2, where God says people are about to die because "I have not found your deeds complete."
38. Titus 1:16. See also 1 John 2:9.
39. 1 Corinthians 13:1-2.
40. Matthew 25:41-42.
41. Matthew 25:44-45. See the entire parable in Matthew 25:31-46.
42. Hebrews 10:24.
43. James 2:20.
44. James 2:14, NLT.
45. Acts 2:37-38,40, HCSB.
46. For more on this side of the paradox, see Hebrews 11:20 and 1 John 3:9.
47. Hebrews 11:6.
48. Matthew 3:8.
49. Ephesians 2:8-9, NLT.
50. Galatians 3:2.
51. James 2:24, NLT.
52. James 2:17, HCSB.
53. Isaiah 64:6. This does not mean that every good deed of an unbeliever (or believer, for that matter) is wrong or sinful. It simply means that these good deeds are totally insufficient *to make up for sin.*
54. Psalm 49:7-9, NLT.
55. 2 Peter 1:10.
56. Hebrews 11:1.
57. Romans 11:6.
58. Galatians 3:3.
59. James 2:18, NLT.
60. Galatians 5:6.
61. 1 John 3:18, HCSB.
62. Philippians 2:17.
63. 1 Thessalonians 1:3. See also 2 Thessalonians 1:11.
64. 1 Timothy 1:4.
65. Hebrews 11:4.

66. Hebrews 11:7.
67. Hebrews 11:8,17.
68. James 2:21-22, NLT.
69. James 2:22-23, NLT.
70. Luke 3:8, NLT.
71. James 2:25.
72. Hebrews 11:23.
73. Hebrews 11:24-25.
74. Hebrews 11:29.
75. See John 10:28-29.
76. See Matthew 21:18-19.
77. Hebrews 6:7-8.
78. Luke 13:8-9, MSG.
79. Isaiah 26:12.
80. Hosea 14:8.
81. Galatians 3:10-11.
82. James 1:22.
83. James 1:25, NLT.
84. Galatians 5:22.
85. This church started on the right path, stating that faith isn't saving faith unless it produces fruit in good works. The church got off the path when it drew the conclusion from this that good works are necessary *preconditions* for salvation, rather than that they are necessary *proof* of salvation.
86. Dallas Willard, *The Divine Conspiracy* (New York: HarperSanFrancisco, 1998), 49.
87. John 6:28-29.
88. John 15:5,8, NLT.
89. John 14:12.

Eleven: We Must Flee Evil, and We Must Fight It

1. See Ephesians 5:8-12.
2. Henrietta Mears, as quoted in R. Kent Hughes, comp., *1001 Great Stories & "Quotes"* (Wheaton, Ill.: Tyndale, 1998), 387.

3. See Galatians 5:1.
4. 1 Samuel 17:47.
5. See Matthew 28:5; Mark 16:4-6; and Luke 1:11-13,28-30. Angels in the Bible seem to get along fine without our help.
6. Romans 12:3.
7. 2 Peter 2:10-12.
8. Proverbs 18:10.
9. Acts 8:1.
10. Luke 4:28-29.
11. Luke 4:30, NLT.
12. Matthew 10:23.
13. 1 Corinthians 6:18.
14. 1 Corinthians 10:14.
15. Colossians 3:5.
16. 2 Timothy 2:22.
17. 2 Timothy 2:23.
18. 1 Timothy 6:4.
19. 1 Timothy 6:11. See also 6:3-5,10.
20. Titus 3:9.
21. 2 John 10-11.
22. See 1 Corinthians 10:13.
23. See Genesis 39:12.
24. Psalm 55:7-8.
25. Psalm 31:20, NLT. See also Psalm 17:8.
26. Psalm 64:2-3.
27. See Proverbs 4:14 and 1 Timothy 6:20.
28. See Psalm 1:1.
29. Psalm 7:1.
30. For more on this side of the paradox, see Psalm 27:5; 32:7; and 143:9.
31. 1 Timothy 6:12. See also 1 Corinthians 9:26.
32. Proverbs 21:22, NLT.
33. Joshua 9:24.
34. Nehemiah 6:10-11.

35. 1 Samuel 17:48.

36. Luke 10:19.

37. Psalm 44:5. See also Deuteronomy 28:7.

38. Ephesians 6:10-13, MSG.

39. 1 Peter 5:8-9.

40. James 4:7.

41. See Matthew 4:1-11.

42. 2 Corinthians 10:4-5.

43. 2 Corinthians 10:4.

44. Ephesians 6:17. See also 2 Corinthians 6:4,7; 1 John 2:13; and Revelation 12:11.

45. For more on this side of the paradox, see 2 Timothy 4:7.

46. See 1 Kings 17.

47. See 1 Kings 19:1-18.

48. See Galatians 5:24.

49. Romans 6:13.

50. James 1:25.

51. Colossians 3:3-4, NAB.

52. Joshua 8:5-7.

53. Romans 12:19.

54. Hebrews 10:25.

55. See Matthew 18:19-20.

56. John 17:15.

57. Hebrews 6:18.

58. Joshua 8:21.

59. See 1 Samuel 7:5-11; 1 Chronicles 5:20; 2 Chronicles 13:14; Psalm 37:39-40; and Isaiah 37:21.

60. Ephesians 5:11.

61. Galatians 2:5.

62. 2 Timothy 3:12.

63. Esther 9:2.

64. 1 Thessalonians 5:17.

65. Matthew 6:7.

66. Luke 6:29.
67. Romans 14:22. The whole of Romans 14 addresses various aspects of this issue.
68. Romans 14:23, NLT.
69. See Exodus 14:14; Deuteronomy 1:30; 3:22; Joshua 23:10; 1 Samuel 17:47; Nehemiah 4:20; and Psalm 35:1.
70. Ecclesiastes 3:8.

Twelve: Innocent As Children but Knowing the Score
1. See Matthew 10:16.
2. Hosea 7:11.
3. See Proverbs 31:8.
4. See Judges 18:7-10,27-28.
5. See Proverbs 3:7.
6. Ezekiel 28:6-7.
7. Matthew 18:2-3.
8. 1 Corinthians 14:20.
9. Psalm 131:2.
10. Matthew 18:3.
11. Mark 10:13-15. See also Matthew 19:13-14 and Luke 18:15-17.
12. Matthew 11:25 and Luke 10:21.
13. Psalm 24:3-4.
14. 2 Peter 3:14.
15. Revelation 2:24. See also Romans 16:19.
16. Proverbs 3:5.
17. Matthew 10:16.
18. 1 Thessalonians 5:22.
19. For more on this side of the paradox, see Psalm 26:6; Matthew 3:16 (where the Holy Spirit takes the form of a dove); and John 1:47.
20. 1 Corinthians 14:20.
21. 1 Corinthians 13:11.
22. Hebrews 5:11-13.
23. Hebrews 5:14.
24. 1 Kings 3:9.

25. Matthew 10:16.
26. Matthew 7:15, NLT.
27. Matthew 7:21, NLT.
28. John 2:24-25, NLT.
29. Jeremiah 12:6.
30. 2 Samuel 22:27 and Psalm 18:26.
31. Luke 16:8.
32. Acts 20:30-31.
33. Romans 16:17.
34. Matthew 10:17, NAB.
35. Matthew 16:6.
36. 1 John 4:1.
37. Proverbs 22:3, MSG.
38. Proverbs 2:11.
39. See Ecclesiastes 2:14.
40. 1 Thessalonians 5:21. See also Ephesians 5:15,17.
41. 1 Chronicles 12:32.
42. For more on this side of the paradox, see Exodus 1:15-20 and Psalm 19:7.
43. 2 Samuel 22:27 and Psalm 18:26.
44. John 3:4-5, NLT.
45. See Ephesians 5:26 and John 16:13.
46. Mark 9:23.
47. Romans 16:19.
48. Psalm 55:6.
49. Psalm 74:19.
50. 1 Peter 2:12.
51. Proverbs 14:33.
52. John 3:14.
53. See Numbers 21:8-9.
54. *Webster's New Universal Unabridged Dictionary*, s.v. "shrewd."
55. Proverbs 30:18-19.
56. See Matthew 18:6-7.
57. See Paul's teaching on this important subject in Romans 14.
58. Proverbs 14:15, MSG.

59. Esther 2:20.
60. Sun-Tzu, *The Art of War,* trans. Ralph D. Sawyer (New York: Barnes & Noble, 1994), 168. See also 2 Corinthians 11:13.
61. 2 Corinthians 11:13.
62. 2 Peter 2:1.
63. Jude 4.
64. James R. Lucas, *Fatal Illusions: Shredding a Dozen Unrealities That Can Keep Your Organization from Success* (Kansas City, Mo.: Quintessential, 2001).
65. See 1 John 4:1-6.
66. Mark 13:23.
67. Ecclesiastes 7:16, NLT.
68. Ecclesiastes 7:18, NLT.

Thirteen: The Center of God's Character

1. Isaac Newton, "Preface to the First Edition," *Mathematical Principles of Natural Philosophy,* Great Books of the Western World, vol. 34, (Chicago: Encyclopedia Britannica, 1952), 2.
2. From Paul Tillich, *Systematic Theology,* vol. 1 (Chicago: University of Chicago, 1951), as quoted in *The Living God: Readings in Christian Theology,* ed. Millard J. Erickson (Vancouver: Regent, 1995), 69.
3. Thomas Aquinas, as quoted in George Seldes, comp., *The Great Quotations* (New York: Pocket, 1967), 852.
4. Luke 10:21.
5. See 1 Corinthians 8:1 and Colossians 2:18.
6. Richard J. Foster, *The Challenge of the Disciplined Life* (New York: HarperSanFrancisco, 1985), 20.
7. Attributed to Theodore Rubin. Found at www.quoteland.com.
8. François Fénelon, *Talking with God* (Brewster, Mass.: Paraclete, 1997), 91.
9. See John 8:3-11.
10. See Acts 5:1-11.

11. The paradox of judging and not judging. *Judge not:* See Matthew
    7:1-5; John 8:11; Romans 14:13; and 1 Corinthians 4:5. *Judge:*
    See Matthew 7:15-16; 1 Corinthians 5:9-13; Titus 3:10; and Revela-
    tion 2:2.

12. The paradox of prayer. *Pray continually:* See Ephesians 6:19 and 1 Thes-
    salonians 5:17. *Condemnation for many prayers:* See Matthew 6:7-8.

13. The paradox of signs. *Sign-seeking is condemned:* See Matthew 12:39;
    16:1; and Luke 1:18-20. *Signs are given by God:* See Judges 6:36-40;
    Isaiah 7:10-14; and Luke 2:12.

14. The paradox of freedom. *Christ frees us:* See Isaiah 61:1; Romans 8:21;
    2 Corinthians 3:17; and Galatians 5:1,13a. *We are God's slaves:* See
    Deuteronomy 10:12; Psalm 2:11; Mark 10:43-44; Romans 6:11-23;
    and Galatians 5:13b.

15. The paradox of works. *Good works in public:* See Psalm 40:9-10; Daniel
    12:3; Matthew 5:14-16; Mark 5:19; Acts 13:47; 2 Corinthians 3:18;
    Philippians 2:15; 1 Thessalonians 1:8; and 1 Peter 2:12. *Good works in
    secret:* See Isaiah 29:13; Matthew 6:1-6,17-18; 8:3-4; 9:30; 14:23; 23:5;
    Mark 6:46; Luke 20:46; and John 6:12.

16. The paradox of distance from God. *Keep your distance:* See Exodus
    19:10-13. *Draw near:* See Hebrews 4:16.

17. The paradox of understanding. *God is beyond understanding:* See Isaiah
    55:8-9. *We have the mind of Christ:* See 1 Corinthians 2:16.

18. The paradox of evil. *Expose deeds of darkness:* See Ephesians 5:11. *Don't
    talk about such things:* See Ephesians 5:12.

19. The paradox of death. *Returning to dust:* See Genesis 3:19. *Standing in
    the flesh:* See Job 19:25-26.

20. The paradox of length of life. *Predetermined lifespan:* See Psalm 139:16.
    Prolonged life: See Psalm 91:16; Proverbs 3:2; 4:10; and Ephesians 6:1-3.

21. The paradox of money. *Love of money as root of evil:* See 1 Timothy
    6:10. *Money as solution:* See Ecclesiastes 10:19. There is a parallel para-
    dox: the paradox of contentment and ambition.

22. The paradox of jealousy. *Jealousy (coveting) is a sin:* See Exodus 20:17.
    God is jealous: See Exodus 20:5.

23. The paradox of strength and weakness: *Be strong:* See Ephesians 6:10. *Seek weakness:* See 2 Corinthians 12:10.

24. Psalm 40:3,5, MSG.

25. As you do, I'd love for you to share your insights and discoveries. You can do so at www.relationshipdevelopmentonline.com.

26. "Meaning-full Translations," an interview with Eugene Nida, by David Neff, *Christianity Today,* October 7, 2002, 49.

Fourteen: Celebrating Our Mysterious Companion

1. N. Graham Standish, *Paradoxes for Living: Cultivating Faith in Confusing Times* (Louisville, Ky.: Westminster John Knox, 2001), 79.

2. Acts 17:28.

3. Colossians 3:3.

4. Psalm 73:23.

5. John 14:23.

6. Isaiah 30:21.

7. Revelation 3:20.

8. John 3:8.

9. Jacques Barzun, *From Dawn to Decadence* (New York: HarperCollins, 2000), 54.

10. Psalm 40:17, NLT.

11. Daniel 2:27-29, NLT.

12. Daniel 2:47, NLT.

13. 1 Timothy 3:16, NLT.

14. Paul Harvey, as quoted in Richard A. Kauffman, "Fenders of the Faith," *Christianity Today,* 5 August 2002, 53.

15. See Psalm 34:3.

16. Luke 24:27, NLT.